FUR TRADE

TO

*Putting the Canada–U.S.
Trade Agreement
in Historical Perspective*

FREE TRADE

FUR TRADE
TO
Putting the Canada–U.S.
Trade Agreement
in Historical Perspective
FREE TRADE

RANDALL WHITE

SECOND EDITION

Toronto & Oxford
Dundurn Press
1989

Design and Production: Andy Tong
Printing and Binding: Gagné Printing Ltd., Louiseville, Quebec, Canada

The writing of this manuscript and the publication of this book were made possible by support from several sources. The publisher wishes to acknowledge the generous assistance and ongoing support of **The Canada Council, The Book Publishing Industry Development Programme** of the **Department of Communications, The Ontario Arts Council**, and the **Ontario Heritage Foundation**.

J. Kirk Howard, Publisher

Canadian Cataloguing in Publication Data

White, Randall
 Fur trade to free trade

2nd ed.
Bibliography: p.
Includes index.
ISBN 1-55002-068-4

1. Free trade - Canada - History. 2. Free trade -
United States - History. 3. Canada - Commerce -
United States - History 4. United States -
Commerce - Canada - History. 5. Canada -
Commercial treaties - History. 6. United States -
Commercial treaties - History. 7. Canada -
Commerce - History. I. Title.

HF3228.U3W35 1989 382.7'1'0971 C89-094186-6

Dundurn Press Limited
2181 Queen Street East
Toronto, Canada
M4E 1E5

Dundurn Distribution Limited
Athol Brose, School Hill,
Wargrave, Reading
England RG10 8DY

CONTENTS

PREFACE & ACKNOWLEDGEMENTS

History books, a diligent young lady tutor in the subject once told me, are not meant to be used in quite the same way as novels.

Some users of this particular book — a kind of hybrid of history and current politics — may want to read the introduction, then only skim the earlier chapters, and concentrate on material closer to the end. Others may want to concentrate on the earlier chapters, and virtually ignore the later ones. Others again may find that some parts of the book pique and sustain their interest, while other parts do not.

For those who like to go the full distance, I have at least worked hard to tell as complete a story as the space available permits, from cover to cover. On the other hand, I have also taken some pains to arrange things for the convenience of more selective readers.

* * *

The concept for the book was suggested by Kirk Howard of Dundurn Press and by Jeanne MacDonald. I am equally indebted to them for much valued advice and assistance with my work on the text, and I owe various notes of thanks to the management and staff at Dundurn Press, especially Ian Low, Andy Tong, and Rashid Farrah.

I am indebted as well to Honor de Pencier for drawing attention to the late 19th and early 20th century Canadian political cartoons of Sam Hunter, that illustrate the text.

The cartoons have been made available for reproduction through the kindness of Mr. Hugh Porter of the Royal Ontario Museum, from the estate of the late Mrs. George Boothe Ferguson (née Margaret Collingwood), adopted daughter of the artist.

I owe similar debts of thanks in connection with Sam Hunter's cartoons to John Crosthwait of the Metropolitan Toronto Reference Library — and to the *Globe & Mail* and the *Toronto Star*, for permission to reproduce some material over which they hold rights on the most generous terms possible.

* * *

A few words about Sam Hunter's now only dimly remembered career can serve as a preface of sorts to the book at large. (And one of my more rewarding discoveries in the larger project has been that the illustrator was an intriguing character.)

When he died, only a few months after the start of the Second World War in 1939, a press report described Sam Hunter as "Canada's outstanding Portrayer of Statesmen" (beings now more commonly known as politicians). He was in his 82nd year, and his life had covered a sweep of the past now lost in the living memory of all generations alive today.

He was born in 1858 in Millbrook, Ontario, a small town in an Irish Catholic countryside near the city of Peterborough. At the Canadian Confederation of 1867, he was nine years old. He spent part of his early adulthood in the romantic late 19th century Northwest, now known as Western Canada; but by the late 1880s he had arrived in Toronto, where he married Rachel Jeanette Brayley, and became, after the age of 30, a widely-admired political cartoonist.

Hunter started drawing pictures about Canadian politics in an era when political cartoons played a more important role in the electorate's perception of its chosen leaders than they do today. On the judgement of his peers, he did his best work for a now long defunct, innovative, and independent-minded Toronto newspaper known as the *World*, owned and edited by W.F. Maclean. He also worked for another now defunct Toronto paper called the *News*, and for the *Globe* (now the *Globe & Mail*). He spent his final years with the *Toronto Daily Star* where, on his retirement at the age of 79 in 1937, he was appointed "cartoonist emeritus."

At the turn of the century he had bought a house on Springhurst Avenue in the old Parkdale district of Toronto, that would serve as both home and workplace until his death some 40 years later. A few years before he had built a cottage on Stoney Lake, in the Kawartha district of Southern Ontario, not far from his hometown. Here he retreated for three months each summer, to remake his peace with the northern wilderness. In this setting he was, an old friend wrote after his death, "attuned to the spiritual world of Thoreau... . Rain or shine, he rambled daily in woods and fields."

At the end of his career, his peers inside and outside the daily press reported: "This country has produced more dashing and daring cartoonists than Sam Hunter, but none more subtle or more likeable." He was an "instructor and entertainer" who was never "nasty, never vulgar, never bitter." He was "always able to bring to his characters something which while pointed was never offensive."

* * *

Like all of us, Sam Hunter was a captive of the prejudices of his time, which were in many respects quite different from those of our time in the late 20th century. To some, his work may bring home the point of the modern Canadian historian Ramsay Cook's quip that the 19th century did not really end in Canada until about 1950.

Yet in other ways the broad issues that form the grist for Sam Hunter's cartoons are quite like the issues that form the subject of this book: they are, as it were, recurrent issues in Canadian history. In this spirit, his illustrations have been used throughout the text, even though, in strict chronological sequence, they cover only about one-quarter of the entire time period under discussion.

There is, as well, no use pretending that the Toronto-Ontario regional point of view in the cartoons is altogether absent from the text they illustrate here. In

Canada today, it seems, no one can lay claim to a national view that does not have some regional overtones — even though to make such bias explicit is at least to aspire to transcend it.

It would be a happy circumstance if Sam Hunter's cartoons also helped offset, in some degree, another kind of bias in the book at large. It has been written during late 1987 and early 1988. At the time of publication it was not clear whether the new Canada-U.S. Free Trade Agreement would be ratified by the U.S. Congress (though most seemed to agree it would be), or how it might be affected by the outcome of an imminent Canadian federal election, or how it might ultimately relate to the fate of its companion Canadian public policy innovation, the "Meech Lake Accord."

The book allocates its greatest space to somewhat more timeless historical material, in a more explicit effort to offset such problems. Yet in the end it remains, like Sam Hunter's cartoons, an ephemeral offering to shifting sands. I can only hope that it stands up at least half as well as the cartoons.

* * *

My particular debts to the various literatures related to the subject are suggested in a Select Bibliography placed at the end. Unless otherwise made clear Statistics Canada and Canada's chief federal electoral officer are the sources for data reported on in tables.

I would like to thank Fred Armstrong of the University of Western Ontario for kindly providing material clarifying Canadian-American trade patterns in the earlier 19th century, and Rex Williams for helpful material on much more recent conditions. I have profited as well from discussions of the issues that the book addresses with The Linsmore Institute and its friends and associates, and from similar discussions with other friends and colleagues who will want to remain anonymous. For various forms of assistance with the modern marvels of computer technology, I am indebted to Patricia Lenhardt and Christopher White.

In a more formal setting, Ron Stagg of the History Department at Ryerson Polytechnical Institute has saved me from some mistakes in historical detail and made many valued suggestions about the first draft of the manuscript, all within lamentably tight deadlines at a very busy time of the year.

Finally, I owe a special note of thanks to the Ontario Arts Council, for its much appreciated assistance with my efforts at writing books.

R.W.
Toronto, April 1988.

PREFACE TO SECOND EDITION

A new final chapter has been added to this second edition of *Fur Trade to Free Trade*, to take account of the Canadian federal election in November 1988, trade statistics published by Statistics Canada in December 1988, and events surrounding the very early implementation of the Canada-U.S. Free Trade Agreement, in the first few months of 1989.

Some minor corrections in the text of the first edition have also been made, but no part of the original 17 chapters has been rewritten in any way.

The fate of the Canada-U.S. Trade Agreement negotiated in 1987 is now somewhat clearer than it was when the first edition of the book appeared. Just what its final form and future will prove to be, however, is still far from certain. Even on the most optimistic assumptions about the agreement's potential for long-term survival, serious judgements about its real economic, political, social, and cultural impacts will not even begin to be possible for at least several years. What has already been said about "an ephemeral offering to shifting sands" applies to the second edition as much as to the first.

I would like to thank all those whose active enthusiasm for the book has made a second edition possible.

R.W.
Toronto, April 1989.

INTRODUCTION

Chapter 1

THE TRADITION OF COMPROMISE

"This is a one-on-one thing," former Alberta Premier Peter Lougheed is reported to have said, shortly after the October 4, 1987 initialing of the draft Canada-U.S. Free Trade Agreement in Washington. "No Canadian will be neutral when it is all over."

A few days later an editorial in the *Toronto Star* took a similar position from the opposite side of the debate. "The question is," the *Star* declared: "are we prepared to continue paying to ensure the kind of society we want? The choice is that basic. It is time for all of us to decide."

This may prove to be how things work out. But anyone who ponders the broad sweep of Canada's past can legitimately raise doubts. From another point of view, moderation and compromise are seared in bold letters on the Canadian soul.

Whatever the ultimate fate of the trade agreement between Canada and the United States scheduled to begin taking effect in January 1989, it will perhaps not be too surprising if the sum of the various regional moods that makes up the current Canadian national mood in fact remains somewhat neutral.

The radical partisans at either end of the debate are right about one thing. It raises fundamental issues. But, chances are, most of us will not come down hard on one side of these issues or the other. We will do what we have always done in moments that call for bold decisions. We will resolutely drive up the middle of the road.

This is what finally happened in the late 1970s debate on another fundamental issue of Canadian life — Quebec nationalism and the French fact. It is what will probably finally happen in the new debate that fate has set before the people of Canada in the late 1980s — on the nature of the relationship between Canada and the United States.

There are continuing reasons for caution in judging the durability of the deal that has been struck. Shortly after a final text for the new agreement had been reached in December 1987, the U.S.-based *Business Week* noted: "Although Congress is expected to approve the deal, the political opposition in Canada, claiming the deal undermines national sovereignty, threatens to abrogate the treaty should the present government fall from power. That's no idle threat: Prime Minister Brian Mulroney's Progressive Conservatives aren't expected to win the next election, which must take place before September 1989."

The first free trade treaty between Canada and the United States — signed back in what now seems the quite remote past of 1854 — was abrogated only a dozen years later. In this case the abrogating party was not Canada but the United States, and the reasons for abrogation were not strictly economic. If the current treaty proves to be as good for Canada as some of its most strident promoters claim, a cynic might not be all that surprised if this particular history were to repeat itself.

A synopsis of the December 1987 final agreement prepared by the Canadian federal government declares: "This is the most important trade agreement Canada has ever concluded. It is the culmination of almost 100 years of Canadian efforts to secure open and stable markets."

In a democratic country, it would be unusual (and alarming) if an international agreement of such scope and importance were not the subject of extended public discussion and debate, over some extended period of time.

The agreement itself includes a number of crucial blanks that are meant to be filled in as it is gradually implemented. In Canada *The Financial Post* has suggested: "It may take years for free trade's final form and effects to be known."

In all these contexts anyone concerned to predict the future (or at least make shrewd guesses about it) might profitably take a long and hard look at the Canadian tradition of moderation and compromise.

The Virtues of the Tradition

It is in the nature of the Canadian tradition of compromise that you must qualify what you mean by it. It cannot, alas, be summarized in a single tight sentence.

Some argue that it is not really the mainstream tradition of Canada as a whole, but only of a particular region. A good case, for instance, can be made for the view that Western Canada has stronger regional tendencies toward polarization and partisanship than, say, Ontario.

Yet before 1980 an equally good case could have been made for the view that Quebec takes its politics more seriously, and has stronger partisan traditions, than any other part of Canada. In the end the people of Quebec resolutely took the middle of the road on the already quite fudged-up question of "sovereignty association." And, if anything, Atlantic Canada is even more full of moderation and compromise than Ontario.

In the Confederation at large, to start with, the tradition implies heeding the advice that Oliver Cromwell urged on one of his followers during the 17th century English Revolution: "For God's sake, man, consider in the bowels of Christ that you may be wrong."

Next, it can be said that the tradition reaches across the barriers of languages and oceans. In 1954, for instance, Winston Churchill, on his last visit to Canada, gave a "Farewell Speech" to the people of the country over the radio airwaves of the Canadian Broadcasting Corporation. He noted that it had been 53 years since he had first visited "the great Dominion — if that expression has not become obsolete." In another ancient tradition of imperial flattery, he commented on the subsequent "tremendous expansion" of "a mighty structure whose future cannot be measured, but will certainly take its place in the first ranks of sovereign communities." Then, with a characteristically prescient eye on both the past and the future, he concluded: "Au revoir, mes amis, Canadiens...C'est un avenir splendide que vous attend demain."

Churchill (a heady model for mere ex-colonials) can help make another point about the Canadian tradition of compromise. Though it deeply believes that politicians are meant to be taken with generous grains of salt, it also believes that in the end politics are important. More than that, they make adventurous careers and avocations for men and women of the world. As Churchill once put it to an intimate audience in his own country: "Politics are almost as exciting as war, and quite as dangerous. In war you can only be killed once, but in politics many times."

Finally, in its best moments the tradition of compromise embraces even its critics. And ever since its modern beginnings in 19th century Canada, it has had its fair share of critics.

In the late 1940s, Harold Innis, then the first Canadian-born Chairman of the Department of Political Economy at The University of Toronto, declared: "As evidence of the futility of political discussion in Canada, there were Liberals who deplored the activities of the federal administration in no uncertain terms but always concluded with what was to them an unanswerable argument — 'What is the alternative?' In one's weaker moments the answer does appear conclusive, but what a comment on political life... ."

In the free trade debate today even an observer who is trying hard to be coldly objective can hear at least some authentically fresh voices (many but by no means most from the West) speaking for a more confident and forthright Canada. They often speak for much of what is strongest and most promising in the future of the country. If the Canadian tradition of compromise really does have an unquenchable instinct for survival, then ultimately it will embrace what is straight and narrow in the arguments of its late 20th century critics.

The tradition of compromise itself, however, will have the very last word, because it flows from the deepest facts of Canadian life. In the late 1980s the political scientist John Wilson has suggested that "whether we like it or not, Mackenzie King had a better understanding of how Canada has to be governed than any other prime minister we have had."

In the spirit of William Lyon Mackenzie King — and in the world of the 21st century that now looms in sight, it is juvenile or worse, not manly, to let your sense of confidence overwhelm your sense of reality. Surprisingly enough to some, Ronald Reagan has aptly put the point in a much more profound context: those who will not accept the inevitability of compromise accept in their deepest thoughts the inevitability of war.

To paraphrase Mackenzie King himself, once called "the Canadian as he exists in the mind of God," in the end we will probably get 'free trade if necessary, but not necessarily free trade.'

The Free Trade Agreement & the Meech Lake Accord

Ultimately the free trade debate in Canada is interesting, and significant, not because of shorter-term economic issues — as important as these always are, but because of its longer-term role in a still larger debate about the future of the Canadian Confederation in the 21st century.

It is no accident, for example, that the Canada-U.S. Free Trade Agreement is recurrently linked in public discussion with the recent Canadian constitutional document known as the Meech Lake Accord. Some in Canada oppose both agreements. Others support both agreements. Still others support one but not the other. (And, it is always worth noting, still others again, in another old Canadian tradition, are not too sure they even want to know where Meech Lake is.)

The Meech Lake Accord itself is in direct descent from the federal Constitution Act 1982. This finally "patriated" all Canada's basic constitutional documents from the United Kingdom (through a long-delayed federal-provincial agreement on a formula for amending the constitution in Canada), and added an entrenched Canadian Charter of Rights and Freedoms to what is now known as The Constitution Act 1867 (formerly The British North America Act 1867).

The Constitution Act 1982 might itself be said to be in direct descent from the 1980 Quebec Referendum, the 1976 Quebec provincial election, and in the more distant past even from initiatives taken by the late 1950s and early 1960s federal governments of the Saskatchewan populist "Chief," John Diefenbaker.

Down the road, additional items remain on the same agenda. Two recent constitutional conferences, for instance, have yet to produce an agreement on the role of the Canadian Indians and Inuit in the modern Confederation. Many of us may find it hard to keep paying attention. But it is a fact that Canada today has at least begun to resolve this fundamental but profoundly difficult issue in the political development of the New World. And its ultimate resolution may have more positive practical implications for our future than we imagine.

Similarly, some argue that the Meech Lake Accord (which finally defines Quebec's role under the 1982 Constitution) will make it more difficult to achieve the elected Canadian Senate that figures prominently in Western Canada's vision of the Confederation in the 21st century. But it is clear enough that the West, as well as Quebec, is carving out a new role for itself in the country. In the not too distant future, this must lead to some kind of major constitutional change in the federal Senate.

Free trade with the United States has a long history as a difficult national issue in Canada. It gave the federal Liberals of the late 19th and early 20th centuries particular trouble; here cartoonist Sam Hunter shows Liberal leader Wilfrid Laurier taking up an awkward middle ground between opposing voices inside his own party.

At a point further down the road, new provinces of some description will be created in Canada's two remaining territories of the far north. And before the process of constitutional renewal is complete, it is even conceivable that it may also include as yet unforeseen agreements to accommodate particular interests in Atlantic Canada or even in Canada's most populous, and least popular, province of Ontario.

The Restructuring Confederation

In the economic jargon of our time, the Canadian Confederation is being "restructured," to meet the challenges and opportunities of a new age.

We are accustomed to hearing about restructuring as a priority for private sector firms and enterprises . It reflects the need to adjust to trends in a rapidly changing global economy. William R.C. Blundell, Chairman of Canadian General Electric, has recently declared: "Canada has demonstrated that it can deal with massive restructuring." (And this is no doubt a good thing, since the new Canada-U.S. Free Trade Agreement will probably bring at least a bit more of it).

We are less accustomed, in Canada, to hearing about the same priority in the context of government and politics. There is also a clear difference between the kind of restructuring involved in the new trade agreement with the U.S. and the kind involved in such things as the Meech Lake Accord. In the one case Canada is restructuring its internal or domestic arrangements, typically in response to largely internal pressures. In the other it is restructuring its external or international arrangements, in response to largely external pressures.

Yet in the highly interdependent world of the late 20th century, these categories overlap. Because the world today is so interdependent, it is perhaps impossible for any country to engage in significant internal restructuring, without ultimately prompting some parallel change in its external relationships.

For Canada, it has long been a simple fact of life that the country's single most important external relationship is with the United States of America. As a new and stronger Canadian Confederation girds its loins for the challenges and opportunities of the 21st century, it makes sense that it should begin the inevitably difficult process of restructuring its external relationships by concluding some kind of trade agreement with the United States.

At the same time, if we are to believe those whom we have for the moment placed in charge of such things, this does in fact mark only a beginning for wider ambitions.

Canada's relationship with the United States, that is to say, is not and has never been its only important external relationship. A reader of the section on "External Relations" in the 1988 *Canada Year Book* (prepared by the federal government's central statistical agency) might come away with the impression that Canada's links with the modern Commonwealth of Nations and "la Francophonie" are at least as significant as its ties to the U.S.A.

Moreover, a reader of the *Year Book* will also discover that: "Since the inception of the United Nations, support for the UN system has been an integral part of Canadian foreign policy." Under the heading "Activities by region," all parts of the world are listed; and we are told that the "Asian and Pacific region" in particular has "emerged as an area of great political, economic, cultural, and strategic significance and interest for Canada".

Several years ago, a Hollywood movie character — a citizen of the U.S.A. played by the irresistible Goldie Hawn — was asked if she had ever lived in a foreign country. She replied that she had lived in Canada for a while. But she supposed that didn't really count, since Canada was "like attached."

This reflects a common U.S. and even more general international perception of Canada. It has its genuine grains of truth, and its Canadian analogues, reflected in the title of a recent Canadian movie — *My American Cousin*. Thus the Preamble to the new Canada-U.S. Free Trade Agreement begins with a reference to "the unique and enduring friendship" between the "two nations" of Canada and the United States.

Yet since the creation of the American Republic in the late 18th century, Canada has also leaned on its external relations with other parts of the world, to help ensure that its unique friendship with the United States does not stray beyond the bounds of what is proper between mere cousins.

This remains a crucial part of the Canadian tradition of moderation and compromise. So the Canadian federal government's commentary to its new agreement with the U.S. stresses that "Canada remains committed to the multilateral trading system and the growth of world trade." Just as the new Canadian Constitution of 1982 was only the first in a series of internal agreements, so the Canada-U.S. free trade deal that takes effect in 1989 (assuming it does endure for at least a while) will be only the first in a series of external agreements — including those associated with the global General Agreement on Tariffs and Trade (more simply known as "GATT").

Economists & Experience in Other Jurisdictions

Within this kind of framework, there are various possible approaches to exploring the implications of the new Canada-U.S. Free Trade Agreement for the Canadian Confederation in the 21st century.

Some economists, for instance, have developed mathematical models to predict the behaviour of such narrowly defined economic variables as employment and income.

Most economists in the most professional sense of the term, in Canada as in similar places, will argue that in principle free trade is a good thing, from the standpoint of "the wealth of nations." Economists working for one kind of client, however, have in fact predicted significant job gains in Canada as a result of the agreement, while economists working for another kind of client have predicted important job losses.

A balanced view would probably be that both kinds of predictions make sense in certain contexts, while most economists believe that job gains will ultimately exceed job losses . An only somewhat less balanced view would be that though many different kinds of economic and other change are certain, it does not make a great deal of sense to spend too much time pretending to predict exact magnitudes in even the key sectors of the Canadian economy. When the Toronto corporate lawyer and former federal Liberal cabinet minister, Donald Macdonald, urged Canadians to make a "leap of faith" in the direction of Canada-U.S. free trade several years ago, he probably summed up the underlying thrust of advice from most professional economists for the layman, as succinctly as is humanly possible.

Another approach is to look at the experience of recent similar trade agreements between other countries. The Canadian federal government's synopsis of the new Canada-U.S. agreement notes four such "previous agreements" as "particularly relevant": the 1960 European Free-Trade Area; the 1965 UK-Ireland Free Trade Agreement; the 1983 Australia-New Zealand Closer Economic Relations Agreement; and the 1985 United States-Israel Agreement.

While each of these might be said to form a precedent of sorts for the new Canada-U.S. agreement, it ought to be obvious enough that none of the relationships involved have genuinely close similarities with the relationship between Canada and the United States.

The 1960 European Free-Trade Area (EFTA), to take the most prominent example in much media discussion, is not quite the same as the 1957 European Economic Community (EC). It was formed to give smaller European countries like Sweden access to the benefits of the EC, while shielding them from the politically worrisome "harmonizing pressures" (as the jargon puts it) of the larger European countries' more rigorous common market.

Yet the modern situation of a country like Sweden with respect to countries like the United Kingdom, France, West Germany, and Italy involves a cluster of social, economic, political, cultural, and historical relationships vastly different from those between Canada and the United States. It is not just like comparing apples and oranges: it is much more like comparing apples with rocks found on the moon.

The History of the Canada-U.S. Relationship

This book takes a broad look at the specific historical development of the relationship between Canada and the United States, from the creation of the American Republic in the late 18th century down to the present. An approach of this sort also has its weaknesses. It has the great virtue, however, of focusing attention on the specific cases in point.

One weakness of a historical approach is that it bumps stubbornly up against the unpopularity of history as a source of wisdom in the late 20th century. Arthur Miller, author of the modern American classic *Death of a Salesman*, has recently bemoaned: "The past has simply ceased in our time."

Yet it is not really the past that has ceased, but only our awareness of the past. For individuals and communities alike, the past is still there, shaping the present and the future, in often ironic ways. Dramatic technological changes — the most profound of which is no doubt the nuclear bomb — have violently shaken traditional senses of history, around the globe. But it remains a simple truth that the past is all there is that is capable of shaping the present and the future.

Arthur Miller has also declared that even today: "To possess the past is to achieve importance." Toward the end of the 1960s, the Canadian Red Tory political philosopher George Grant introduced the subject "Canadian Fate and Imperialism" by proclaiming: "To use the language of fate is to assert that all human beings come into a world they did not choose and live their lives within a universe they did not make."

In the global village of the late 20th century, there is no point in pretending that the particular Canadian universe which we of the generations alive today did not make has some unusual significance. The roots of Canadian patriotism are more subtle than that . Canada is a country that has just grown up like Topsy (a phrase in fact adapted by Harriet Beecher Stowe from the writings of Thomas Chandler Haliburton, creator of the foxy old Nova Scotia trader, Sam Slick). The United States, of course, has a quite different kind of past. Part of the rationale for the historical approach is that it makes the often rather smoky differences between Canada and the United States unusually clear.

In the end, sensible people, George Grant has also suggested, value the past principally for the light it can shed on the present and the future. The first part of what follows presents ten successive snapshots of the evolving relationship between Canada and the United States, and its impact on Canadian development — from the American War of Independence down to the last government of Pierre Trudeau in the early 1980s. The second part uses this exercise to explore the current debate over Brian Mulroney's Canada-U.S. Free Trade Agreement of the late 1980s. A brief concluding section suggests some implications for the the Canadian Confederation in the 21st century.

The premise is that this particular approach provides hard information which can help make the complexities of the present at least a little clearer — while covering some important ground that is seldom covered in more analytic kinds of treatment. Alas, it cannot even pretend to offer simple solutions or straightforward, unambiguous answers to often difficult human questions. Within the framework handed down by the past, each generation must make its own history for itself.

Finally, the book is unapologetically subject to a caveat that the very sensible English historian George Clark expressed very clearly in his early 1970s survey of the much longer history of England and "such neighbouring communities as Wales, Scotland, Ireland, and France." The reader "has his own view of human nature and he has every right to bring it to bear. The conditions on which he is entitled to disagree with the historian are the same as those on which he is entitled to disagree with his next-door neighbour about current affairs."

PART ONE:
THE LONG ROAD
BEHIND US

A. Ancient History

Chapter 2

"THE POSSESSION OF THIS COUNTRY MUST FINALLY BE DECIDED BY THE SWORD."

W here you begin the path of Canadian history that ultimately leads to the Canada-U.S. Free Trade Agreement of the late 1980s depends on your purposes. A narrow, shorter-term purpose, concerned much more with economics than with politics and economics together, might start with the Canadian federal elections of 1911 or 1891. The broadest purpose would begin with the beginnings of Canada itself.

This book takes some account of Canada's earliest beginnings through a few subsequent flashbacks. It is part of the difference between the two countries today, however, that Canada has diffuse, almost organic origins which stretch comparatively far back into time, while the United States has a clear-cut, self-willed moment of birth, with a precise date. And this modern American moment of birth marks the real beginning of the modern relationship between Canada and the United States.

In this spirit we can start by stepping into history, as it were, on a frosty morning toward the end of March 1776, as a party of five men set out from the city of Philadelphia for the city of Montreal. Today you can make the trip by air in a few hours. In the raw world of late 18th century North America it took about a month, by water and land.

The most eminent member of the group was Benjamin Franklin — a 70-year-old partisan for the cause of the thirteen United Colonies in British America, and a delegate from Pennsylvania to the Continental Congress at Philadelphia. The other four members of the party were less illustrious. Samuel Chase was a Sons of Liberty partisan in his mid-30s, and a delegate to the Continental Congress from Maryland. Charles Carroll of Carrollton (as he liked to be called) was a Maryland nabob, descended from Irish Catholics and educated in France. The Rev. John Carroll was a cousin of Charles Carroll, and a Jesuit priest. Fleury Mesplet, a French printer, had been attracted to America by what he thought was the revolutionary cause of the Continental Congress.

There was a carefully crafted logic to the composition of the group. In February 1776 the Congress, after some considerable debate, had appointed Franklin, Chase, and Charles Carroll special commissioners, with responsibility for doing everything in their power to promote a union between the thirteen rebellious English colonies and the old French colony of Canada in the far north.

At the time Canada was still a place where the overwhelming majority of the white inhabitants were French-speaking Roman Catholics. A few British and Anglo-American merchants had moved to Montreal and Quebec City in the wake of the British Conquest of Canada (more commonly known to American colonials as the French and Indian War), which had ended only 13 years before. But for at least another generation "Canadian" would remain largely reserved for French Catholics, born among the Indians in the most northern part of North America.

In the sea of New World Protestantism south of the St. Lawrence River, Maryland was virtually the only English colony where the Roman Catholic Church had any notable foothold. And, according to the republican activist John Adams, the Maryland notable Charles Carroll "had a liberal education in France," was "well acquainted with the french Nation," and spoke "their language as easily as ours."

In the same spirit the three commissioners appointed by the Continental Congress had decided to take the Rev. John Carroll and Fleury Mesplet along with them. Charles Carroll's Jesuit cousin was a response to earlier urgings from the Congressional general, Charles Lee: "If some Jesuit or Religieuse of any other Order (but he must be a man of liberal sentiments, enlarged mind and a manifest friend of Civil Liberty) could be found and sent to Canada, he would be worth battalions to us."

The French printer Fleury Mesplet was to tell the people of Canada about the Continental Congress and its cause in their own language. To fulfil his mission he lugged a printing press all the way from Philadelphia to Montreal.

Canada in the Spring of 1776

The five travellers had not left Philadelphia without advance preparation. In November 1775, buoyed by their earlier successes at Lexington and Concord, the rebellious forces of the Continental Congress had taken the Montreal area from British troops, and laid seige to Quebec City, to the east along the St. Lawrence River.

Among other things, strategists of the Continental Congress feared some revival of the bloodiest of all North American Indian uprisings, known as the Conspiracy of Pontiac, that had erupted in the north immediately after the British Conquest of Canada. More to the point for Benjamin Franklin and his fellow commissioners, their supporters in the Congress hoped that many French Canadians would see invading American Patriot forces as liberators from British Tory tyranny.

The hope was not altogether vain. In the Montreal area there was some initial support for the Congressional cause among the Canadian *habitants* — partly New World versions of French peasants, and partly unusual kinds of independent North Americans. Yet the fledgling Congressional forces were unable to pay many of their bills in Canada. What later English Canadians would call "the monkish atmosphere of Lower Canada" frightened some young Anglo-American soldiers into believing that they were in "the dwelling place of Satan."

Moreover, the guiding lights of the only recently conquered French Canadians were the *seigneurs* (a pale colonial imitation of the pre-revolutionary nobility in France) and, above all else, the Roman Catholic clergy. They remembered that before 1763 generations of Catholics from New France and Protestants from New England had periodically been at each others' throats, in company with assorted nations of proud Indian warriors. Of much more immediate consequence, in 1774, the British Parliament in London, England had passed the Quebec Act. It recognized, in effect, the privileged position of the Catholic Church in the French Canadian state. And it prescribed French rather than English civil law in the administration of a new British Canada.

In the deliberations of the French Canadian leaders, the Quebec Act prompted a strategic attraction but little serious sentiment for what later English Canadians would call "the British connexion." (Much later the early 20th century nationalist, Henri Bourassa , would declare: "we had to choose between the English of Boston and the English of London. The English of London were farther away and we hated them less.")

In another part of the community, the economically dynamic element in Canada before the British Conquest had been the ostensibly noble merchant adventurers and explorers of the far-flung Canadian fur trade: men like the Sieur de La Salle, Count Frontenac, the Sieur de La Mothe Cadillac, and the Gaultier de Varennes et de La Vérendrye. Yet, though French and Métis *voyageurs* and clerks remained important in the fur trade even after the Conquest, for the most part the old French economic leadership was rather quickly replaced by the British and Anglo-American merchants who began to settle in Quebec City and especially in Montreal.

In 1776 some among the new British merchants of Canada were attracted to the ideals of Benjamin Franklin and the Continental Congress, and many were irked by the pro-French Catholic provisions of the Quebec Act. They were pleased, however, by the Act's generous definition of the Canadian fur trade territory (which included substantial parts of what is now the U.S. Midwest). They were pleased as well by its implicit support for the Indians of the interior, who had played an indispensable role in the growth of the fur trade since the 1600s.

In fact, in the Conspiracy of Pontiac, inspired by a war chief of the Ottawa nation, the Indians of the northern interior had already fought their own war in defence of the Great Lakes and northwestern fur trade territory — and made agreements with the British Crown on how the territory was to be managed. As Harold Innis would much later observe, in 1930, "the Indian and his culture were fundamental to the growth of Canadian institutions."

The British merchants of Montreal also knew that they depended on the advanced metropolitan economy of the European mother country to supply the kind of trade goods that the Indians would most willingly exchange for furs. The markets for the furs themselves were still in Europe, not North America. In 1776 it was not in the interests of the new British merchants of Canada to stand up too boldly for the Continental Congress in Philadelphia.

The Continental Congress Retreats

Given all these circumstances, it is not surprising that Franklin, Chase, the two Carrolls, and Fleury Mesplet met with a somewhat cool reception when they finally arrived in Montreal on April 29. Their problems began as soon as they tried to board the ferry boat across the St. Lawrence River. On learning their identity, the ferry operator refused to grant passage without immediate payment in hard cash.

Once lodged with Congressional forces in Montreal, the commissioners began to grasp the more detailed difficulties that confronted the cause of the Continental Congress in Canada. They wrote home that they were "pestered hourly" by creditors, and spent much time appeasing angry Canadians from whom Congressional forces had requisitioned provisions or services without pay. Fleury Mesplet set up his printing press in the basement of the Chateau de Ramezay. Yet even in French news of the American Patriot revolution was not eagerly awaited.

The Montreal clergy asked the Rev. John Carroll, the Jesuit priest from Maryland, to name even one colony among the thirteen where the Roman Catholic clergy had anything equal to the privileges recently granted the clergy of Canada by The Quebec Act. John Carroll replied that the three commissioners from Philadelphia were making a particular promise to allow Canadians "the free and undisturbed exercise of their religion." Then the Montreal clergy asked how he reconciled this promise with a recent public document of the Continental Congress, accusing the Roman Catholic Church of "impiety, bigotry, persecution, murder and rebellion throughout every part of the world."

On May 10 it was learned in Montreal that the Congressional forces at Quebec City had finally been turned back by British troops, and were retreating out of Canada to points south. The 70-year-old Benjamin Franklin was worried about his health in the confusion of an 18th century city under wartime conditions. Already it was clear to him that, for the moment at least, there was no point in pursuing the cause of the Continental Congress in Canada through diplomacy. He decided to return to Philadelphia.

Chase, the Carrolls, and Fleury Mesplet stayed in Montreal until the end of May. They agreed with Franklin, however, that it was not possible to recruit a credible Canadian delegation to the Continental Congress in Philadelphia.

As Sam Hunter saw it, the Roman Catholic clergy of Quebec, who played an important role in keeping Canada out of the new American Republic in 1776, also ploughed furrows in the anxious brow of Wilfrid Laurier well over a century later. Even in the 1940s, the English Canadian political scientist Alexander Brady would write that in French Canada the "village church is...the symbol of social unity, while over the years the message of the hierarchy to their flocks has varied little...be calm and stoical, till your fields, raise God-fearing children, do not surrender your language or your culture."

Before leaving at the end of May, Charles Carroll of Carrollton had written home: "the possession of this country must finally be decided by the sword."

By this time British forces were moving to relieve Montreal, both from Quebec City to the east and from the upper St. Lawrence-Great Lakes region to the west. In June the occupying Congressional forces left Montreal for a last unsuccessful battle with the British at Three Rivers. Then they retreated southward to Lake Champlain, where they arrived safely, just in time for the July 4 Declaration of Independence.

The possession of Canada had been decided in favour of the British Empire.

North American Geopolitical Economy

The American Republic that won its independence from the British Empire in the late 1770s and early 1780s represented only 13 of the present 50 states of the Union — huddled along the Atlantic coast of America today. The United States of America that won international recognition at the Peace of Versailles in 1783 stretched no further west than the Mississippi River. It did not include Florida, or the southern parts of present-day Alabama and Mississippi, or any of present-day Louisiana. It would not include Texas or California for another two generations. Alaska and Hawaii only became the 49th and 50th states of the Union in 1959.

In a miniaturized version of similar principles, the United Province of Canada that would begin Canada's much longer and more complicated evolution from colony to nation in the 1850s and 1860s included only the southern parts of present-day Quebec and Ontario (or, more accurately perhaps, on the old French understanding of what "Canada" meant, Quebec, Ontario, and significant chunks of present-day Manitoba, Saskatchewan, and Alberta). The original Canadian Confederation of 1867 added only Nova Scotia and New Brunswick. Newfoundland did not become Canada's 10th province until 1949.

In the midst of such similarities, there is at least one intriguing difference between the experience of Canada and the U.S.A. In the U.S. the most easterly, Atlantic-oriented parts of the country are where the country began. In Canada the country began along more central inland water routes. Its most easterly, Atlantic-oriented parts only joined subsequently, like its most westerly, Pacific-oriented parts.

This has various arguable implications for the most northern part of North America today. In 1776 it meant that there was another part of modern Canada that, for its own reasons, declined to become involved in the historic experiment of the American Republic. It was then known as Nova Scotia (the Latin for New Scotland); but it included present-day New Brunswick; and it speaks in history as we understand it today for what were even then known as Prince Edward Island and Newfoundland.

Though the neutral Yankees and the American Loyalists of Nova Scotia joined the Canadian Confederation in 1867, Newfoundland would remain aloof until 1949. For Sam Hunter in the early 20th century, this did not help the inhabitants of the rock in dealing with aggressive U.S. Atlantic fishing interests. The bearded figure in this cartoon is U.S. Senator Henry Cabot Lodge, and the original caption reads: "That boy Bond of Newfoundland seems to have overlooked the fact that I cut a great deal of ice here."

Acadians, Loyalists, & Neutral Yankees

In fact, as in Central Canada, the French were in Atlantic Canada first (and, as everywhere in the New World, the Indians were first of all). Champlain, "the Father of New France," began his first colonizing ventures on the shores of the Bay of Fundy in 1604.

Old Acadia, however, the Atlantic part of the French empire in America, was a highly unstable place. It was a strategic site for transatlantic shipping, peculiarly attractive to attack from the sea, and peculiarly isolated from surrounding territory. Europeans who settled there found it prudent to be politically discreet. From an early date what France claimed as Acadia, England also claimed as Nova Scotia. After generations of recurrent conflict, "the neutral French of Acadia" had officially fallen under British rule by the Treaty of Utrecht in 1713.

What the British called Nova Scotia then became the northern frontier of the Thirteen Colonies on the more southerly Atlantic seaboard, and attracted migrants from New England. The migrations accelerated after 1755, when many French-speaking Acadians were tragically expelled from the region by British imperial officialdom (helping to create, among other things, the Cajuns of modern Louisiana).

The new English-speaking settlers found themselves in a similar position to that of their predecessors. As the 20th century historian John Bartlet Brebner would put it, the neutral French of Acadia were joined by "the neutral Yankees of Nova Scotia."

In 1776 these neutral Yankees in the most northern parts of North America were not so much hostile as remote from and indifferent to the cause of the Continental Congress in Philadelphia. Their natural leaders, insofar as they had any at all, were the British merchants of Halifax. They presided over a fishing economy that had special links with the Channel Islands between England and France across the ocean, and they played a strategic role in imperial trade with the British West Indies. Like the new British fur trade merchants of Canada, they had few interests in standing up boldly for the ideals of the American Patriots.

To resolve any lingering doubts, in March 1776, not long before Benjamin Franklin and his fellow commissioners left Philadelphia for Montreal, the early successes of the Congressional cause in the heart of New England had prompted British forces to evacuate Boston and set sail for Halifax. They did not travel alone.

Political causes never elicit uniform reactions from the people whom they pledge to serve. The American historian Samuel Eliot Morison (with personal roots in the New England of the first half of the 20th century) has estimated that as much as 50% of the population in the Thirteen Colonies was effectively neutral in the American War of Independence, while some 10% remained loyal to the British Crown. Canadian opinion on the subject, as one might expect, tends to place the proportion remaining loyal rather higher.

Regrettably or otherwise, there were no opinion polls in the 18th century. Yet, whatever the ultimate unknowable truth may be, when British forces left Boston for Halifax in March 1776, they took as many as 1,000 American Loyalists with them. The Loyalist migrations into the most northern parts of North America, which would swell in the 1780s (and would be especially important in what is now Atlantic Canada), had begun.

Among many other things, Canada would become a place not just for English-speaking people who were indifferent to the cause of the Continental Congress, but for those who had actively opposed it as well — and for those who believed, in the much later words of the modern Canadian historian Carl Berger, that "republicanism" was "the mother of disobedience, lawlessness and vulgar materialism."

The War of Independence Settlement

Military aid from the Kingdom of France played an important part in the birth of the new American Republic. France was no longer the greatest power of Europe that it had been at the start of the 18th century. But it was strong enough to avenge its still recent loss of Canada (and parts of the Indian subcontinent in South Asia) to the British Empire. Ironically, however, as the increasingly global imperialism of Europe reorganized itself in the late 18th century, in North America the old English Thirteen Colonies left the British Empire, but the old French Canada remained in its embrace.

At the Peace of Versailles in 1783, the British government sacrificed the most southwesterly part of the Canada of the Quebec Act to the interests of making a fresh start with its wayward American children. Though what are now the states of Ohio, Indiana, Michigan, Wisconsin, and Illinois were once a covetously defended territory of the French and Indian fur trade through the St. Lawrence River, they became part of the new United States. Yet most of old French Canada remained intact.

Of more consequence for the longer term, virtually all the then known territory in the most northern part of North America remained in the hands of the British Empire — from Nova Scotia and what is now Atlantic Canada in the east, to the Prince Rupert's Land of the Hudson's Bay Company in what is now Western Canada.

Finally, though no one knew it at the time, when it opted out of the new republic old Nova Scotia (and modern Atlantic Canada at large) in effect opted into a new Canada. The formal decision would not be made for another three generations. But the die had been cast. From the early 17th to the late 18th century, Canada had been the only sizeable and well-rooted alternative to the Thirteen Colonies in North America north of the Gulf of Mexico — and this would count for the future.

The first constitution of the new American republic, known as the Articles of Confederation and taking official effect on March 1, 1781, implicitly recognized the potential significance of Canada's position, and (as a modern Canadian might see it at least) tried to deal with the problem. The document contained 13 different articles, nicely matching the symbolism of the old Thirteen Colonies and the new 13 founding states of the union. Article XI read: "Canada acceding to this confederation, and joining in the measures of the united states, shall be admitted into, and entitled to all the advantages of this union: but no other colony shall be admitted into the same, unless such admission be agreed to by nine states."

Chapter 3

A NEW MOSAIC

The Canada that did not become part of the United States of America in 1776 already had a comparatively long history behind it. In its most distant past Jacques Cartier had sailed up the St. Lawrence River in the early autumn of 1535. At this point the banks of the river were inhabited by Iroquoian Indians, and Cartier had called the place "the province of Canada," after the local Iroquoian word for village.

Though the name Canada evokes the breathtakingly tough and rugged aboriginal wilderness cultures of northern North America, the first people to call themselves Canadians (or, more exactly, *les canadiens*) were the French-speaking European settlers of the lower St. Lawrence valley. Transient fur traders and fishermen were active in the Gulf of St. Lawrence in the 16th century. But permanent French settlement in the valley did not begin until Champlain founded Quebec City in 1608 — just one year after the beginnings of more southerly English settlement in Virginia, and only a dozen years before the *Mayflower* and the start of the more northerly English settlements of New England.

Climate and geography made Canada not at all as hospitable to large-scale European agricultural settlement as the regions further south. Geography and climate quickly lured the French in Canada into the interior of the North American continent.

The crucial industry of early Canada was the French and Indian fur trade. By the middle of the 18th century, some 60,000 French Canadians, strung out along the shore of the St. Lawrence River between Quebec City, Three Rivers, and Montreal, formed an anchor for the trade. They looked east to the Atlantic Ocean and western Europe, where furs were sold for sometimes remarkable profits. They looked west to the Great Lakes, a gateway to the intricate inland waterways of the North American interior, where the fur resource was stored.

Many of the inland waterways were only navigable via the Indian transportation technology of the canoe and portage. To survive buying furs from the Indians in the interior (with trade goods from Europe), you had to become adept at their languages and politics. For some voyageurs the best romance of the wilderness was to marry an Indian. The half-breed native culture of the Canadian Métis became both an important part of Canada's first resource economy, and an extreme expression of multiracialism in early Canadian society.

After a century and a half of growth and development, there were far fewer white people in French Canada than in the English Thirteen Colonies (which had a total population of more than a million people by the middle of the 18th century). In alliance with a wide assortment of Indian nations, however, the French in North America commanded a much vaster sweep of territory.

As early as the 1640s, the Jesuits had built a Roman Catholic mission among the Indians at Huronia in what is now central Ontario. By the 1680s La Salle had travelled from the St. Lawrence valley to the Mississippi River, and then down the Mississippi to the Gulf of Mexico. By the early 1700s Cadillac, earlier a protegé of Count Frontenac, Governor of Canada, had founded Detroit between Lake Erie and Lake Huron. And by the 1740s La Vérendrye had reached the Rocky Mountains in what is now Western Canada.

The empire at its height did not last long, but it was a remarkably far-flung and exotic collection of trading posts, French forts, and Indian villages — located on inland waterways and anchored by the St. Lawrence valley at one end and then, after 1718, by New Orleans at the other. Its most northerly reaches were destined to survive, and continue their development, in a new form.

The Northwest Company & the Golden Age of the Fur Trade

As early as 1713 France had lost most of the Atlantic part of its American territory in Acadia to the British. Then in 1763 it lost Canada to the British, and Louisiana (the region of the lower Mississippi valley) to Spain.

Yet the British Conquest of Canada did not end the Canadian fur trade. The higher management of the business merely shifted from the old ostensibly noble French commercial adventurers, based in the lower St. Lawrence valley, to the new British and Anglo-American merchants of Montreal and Quebec City, based in the lower St. Lawrence valley.

The loss of Louisiana in 1763 was not important. It was already more under the sway of New Orleans than Montreal, and the best furs were to be found in the colder climates of the north. The loss of the most southwesterly parts of Canada (even as defined under the British Quebec Act) at the Peace of Versailles in 1783 was more irksome, but it concentrated the minds of the merchants of Montreal on the more remote Canadian northwest, that La Vérendrye and his Indian guides had begun to open up in the 1740s.

*The greatest prize of the Canadian fur trade was the pelt of the beaver - **castor canadensis**. Long after the golden age of the fur trade had ended, Hunter sometimes used the beaver to depict the typical citizen of Canada in his cartoons. The original caption for this one reads: "and those whose business it is to protect me are the men who set the biggest traps."*

By the end of the American War of Independence in the mid-1780s the Canadian fur trade had come to be dominated by a large but highly decentralized and adventurous business organization, known as the Northwest Company and headquartered in Montreal. It was an enterprise steeped in bold expansionism. In 1793 Alexander Mackenzie, a sometime partner, became the first white man to travel from east to west across the North American continent. He blazed a new trail for the Canadian fur trade, along the inland waterways of the northern North American interior, and he wrote on a rock at the edge of the Pacific Ocean, in vermilion and grease: "Alexander Mackenzie, from Canada, by land."

By the early 1800s the Northwest Company, which socialized at the Beaver Club in Montreal, had brought the Canadian fur trade into its golden age. Though the company itself would disappear into a merger within a few decades, it presided over the birth of the modern east-west transcontinental Canadian economy.

It was also, Harold Innis would write in the 1930s, "the first organization to operate on a continental scale in North America," and in several respects "the forerunner of the present confederation" in Canada today. The modern Bank of Montreal, the oldest Canadian bank still in business, was founded on the profits of the fur trade in the old Northwest.

The Evolving Pluralist Society

In the later 17th century two dissidents from the French fur trade in Canada, Pierre Esprit Radisson and Médard Chouart des Groseilliers, had gone to London, England to seek financing for a new trade in the far north, based not in the St. Lawrence valley but on the sub-Arctic shores of Hudson Bay. This had led to the establishment of the Hudson's Bay Company in 1670.

The Hudson's Bay Company became an English enterprise that competed with the French of the St. Lawrence valley for the trade of the far Northwest. After the Conquest it competed with the Montreal-based Northwest Company. In 1821, as the resource economy of the fur trade in the Great Lakes was giving way to agricultural settlement and a new resource economy of lumbering and wheat, the Northwest Company merged with the Hudson's Bay Company.

The English-speaking presence in what is now Atlantic Canada stretches back still farther. St. John's, Newfoundland was established as a shore base for transient English fishermen as early as 1504. The first European courts of law in the New World were established at Trinity, Newfoundland in 1615.

In the earlier 18th century English-speaking elements in the early Canadian mosaic were strengthened, when the neutral Yankees of Nova Scotia joined the neutral French of Acadia. In the late 18th and early 19th centuries, similar migrants on the westward-bound Anglo-American settlement frontier would be a formative influence in the early development of modern Ontario and, much later, Western Canada.

The United Empire Loyalists (or, in another lexicon, British Tories), who began to move north in numbers at the end of the American War of Independence, played a politically significant role in the late 18th century history of both Atlantic and Central Canada. In 1784 they prompted British imperial official-dom to create the province of New Brunswick in the western half of old Nova Scotia, where Loyalists were particularly numerous.

Under similar pressures, in 1791 old Canada was divided into a predominantly French-speaking eastern part known as Lower Canada (where the French Catholic institutional trappings of the Quebec Act lived on), and a predominantly English-speaking western part known as Upper Canada (which was given English civil law and, to begin with at least, an Anglican Protestant ruling oligarchy). Though perhaps five times as many Loyalists migrated to old Nova Scotia as to what is now Central Canada, they might also be said to have prompted the creation of modern Ontario and Quebec.

Both the Loyalists and the neutral Yankees who moved north were predominantly English-speaking, but not uniformly white Anglo-Saxon Protestant. Among the Loyalists of early modern Ontario were the pro-British factions of the Six Nations Iroquois from northern and western New York. Some among both Loyalists and neutral Yankees were of German or other continental European descent. And some brought black slaves to both Nova Scotia and Ontario (virtually all of whom would be, under the urgings of British imperial officialdom, at least legally liberated by the early 19th century).

By the 1820s a new wave of British immigration to what is now Canada (as well as the United States) was in progress. It brought Scotch, Irish, and Welsh as well as English, Catholics along with Protestants, and even some Jews. Much, much farther back in time, the Indians (who would remain visible longer in Canada than in the United States, and are still proportionately more numerous in Canada today) had themselves originally migrated to the New World from Asia.

Another Kind of Democratic Vista

By the early 19th century Canada had become a notably heterogeneous place. Economically it had much to do with the global trading network of the British Empire. Yet culturally it had already reached a point described much later in a mid-20th century Canadian political science textbook, which observed that the country's "continued existence has been largely experimental, and its future depends chiefly on the capacity of the people to tolerate marked dissimilarities and yet cultivate mutual interests and loyalties. If this cannot be done in a democratic, New World environment, it cannot be done anywhere."

In the early 19th century, the most northern part of North America could not be described as democratic. After the precedents of the British mother country, the language of democracy in "British North America" would restrain itself until the late 19th century.

Even British North America in the far north, however, was in North America, not Europe. Its democratic revolution — in a characteristically muted style — took place after that of the United States, but still before that of the

United Kingdom. For all practical domestic purposes, what is now Canada had won its own democratic governments by the middle of the 19th century.

Even in Canada the achievement of democracy involved some violent conflict. It came in two somewhat contrasting bursts, separated by a quarter of a century, and it was not in either case dramatically bloody. Yet during the first half of the 19th century Indians, French-speaking people, and English-speaking people (mostly white, but a few black as well) risked and in some cases gave their lives for what would very gradually become a somewhat complicated new country.

Following pragmatic channels, a modern democratic Canadian people — extending and enriching the heritage of *les canadiens* in the old lower St. Lawrence valley — began to struggle haphazardly into existence. Much later, in the late 1960s, the Canadian literary critic Northrop Frye would capture some of the particular end result when he wrote: "democracy has to do with majority rule and not merely with enduring the tyranny of organized minorities. It would not be conservative or radical in its direction, but both at once."

War Along the Border

In one view of political reality in the early 19th century, any serious modern Canadian democracy logically implied annexation to the still quite novel U.S.A. — the 19th century laboratory of what the French aristocrat Alexis de Tocqueville would celebrate as *Democracy in America* in the 1830s. Though this view conveniently ignored the peculiar institutions of the black slaveholding American South, it was only common sense to many in rapidly expanding parts of the U.S. Northeast and (especially) the new U.S. Midwest.

The closest approximation to a major historical event that might be said to have spelled at least the beginning of the end for the American annexationist view of the Canadian democratic future is the War of 1812, fought between a still very youthful United States of America and the United Kingdom of Great Britain and Ireland, and its empire overseas.

The War of 1812 (or, more exactly, 1812-1814) has a place in the tender annals of early American as well as early Canadian patriotism. As recently as the 1920s Wisconsin was only one of various U.S. states to pass laws declaring: "No history or other textbook shall be adopted for use...which falsifies the facts regarding the War of Independence, the War of 1812, or defames our nation's founders."

From a Canadian standpoint, the crux of the war is that it included a U.S. invasion of Canada which failed (or might even be said to have been defeated), just like the Continental Congress's earlier failed invasion of the Montreal and Quebec City regions in 1775-1776.

A key element in the background to the invasion was the northwesterly expansion of the Anglo-American settlement frontier in the late 18th and early 19th centuries. This had brought into the new predominantly English-speaking British Upper Canada (created to accommodate the Loyalist migrations of the

1780s) another wave of the same neutral Yankees who had moved into Nova Scotia a generation or more before (or who would start to move into the Mexican province of Texas a generation or so later).

On the eve of the War of 1812 these new neutral Yankees in Southern Ontario outnumbered the slightly older Loyalists: on one sometimes contested estimate — nonetheless reported by Gerald Craig, the modern historian of old Upper Canada — by as much as four to one. Yet, though invasion attempts at various points by U.S. forces made some headway in 1813, they were finally turned back by heterogeneous assortments of old Loyalist militiamen, Indian allies of the Crown, feisty fur traders, loyal blacks (grateful for even merely legal liberation from slavery), a few French Canadians, and (above all else) seasoned professional soldiers of the British Empire.

A few neutral Yankee frontier migrants left Upper Canada on the eve of the war, and joined invading U.S. forces as irregulars, in some cases out to settle old private scores. For the most part, however, on both sides of the border militia regiments were dominated by family farmers, who were eager to return to their families alive, and did their best to avoid serious fighting. At one point in the Battle of Queenston Heights the New York militia, recalling that it was not required to fight outside its own state, declined to accept an order from its leaders to cross the Niagara River and attack "the British" on the other side.

In the shortest term the defeat of the attempted American invasion of Canada in the War of 1812 was a victory for the most conservative forces in both the Canada and the wider British North America of the early 19th century. Even in the longest term, it helped ensure that the ultimate Canadian democratic rule of the majority would be, as Northrop Frye would much later put it, both conservative and radical at once.

At the same time, the war was also a crucible for nascent popular Canadian sentiments that would finally transcend polarizations between conservatives and radicals — and would embrace an English as well as a French-speaking people. Before 1812 Canadian was still largely a term reserved for French Roman Catholics, in what is now Quebec and in the more westerly fur trade interior of the Great Lakes. After 1815 there would be both French-speaking "*Canadiens*" and English-speaking "Canadians."

Economic Development & Political Change

Somewhat ironically, the peaceful conclusion to the War of 1812 gradually stimulated British North American trade relationships and rivalries with the U.S.A. Along with a new east-west Canadian political future, the 1820s ushered in old north-south economic pressures and new commercial opportunities, earlier offset or thwarted by the long period of British-American hostility that had followed the War of Independence.

Moreover, by the early 19th century Canada had begun to evolve beyond the earlier bastion of the fur trade, with an Atlantic fishery to its east. British North America's own variation on the continental Anglo-American agricultural

In a somewhat complicated and even ironic sense, the War of 1812 might be said to mark the earliest beginnings of a late 19th and early 20th century cartoon character known as Jack or sometimes Johnny Canuck — another image of the typical Canadian, analogous to Uncle Sam in the U.S. and John Bull in the U.K. Hunter was far from the only cartoonist to use the character, but he drew him with a special flair.

settlement frontier (a phenomenon that, socially and economically, included even the Loyalist migrations of the 1780s) was rising. In both Atlantic Canada and French and English Central Canada the needs of the British Royal Navy had stimulated a new northern lumbering industry, that would soon find fresh opportunities in the buoyant if often erratic markets of a rapidly growing American Republic.

Economic development helped create new pressures for political change. They pointed in at least some of the directions suggested by de Tocqueville's democracy in America, whose influence soared in the U.S. itself during Andrew Jackson's presidency from 1828 to 1836 (and, for that matter, had some European parallels in the movement that inspired the first Reform Act of 1832 in the United Kingdom).

In both Upper and Lower Canada the status of British Tory ruling oligarchies, fostered by the mercantile and Loyalist migrations of the late 18th century, was initially strengthened by the War of 1812. Parallel developments took place in what is now Atlantic Canada.

Though opposed on principle to popular self-government, the Tory oligarchs had some high-minded ambitions of their own. Beginning a critique of the American dream that would be raised to its full profundity by the Red Tory political philosopher George Grant about a century and a half later, John Beverley Robinson, noble Chief Justice of Upper Canada (and a descendant of the loyal Virginia planter aristocracy), declared: "trade and revenue are not all that constitute the happiness of a people...by endangering other objects in the hope of benefiting these, we may find that we have purchased even wealth at too high a price."

By the later 1820s, however, factions of Reformers more unreservedly enthusiastic about economic growth and popular self-government in the New World had arisen in all parts of British North America. In English-speaking settlements they drew on the frontier ethos of the neutral Yankees, and the aspirations of immigrant British levellers and democrats. In the still overwhelmingly French Catholic St. Lawrence valley, they also raised voices on behalf of older Canadians who, despite the Quebec Act, remained a restless, conquered people.

Conflict between Tories and Reformers reached a peak in the Canadian Rebellions of 1837. In predominantly French-speaking Lower Canada the rebel *Patriotes* were led by Louis Joseph Papineau, an old seigneur's son inspired by the democratic ideals that de Tocqueville had recently written about, and by the dream of a French republic in the North American New World. In predominantly English-speaking Upper Canada rather less vigorous forces of armed rebellion were inspired by "The Firebrand", William Lyon Mackenzie — a radical Reformer born in Scotland, with at least some irascible political enthusiasms for "the American model."

On the face of things, the rebellions were far from successful. Both Papineau and Mackenzie escaped to the United States. Mackenzie landed in Buffalo, New York, where he was initially lionized by American sympathizers. Then, in 1838, several haphazard American Patriot invasions of Upper Canada proved even less successful than the Rebellion of 1837. A few other radical Reformers went into exile in the U.S.; some in Lower Canada lost property (for which there would later be public compensation); in Upper Canada Samuel Lount and Peter Mathews were hanged for treason.

Yet by 1839 it had become clear that, though Papineau and Mackenzie had not come at all close to achieving their own particular objectives, they had helped convince British imperial officialdom that change in the government of the Empire's remaining North American colonies was overdue. Canada would not have the kind of democracy in America that prevailed in the U.S.A., but it would have a democracy of its own.

It would take another decade for the process of change to reach its ultimate fruition: but on the moderately bloodstained battlefields of 1837 the Canadian democratic tradition of moderation and compromise had begun to set down roots.

Chapter 4

THE FIRST FREE TRADE TREATY

A lmost a dozen years after the earliest fighting of 1837, on the evening of April 25, 1849, the first democratic assembly of The United Province of Canada was working into the night inside its colonial parliament building in downtown Montreal. Around 9 PM the elected members, dominated by an alliance of French and English Reformers, heard an angry mob on the street outside. Shortly after, stones shattered the building's high glass windows.

Then, the late 20th century Canadian historian Jacques Monet tells us, "the door burst open and Tory rioters flooded into the room, smashing furniture and breaking lights. In the confusion was heard a shout of warning — Fire!" Determined to remain calm , the members promptly passed a formal motion of adjournment and filed out of the now burning building to safety.

The incident marked the peak of the last virulent protest against the rise of democratic self-government on the British parliamentary model, in the 19th century colony of Canada. Characteristically, the protest came from within the colony, and not from the mother country .

Its most long-lasting effect was to ensure that Montreal, where the various political and cultural solitudes of Canada lived in closest proximity, would never again be a capital city for any Canadian government. For most of the remainder of its short, stormy existence, the capital of the United Province of Canada would rotate between Quebec City, the old French Canadian capital on the lower St. Lawrence River, and Toronto, the rising new English Canadian western frontier metropolis in the heart of the old fur trade interior.

The United Province itself, established in 1841, had been British imperial officialdom's response to the Rebellions of 1837.

Originally, it was intended to bring somewhat less than so-called responsible government — the moderate colonial Reformer's adaptation of British parliamentary principles to the democratic aspirations of the New World. In a reversal of the Quebec Act of 1774, it was also intended to promote the gradual anglicization of French Canada, through the union of the old predominantly French Lower Canada and the predominantly English Upper Canada (or, broadly, modern Quebec and Ontario). Only in this way, officials of the mid-19th century British Empire had come to conclude, could the strong French-English antagonism that had marked the Rebellion in Lower Canada be resolved.

In fact, during the first half of its short quarter-century lifetime the United Province became an incubator for an even stronger French and English Canadian Reform alliance, with rather different ideas of its own. By 1848 (also a year of revolution in continental Europe, that produced the first democratic assembly of the Second French Republic), the alliance had won full democratic self-government in domestic affairs, and reaffirmed the rights and privileges of French-speaking Roman Catholics in the earliest beginnings of a new Canadian state.

It was, in effect, co-premiered by Louis Hippolyte Lafontaine of Montreal in Canada East and Robert Baldwin of Toronto in Canada West. Lafontaine had been a somewhat more moderate follower of Papineau in the 1830s. Baldwin had been a distinctly more moderate colleague of Mackenzie's, who disagreed with the Firebrand both about the resort to violence in 1837 and the impossibility of attaining Reform objectives within the framework of the British Empire.

Though he set some of his children to the task, Baldwin himself never quite managed to learn French. But he and Lafontaine (who, like most French Canadian leaders since the Conquest, spoke both French and English) became close personal as well as political friends. Of much greater consequence for the future, they offered at least the beginnings of an answer to a recurrent question for any modern Canadian democracy: how can French-speaking and English-speaking people combine in a single national political system?

Imperial Free Trade

The achievement of Lafontaine and Baldwin in the United Province of Canada was facilitated by dramatic changes in the economic structure of the British Empire during the decade of the 1840s.

More than two generations before, Adam Smith in Edinburgh had launched the new academic gospel of economics, with the publication of *The Wealth of Nations* in 1776 (the same year as the American Declaration of Independence). Among other things, the gospel proclaimed that trade barriers between nations had the ultimate effect of reducing profits and increasing prices inside each nation.

Seventy years later, in 1846, the United Kingdom repealed its historic "Corn Laws," and began to dismantle the ancient protected trading system of the British Empire, in favour of a bold new policy of imperial free trade. The "mercantilist" empire that had begun to take shape under Oliver Cromwell's English Commonwealth of the mid 17th century had been based on a system of tariffs or duties on agricultural and other products, navigation laws, and related policies, through which the British government closely regulated trade between the mother country, its growing list of overseas colonies, and foreign countries. In the new free-trading empire of the mid 19th century, the British government would take a back seat to the unregulated market forces of an expanding international economy.

For all the remaining British North American colonies, this had the benign effect of removing a crucial objection to colonial self-government in the eyes of imperial administrators. There was no longer a need to worry that colonial democracy might thwart effective central management of the protected imperial trading system.

Yet imperial free trade also had less benign economic impacts. Since even before the American War of Independence, the British merchants of both Halifax and Montreal had built their businesses on the protected imperial British trading system. By the middle of the 19th century the merchants of Montreal had left the old resource industry of the fur trade for the new resource industries of lumbering and wheat. The old canoe and portage interior transportation system of the Indians had been enriched by a new system of European-engineered St. Lawrence River and Great Lakes canals. But the structure of the Canadian economy still leaned on protected relationships with imperial markets that had been established after the British Conquest of Canada in the 18th century.

Moreover, the rapidly growing United States of America saw no advantage in any bold gestures toward free trade on its own part. It was increasingly protectionist, under the rising influence of the neo-mercantilist "American System" originally devised by Henry Clay . British Empire free trade meant that U.S. business would have the same access to the markets of the Empire as Canadian business, while Canada still faced tariff and other trade barriers when it sold into the markets of the U.S.A.

Under these circumstances, it was thought, Canadian business could not hope to remain competitive. In the late 1840s, international economic life went through a tough adjustment process in the wake of British Empire free trade. Some among the British merchants of Montreal swallowed their ancient professions of loyalty. They drew up a petition urging the kind of union of Canada and the United States that Benjamin Franklin and his colleagues from Philadelphia had proposed more than 70 years before.

The solution of the French and English Reform alliance in the United Province of Canada was more in keeping with the aspirations of party politicians who were laying the earliest foundations of a new democracy in the north of North America. After some five years of erratic negotiations with reluctant branches of the American government, it led to the first free trade agreement between Canada and the United States — the Reciprocity Treaty of 1854, which provided for free trade in resource products between the United States of America and all the colonies of British North America.

The Reciprocity Treaty of 1854

Domestic self-government and colonial democracy still implied strong imperial supervision in external relations. The chief negotiator of the Reciprocity Treaty of 1854 was Lord Elgin, appointed British imperial Governor of the United Province of Canada. At the same time, by the unwritten terms of the agreement struck in 1848, Elgin had bound himself to pay close heed to whatever advice was offered by his French and English Reform cabinet even on such matters as trade policy, broadly on the model of a colonial constitutional monarch.

Lafontaine and Baldwin had begun reciprocity negotiations with the United States in 1849. Baldwin's side of the alliance in particular spoke not just for the merchants of Montreal, but also for a rising mercantile community in Toronto with special interests in American trade.

The rapidly growing cities south of the Great Lakes were providing warm markets for the lumber and wheat of a bubbling "Canada West," that was also growing very rapidly itself. Even without a trade agreement, Toronto business was developing extensive American connections, and ties to New York City financial interests that rivaled its ties to British financial interests based in Montreal.

By 1851 Lafontaine and Baldwin were older men who had spent more than a quarter of a century in the unusually bitter wars of Canadian politics in the 1820s, 1830s, and 1840s. Though they would continue their personal friendship, they jointly retired from public life. The leadership of the French and English Reform alliance passed to two longstanding colleagues, Francis Hincks and Augustin-Norbert Morin.

Hincks had run a pro-Reform Bank of the People in Toronto during the 1830s, and had subsequently served as finance minister under Lafontaine and Baldwin. Even in this setting, free trade in resource products with the United States had been Hincks's particular enthusiasm, and he was in Washington with Lord Elgin for the final successful negotiations in 1854.

It had taken time, skill, luck, and concessions to coax a quite cool American federal government into a reciprocity treaty. Many U.S. politicians felt that if the British North American colonies wanted free trade with the United States they should simply join the republic, as some among the merchants of Montreal had proposed. Getting an agreement finally required: a promise of free American access to the St. Lawrence River waterway and the British Atlantic fisheries; the votes of Southern U.S. Senators, who believed Lord Elgin's argument that free trade would actually thwart prospects of the far northern colonies' applying to join the Union, and upsetting its delicate pre-Civil War balance between free and slave states; and even periodic gentle displays of military might from what was still the greatest empire since Rome.

Yet after some five years of negotiation the new, emerging Canadian democracy would have, for a while at least, the best of both worlds. It would develop in its own way politically, and at the same time participate fully in the rapidly expanding economy of the North American continent.

The figure in the centre is not Lord Elgin but Lord Grey (or, more strictly, "Earl Grey, G.C.M.G." - donor of Canadian football's Grey Cup). Though he became Governor General of Canada almost exactly half a century after the Reciprocity Treaty of 1854, his message in this Sam Hunter cartoon also reflects the thrust of imperial policy for British North America in the optimistic early years of British Empire free trade: "Uncle Sam, shake hands with Jack Canuck. Now you two blades can settle your business without troubling the old gentleman." (The old gentleman is John Bull himself, off in the left-hand corner of the drawing.)

The British Atlantic Provinces Before Confederation

It was a milestone on the road to the Confederation of 1867 that, along with the United Province of Canada, the British Atlantic provinces of Nova Scotia, New Brunswick, Prince Edward Island, and Newfoundland were also part of the Reciprocity Treaty of 1854.

Similarly, the 1850s mark the real beginnings of the railway age in the most northern part of North America. Some new railroads linked various parts of British North America up with various parts of the U.S.A. Yet another of Francis Hincks's enthusiasms in the early 1850s was an Intercolonial Railway, that would eventually link the United Province with the British Atlantic provinces on its eastern frontiers.

Ordinary life in the Atlantic provinces remained quite remote from ordinary life in the United Province of Canada. But then ordinary life in the predominantly French-speaking eastern section of the United Province also remained quite remote from ordinary life in its predominantly English-speaking western section. Moreover, the Atlantic provinces had their own residual French fact — most notably among the surviving heirs of old Acadia concentrated in New Brunswick. And, as in United Canada, on the rugged seacoasts of the British North American Maritimes the 1840s had brought colonial self-government, and new democratic ambitions.

The region's leading apostle of colonial democracy was Joseph Howe — the "Tribune of Nova Scotia" (or, in the language of his late 20th century biographer, the "Conservative Reformer"). Early in 1848, under Howe's guidance — and in tandem with developments in the British colony of Canada, the British colony of Nova Scotia lived through its own quiet and orderly democratic revolution. In the assembly at Province House in Halifax the Reformers voted the Tory oligarchs out of office, and installed a government of their own, with a cabinet dominated by Howe, J.B. Uniacke, and William Frederick DesBarres.

Howe was particularly proud of the revolution's extreme moderation. Nova Scotia's democratic transformation was "elevated, intelligent, peaceful.... She shed no blood, like Canada." She also set the pace for even more moderate transformations in the other three Atlantic provinces: in 1851 in Prince Edward Island, in 1854 in New Brunswick, and in 1855 in Newfoundland.

At this point the new democratic politicians of the region were seeing their political future more in some form of Maritime union, rather than union with the United Province of Canada.

Howe himself felt that what had by the early 1850s become an astoundingly buoyant economic boom in the United Province owed much to the political union of the old Lower and Upper Canada. But he envisioned bringing a similar prosperity to Nova Scotia through political union with New Brunswick, Newfoundland, and Prince Edward Island. And when he talked about promoting "the honor, the prosperity, and elevation, of our country," he still meant Nova Scotia alone.

In the new era brought on by British Empire free trade, however, all the parts of British North America in the far north were following common trends.

By the mid-1850s the haphazard path of modern Canadian history begins to show the future of Atlantic Canada, emerging more clearly from the quiet decisions of surviving Acadians, British fishermen, neutral Yankees, and American Loyalists in 1776.

Early Western Canada

By the 1850s the haphazard path of modern Canadian history also begins to show the future of Western Canada: site of the last sunset of the ancient British, French, and Indian fur trade in the 19th century.

The ties of what was then known as the British Northwest with the Canada of the St. Lawrence River and the Great Lakes stretched back to La Vérendrye and the French regime. They had been expanded by Alexander Mackenzie and the Northwest Company in the 1790s and early 1800s.

In 1811 the British philanthropist Lord Selkirk, undaunted by two earlier failed attempts to establish colonies of Scottish crofters and Irish cotters in Prince Edward Island and Upper Canada, had acquired a grant of 120,000 square miles of land along the Red River from the Hudson's Bay Company. A few months after the start of the War of 1812, Selkirk's agent, Miles Macdonnell, established a settlement of Scottish and Irish labourers, a mile below a Northwest Company fur trading post at the confluence of the Red and Assiniboine Rivers, in what is now Winnipeg, Manitoba.

For more than a generation the settlement struggled in a world still dominated by French and English fur traders, Métis, and Indians, all still eager to defend the final refuge of the romantic wilderness commerce in the far north. Like the fur traders and the Métis and the Indians, for years Selkirk's colonists depended on the prairie buffalo hunt for much of their food supply.

By the 1850s, however, even life in the romantic Northwest had begun to glimpse more settled new horizons. In 1849 the U.S. federal government established the Territory of Minnesota to the south of the Red River settlement. The Anglo-American agricultural frontier that had earlier spilled over into what is now Southern Ontario, was spilling over into what is now Manitoba.

Back east the old fur merchants of Montreal were not too much more than a memory. Even with the north-south promptings of the Reciprocity Treaty of 1854, however, some among the new wheat and lumber merchants in Montreal, and especially in the rising inland Great Lakes metropolis of Toronto, were reviving the fur-trade vision of a transcontinental east-west commerce in the most northern part of North America.

In 1856 George Brown, founder of the Toronto *Globe* and a rapidly rising star in a new, more radical English Canadian Reform firmament, advised his readers: "Let the merchants of Toronto consider, that if their city is ever to be made really great — if it is ever to rise above the rank of a fifth rate American town — it must be by the development of the great British territory lying to the north and west." The next year a detachment of Royal Canadian Rifles was sent to the Red River district, to bring some order to the incursions of the Anglo-American frontier.

In 1857 the democratic colonial government of United Canada also sent the engineer S.J. Dawson and Henry Youle Hind, a Toronto professor of chemistry and geology, into the Northwest on a mission of exploration. The British imperial government dispatched a parallel expedition under Captain John Palliser. These exploring parties, which confirmed that there was some genuine potential for agricultural settlement on the more southerly prairies of the region, were soon followed by an advance guard of English Canadian settlers from what is now Southern Ontario. In 1859 William Buckingham and William Coldwell, former employees of George Brown's *Globe* in Toronto, moved to the Winnipeg area and established a newspaper known as the *Nor' Wester*.

Back in the mother country a select committee of the British House of Commons studied the future of the Northwest. It recommended that the way be cleared for the ultimate acquisition of the Red and Saskatchewan River valleys by the United Province of Canada. It also recommended that crown colonies be created on Vancouver Island and on the Northwest Pacific slope.

Movement in this last direction had begun in 1849, when the Hudson's Bay Company had been granted Vancouver Island, on the condition that it establish "settlements of British subjects thereon within five years."

Here too an exotic Pacific branch of the Anglo-American frontier (already poised to absorb large chunks of Mexico) had been spilling over the boundary between the U.S.A. and the British territories of the far north — itself only finally resolved by the Oregon Treaty of 1846. Following the recommendation of the select committee in the mother country, in 1858 the crown colony of British Columbia was created on the Northwest Pacific slope.

In 1866 British Columbia would absorb the separate colony of Vancouver Island, and mark the beginning of the end for the domination of the fur trade and the Hudson's Bay Company, even in the old British Northwest.

Cultural Impacts of Free Trade

British imperial impulses, as well as embryonic Canadian national ambitions, were mixed in with the Canadian expansionist mood of the 1850s — symbolized at one end by Francis Hincks's schemes for an Intercolonial Railway to the Atlantic provinces, and at the other by Dawson and Hind's western journey of exploration in 1857. Yet in the late 20th century it is hard not to notice that the mood also took shape in the context of the Reciprocity Treaty of 1854.

The treaty provided for free trade between the U.S.A. and the British North American colonies in resource products only (fish, lumber, wheat, and even furs). Though it can be said to have mildly stimulated infant northern industry in a more general way, it had no direct impact on such fledgling manufacturers as the farm machinery makers Daniel Massey and Allanson Harris, in what was still not quite yet called Southern Ontario.

Yet it did help give a haphazardly emerging modern Canadian political community its own experience of what was perhaps the greatest burst of North American economic expansionism and democratic optimism — what the English writer George Orwell would much later call "the golden age of America...when wealth and opportunity seemed limitless, and human beings felt free, indeed *were* free, as they had never been before and may not be again for centuries."

There was, it seems clear enough, some increase in American cultural influence in Canada as a result of the treaty. But American cultural influence had also been a fact of life in the British North American colonies (and particularly in the predominantly English-speaking ones) long before the treaty was signed.

In Lower Canada it was thwarted though not altogether repulsed by the French language and the Roman Catholic Church. Elsewhere it was offset somewhat by the red military coats, public institutions, public officials, and recent metropolitan migrants of the British Empire, or even, at the edges of settlement frontiers, by the all too quickly fading nobilities of the Indian allies of the Crown.

Moreover, by 1850 there were more than 23 million people living in the American Republic, and less than 2.5 million in all the British North American colonies. Even if anyone had been interested, cultural aspirations that were becoming economically realistic for the much larger place were still beyond the reach of the smaller one.

In 1850 Henry Thoreau, the "transcendental economist" of Concord, Massachusetts, took a trip up north and made some notes, later published as *A Yankee in Canada*. He was impressed by the Church of Notre Dame in Montreal, "said to be the largest ecclesiastical structure in North America." He was struck as well by the ubiquity of British soldiers, whom "the inhabitants evidently rely on...in a great measure for music and entertainment."

He felt that at least the Roman Catholics of French Canada were "capable of reverence," while "we Yankees are a people in whom this sentiment has nearly died out." Montreal, Canada's largest city, was "growing fast like a small New York." The names of its public squares "reminded you of Paris...and you felt as if a French revolution might break out any moment." But he also reported: "I inquired at a principal bookstore for books published in Montreal. They said that there were none but schoolbooks and the like; they got their books from the States."

American Political Culture & Canadian Politics

There was, however, another side to the coin; and this side would count the most for the future. Ironically enough, the influence of American political culture in the 1850s also helped set the United Province of Canada firmly on the road to the wider Canadian Confederation of 1867.

In the predominantly English-speaking western section of the Province the final achievement of colonial democracy, and the new enthusiasm for doing

U.S. influence on Canada during the reciprocity or free trade era of 1854-1866 had precedents in the past, and it would echo into the future, even without a free trade agreement. This Hunter cartoon from a generation later shows Uncle Sam happily influencing Ontario Premier Oliver Mowat and the federal Liberal politician John Charlton — both of whom would support unsuccessful efforts to negotiate a second Canadian reciprocity treaty with the United States.

business with the United States, helped prompt a great rise in the political fortunes of the more radical strains in the Reform movement. Mackenzie and other leaders of the 1837 Rebellion returned from exile south of the border, in the midst of new political enthusiasms for the American model.

Though now old men who could no longer lead, they helped inspire the radical Reform faction that dubbed itself the "Clear Grits" — lodged with particular strength in the Great Lakes peninsula of modern southwestern Ontario (which had much in common with the booming agricultural frontier of the American Midwest). The Clear Grits established a Toronto newspaper called *The North American*, and vigorously pressed for measures that would bring Lafontaine and Baldwin's reforms much closer to de Tocqueville's ideals of democracy in America.

In the interests of "the British connexion" that more than a few English and even some French Canadians still thought important (for one reason or another), by the late 1850s George Brown and his *Globe* had managed to tame the Clear Grits , through a skillful weaving of enthusiasms for high finance in New York City, the Canadian variation on "the rural population, the reading population who rule in the United States," and the liberal cosmopolitanism of the British Empire in the new era of imperial free trade.

Yet even the moderating skills of George Brown could not prevent the new Grit Reform agenda from rubbing against majority sentiment in the predominantly French-speaking eastern section of the United Province of Canada. As in the somewhat different though related case of Benjamin Franklin and his colleagues in 1776, a key stumbling block was the enormous popular influence of the Roman Catholic clergy in the continuing survival of a distinctive French Canadian culture. For George Brown old Lower Canada was in the grip of a "Priestocracy," almost as offensive as the "Slavocracy" that ruled in the American South.

Brown's British Empire moderation of the Clear Grit program did ultimately make him the dominant political leader in the predominantly English-speaking western section of the United Province. But his preferred French-speaking allies in the eastern section were the moderately anti-clerical adherents of a new French radical Reform faction known as "Les Rouges," led by Antoine-Aimé Dorion who (as the 20th century English Canadian historian J.M.S. Careless has put it) "dreamed rosily of a French democratic nation within the republican sisterhood of the American states."

The French Catholic clergy would not accept Dorion, and their influence was such that he could never manage more than a slim minority of French Canadian electoral support. The upshot was that the French and English Reform alliance could no longer form governments for the United Province as a whole.

The Confederation of 1867

The ultimate beneficiaries of North American radicalization in the English Canadian Reform movement were George-Etienne Cartier and John A. Macdonald. Cartier was an urbane, Montreal business lawyer leading a new conservative faction of French "Bleus," that won the blessings of the Catholic clergy. Macdonald was an immensely shrewd heir of the Upper Canadian Tory oligarchs from "the loyal old town of Kingston," Canada West, who had a legendary capacity for alcohol, and who understood how English conservatives ought to trim their sails in the new colonial democracy.

Even this so-called Liberal-Conservative combination, however, could not form durable majority governments within the framework of the United Province itself. Just as Brown and Dorion stumbled over their lack of French support in the east, Cartier and Macdonald were typically hard pressed for English support in the west.

From the mid-1850s to the mid-1860s the new democracy of the United Province of Canada went through 10 different governments in as many years. By the early 1860s it had become clear that a genuinely democratic union of French and English Canadians was politically unworkable.

The practical solution was a new Confederation that gave each of the old provinces of Upper and Lower Canada its own regional or provincial government for cultural and related purposes, while retaining a federal government for common political and economic purposes — a variation on the model of the great republic to the south. To keep faith with the expansionist mood of the 1850s, the new Confederation would also assume responsibility for the old British Northwest from the Hudson's Bay Company, and invite the participa-

Despite Uncle Sam's influence and the Reciprocity Treaty of 1854, the Canadian beaver took a step forward into his own future with the Confederation of 1867. Hunter's cartoon here, addressed to a revival of the issue in the early 20th century, is apt enough. The somewhat smug-looking beaver is saying: "I may have a very fresh appearance and a large inviting tail but he's not going to salt me this season."

tion of the British Atlantic provinces and the new colony of British Columbia on the Pacific coast.

It would be Macdonald and Cartier's Liberal-Conservative coalition (whose very name highlights the growing richness of the still youthful tradition of compromise) that would ultimately make the new Confederation work. An early enthusiast, and Macdonald supporter, had been Alexander Tilloch Galt, political friend to the merchants of Montreal. At the same time, it was George Brown, visionary Reform publicist for the merchants of Toronto, who proposed the concept in its final form, in the late spring of 1864. Only a few years before, while arguing that Canada's sympathies belonged with the North not the South in the American Civil War, Brown had informed the readers of the *Globe*: "We too are Americans. On us, as well as on them, lies the duty of preserving the honour of the continent. On us, as on them, rests the noble trust of shielding free institutions."

The ensuing Canadian Confederation debates began during the late summer of 1864 at Charlottetown, Prince Edward Island, formally tacked on to a conference on the potential for union among the British Atlantic provinces. In the end, on July 1, 1867 — three days before the traditional date for the celebration of the birth of the American Republic — the United Province of Canada and the Provinces of Nova Scotia and New Brunswick officially created "The Dominion of Canada," the first self-governing, colonial democratic state in the British Empire.

With adjustments in many new directions, the Canada of the French and the Indians in the 17th and 18th centuries would survive the age of progress in the 19th century, and go on to meet the 20th-century age of anxiety.

Chapter 5

THE NATIONAL POLICY

AccORDING to the early Canadian nationalist William Caniff, the Canadian Confederation of 1867 would not have been possible if the Reciprocity Treaty of 1854 between the United States of America and the British North American colonies had remained in effect. This is only one man's opinion, and it must at least be set beside the simple truth that Canadian politicians who strongly supported the Reciprocity Treaty with the United States also played important roles in designing and promoting the 1867 Confederation.

The treaty of 1854, however, did provide for abrogation by either party after an initial period of 10 years. In 1866, not long after the initial period had expired, the government of the United States abrogated the treaty. Even if William Caniff is completely wrong, it is also a simple truth that American abrogation of the Reciprocity Treaty did help keep some more reluctant partners at the Confederation bargaining table.

The customary explanation of the American abrogation of the Reciprocity Treaty in 1866 stresses resentment in Washington over British Empire and British North American conservative sentiment for the vanquished Confederacy of the South in the American Civil War. This points to an even more important external influence on the Canadian Confederation of 1867. The Civil War began in 1860 and did not end until 1865 — the year after George Brown made the decisive proposal which began the Confederation debates among the British Atlantic provinces and the United Province of Canada.

From one angle, the American Civil War is the great progressive act of the American Republic. Black America would not really begin its liberation for another century. But the war put an end to slavery as a legal institution in any part of the United States. It erased the most obvious blot on the new Republic's historic pretensions as a model for a new kind of democratic political system.

From another angle, as Abraham Lincoln himself urged, the war was not fundamentally about eliminating black slavery. A century later (in the 1960s)

Like many Americans, in the 1930s Sam Hunter linked the Civil War legacies of Abraham Lincoln with Franklin Roosevelt and the New Deal. Yet "Father Abraham" was a Republican not a Democrat. In the 1980s the self-confessed "disturbing presence on the American scene," Gore Vidal, has urged that Lincoln was more concerned with perfecting the American Union than abolishing slavery. Vidal has also written: "nothing that Shakespeare ever invented was to equal Lincoln's invention of himself, and in the process, us." Whatever the case, in the late 19th century the new United States of America that Abraham Lincoln set in motion did not have much use for the new Canadian Confederation on its northern frontier.

the Harvard professor Barrington Moore Jr. would declare ("after much uncertainty") that it was in fact "the last revolutionary offensive on the part of what one might legitimately call urban or bourgeois capitalist democracy." More simply, the defeat of the South cleared the way for the triumph of the industrial revolution in America, and the ultimate carrying of this revolution to heights as yet unfathomed in its European birthplace.

The American Civil War was also the first modern war of mass destruction, driven by the first wave of the new industrial technology (including hot-air balloons — the advance guard of modern air travel). It forged a new American identity, in the bloody crucible of a "brothers' war": thin, hard, centralizing, relentlessly expansionary, and profoundly nationalistic.

The new identity turned away from de Tocqueville's fundamentally decentralized democracy in the America of the 1830s, with its stress on the "necessity of examining the condition of the states before that of the union at large." The victorious Republican party of Abraham Lincoln also deeply believed in high tariffs as a lever for American industrial expansion, in the tradition of Henry Clay and the American System.

In such an ardently protectionist and more uniform American union there could be no place for a free trade treaty with the British North American colonies. The new American national mood cast a harsh light as well on the new Canadian Confederation. Having just fought the first war of mass destruction in history to prevent the creation of a reactionary new confederacy in the American South, the "Radical Republican" heirs of Abraham Lincoln did not look kindly on the creation of what they saw as a reactionary new confederacy in the Canadian north.

Key members of the postwar U.S. administration, the American historian Samuel Eliot Morison tells us, "adhered to the old Ben Franklin doctrine that a division of North America was 'unnatural'... . Without countenancing aggression against Canada, they hoped that the British provinces would join the American Union voluntarily."

Shortly after July 1, 1867, a joint resolution of the U.S. Congress declared that the constitutional monarchy which overlay the new democracy of the Dominion of Canada might very well contravene the Monroe Doctrine of 1823 — through which the American Republic asserted its intention to shield the Western Hemisphere from any further encroachments by the colonial empires of Europe.

A Mari Usque Ad Mare

The attitude of the post Civil War U.S. political leadership toward the new Canadian dominion helped ensure that its founding moments would be orchestrated largely by those Canadian politicians who least admired the historic experiment of the American Republic, and this helped make John A. Macdonald a principal architect of the 1867 Confederation bargain.

Macdonald's early career had rested on his ally Cartier's reliable French Catholic majority in what became Quebec in 1867. After Cartier's death in 1873

Macdonald himself managed to keep a grip on French Catholic support without so prominent a Quebec ally. But his later career leaned on the memory of his earlier partnership with Cartier — a conservative successor to the French and English Reform partnership of Lafontaine and Baldwin in the old United Province of Canada.

Whatever else, John A. Macdonald was skillful in the particular power mongering required to hold together an extremely diverse new country — in an age when popular government was notably robust, and all forms of patronage were vital lubricants in democratic political development. Moreover, his more visceral dealings were underpinned by a stubborn, clear, and centralizing vision of the new federal political system that was, to the extent required, capable of countervailing the aggressive new nationalism of the United States after the Civil War.

For Macdonald the American Civil War itself showed that a decentralized federal system which stood up for regional rights would inevitably be unstable on the North American continent. He placed a high value on stable government — perhaps especially because he had seen so little of it in the United Province of Canada. He saw the new provincial governments of the Confederation as little more than "glorified county councils," fundamentally subservient to the federal parliament at Ottawa.

There was considerable support for this view in what passed for a Canadian Constitution — a piece of British legislation known as the British North America Act, which Macdonald had a strong hand in drafting. Yet in this respect as in others the new Canada would stray from his design. In a society of great geographical, cultural, and almost every other kind of diversity, the Canadian Confederation would develop a notably decentralized federal system, modeled on the United States before, not after, the American Civil War (while the highest courts of the British Empire would ensure that the British North America Act could be interpreted to accommodate the trend.)

In the immediate post-Confederation era, however, all this was in the future. Newfoundland would not join the four original partners of Nova Scotia, New Brunswick, Quebec, and Ontario until 1949. But by the time of Cartier's death in 1873, he and Macdonald had managed to stick together a new Canadian federal government that included even such figures as Joseph Howe of Nova Scotia — who had initially been aghast at the prospect of belonging to a French and English "catarmaran of a Confederacy," with its capital city at Ottawa on the border between Ontario and Quebec: a place "with an Indian name, and any quantity of wilderness and ice in the rear of it."

By 1873 a new Canadian Northwest Territories and a new province of Manitoba had also been established in the old western realm of the Hudson's Bay Company. The Pacific colony of British Columbia and the Atlantic colony of Prince Edward Island had become new provinces in the Confederation. The Dominion of Canada was in business, as its new Latin motto declared: *a mari usque ad mare* (or, in one of the new country's two customary languages, "from sea to sea").

Macdonald & Free Trade Before the Mid-1870s

Up to the time of Cartier's death in 1873, John A. Macdonald was not noted for any particular opposition to reciprocity or free trade with the United States.

Like other Canadian politicians of the Confederation era, he had supported moves to forestall the U.S. abrogation of the 1854 treaty while the Confederation bargain was still being struck. He supported an early unsuccessful move for re-negotiation in 1869. When he accompanied the British delegation at the 1871 Treaty of Washington (which, among other things, led to the departure of British imperial armed forces from Canadian soil) he tried unsuccessfully to have a renewal of the old abrogated arrangement placed on the agenda. At this particular juncture his finance minister was Francis Hincks, a driving force behind the treaty of 1854.

Even in the Northwest, the new Canada was leaving the old resource economy of the fur trade behind. But Macdonald appreciated that the new economy, dominated by fish, lumber, and wheat (with mining in the wings) still depended on comparatively small numbers of people, taking resources from a very large territory. To prosper, Canada still had to sell at least a significant share of its resources to markets outside its own boundaries.

In an earlier era the French and then the British empires had held the key markets. As the rapidly growing American Republic began to industrialize in the early 19th century, however, its markets became increasingly important, stimulated by the great advantage of being much closer at hand. Set beside British Empire free trade in the 1840s, the attractions of buoyant U.S. markets had given many among the merchants of Halifax, Montreal, and Toronto strong interests in Canadian-American free trade .

Moreover, in the wake of the Civil War, an enormous new burst of North American economic growth based on the new industrialism loomed in sight — characterized somewhat later in mid-American folklore as "The Great Barbecue." Even the most northern North Americans, who could feel the same heartbeat of the continent as their cousins to the south, could sense what was coming. Few Canadian democratic politicians felt that the all-male small property owning electorate of the new Confederation (which at the time included the great majority of the adult male population) wanted to sit the barbecue out.

For close to a generation, the northern economy had already been tilting strongly in continental directions. In 1870, federal statisticians reported, only 38% of the new Canada's exports went to the United Kingdom, with an additional 3% going to other parts of the British Empire. An additional 8% went to other parts of the world beyond North America. But a full 51% went due south, to the markets of the U.S.A.

George Brown's Failed Reciprocity Treaty of 1874

In 1874 a new Canadian federal government, led by politicians with greater admiration for the American Republic than John A. Macdonald, had slightly more success in reviving the Reciprocity Treaty of 1854.

The Liberal-Conservatives guided the first half dozen years of the Confederation. Then a new federal Reform (or Liberal-Reform) party fell into office, and confirmed its good fortune with a convincing victory in the election of 1874. One of its first actions was to send George Brown, now honourifically seated in the new appointed body of the Canadian federal Senate, to negotiate a second Canadian-American free trade treaty in Washington.

At this point the high tide of Radical Republicanism in the U.S. was ebbing somewhat. Unlike the Liberal-Conservatives, George Brown and his Grit Reformers had been warm supporters of the North in the Civil War. The *Globe* in Toronto had often reported war news under the heading: "The American Revolution." Even in the midst of the war, there had been American supporters of Canada-U.S. free trade — particularly in the old lost French Canadian southwest of the upper Great Lakes and Mississippi valley.

Brown actually managed to arrive at a draft treaty with the administration in Washington, after reluctantly agreeing that in key areas of trade policy Canada would discriminate against the United Kingdom in favour of the United States. Yet this was not enough to persuade the post Civil War American Senate. The Southerners who, wisely or otherwise, had believed Lord Elgin's argument that a Canada-U.S. free trade treaty was the best way of keeping Canada out of the Union in 1854, were gone. The draft treaty went into limbo on the agenda of the Senate Foreign Relations Committee; there was not enough support to even vote on the deal that Brown had struck with administration officials.

It was now clear that even the Canadian Reformers, who had studied at the feet of democracy in America, could not get a new free trade treaty between a new Canadian Confederation and the post-Civil-War U.S.A.

The gloom was thickened by the international financial panic of 1873, which had precipitated a major stock market crash in New York and would prompt a depression lasting for much of what remained of the 1870s. Recurrent financial panic and alternating periods of boom and bust had punctuated the course of North American economic growth in the first half of the 19th century. But the crash of 1873 marked a new watershed.

In the United States most of the ground for the great industrial expansion of the late 19th century had already been cleared by the Civil War. In the spirit of the 20th century economist Joseph Schumpeter's theory of "creative destruction," however, some stubborn, remaining obstacles were disposed of in the depression of the later 1870s. More than 10,000 U.S. businesses went bankrupt, and such supremely aggressive men as Carnegie, Vanderbilt, and Rockefeller began to consolidate new corporate industrial empires.

In Canada, a veteran official of the Bank of Commerce would later write: "During these years, 1873-78, a manufacturing plant or establishment could scarcely be given away — timber limits were practically unsaleable, water powers were considered of small and decreasing value." As the continental creative destruction deepened, the question became: what would happen to the Dominion of Canada?

The Image of National Development

It was in this context that John A. Macdonald, for the moment a political leader on the opposition benches in the still quite new neo-Gothic Canadian federal parliament buildings at Ottawa, came up with the concept of "The National Policy" (or as it would often be put in the press of the day, "the N.P."). It would help him win the federal election of 1878, and remain prime minister of Canada from then until his death in 1891.

During the 1878 election campaign a well-known Liberal-Conservative wit, Alonzo Wright, confided to some friends: "Well, if we get in, J.M. Currier must be in the cabinet...so far as I know at present, J.M. Currier is the only man who thoroughly understands the N.P." In fact, though it might be said to have begun strictly as a tariff program, it would eventually become a political slogan for a broader vision — drawing on a few already widely known themes, a few policies that John A. Macdonald creatively borrowed or inherited, and some that any Canadian federal government would have had to pursue in any event.

The unifying inspiration was the old transcontinental romance of the Canadian fur trade, headquartered in Montreal. From at least one point of view, this was no more and no less than the unifying inspiration for the Canadian Confederation itself.

To start with, though the merchants of Montreal had left the fur trade behind by the mid-19th century, the Beaver Club and the Bank of Montreal still remembered its tough spirit of commercial adventure, and they were willing to be revitalized by injections of new blood from Halifax. Even the upstart merchants of Toronto had learned the gospel of Canadian westward expansion from George Brown and the Grit Reformers, and they had already established outposts in the new province of Manitoba.

If it was to be divided economically from its cousins to the south by high U.S. tariff walls, the new Canada did have an immense geographic territory of its own. This was somewhat deceptive, since the most northern part of North America contained large tracts of rugged rock and wilderness hostile to human habitation. But the country could easily support many more people than it had in the 1870s.

As Dawson and Hind and the Palliser expedition had shown in the late 1850s, the new Northwest had agricultural potential comparable to that of the booming mid-19th century wheat economy in Southern Ontario. If Canada's access to the Great Barbecue to the south was to be blocked, it could at least have a miniaturized North American prosperity of its own.

The Canadian Pacific Railway

The historic transportation system of the fur trade had been built around the complex waterways of the Canadian interior, and the Indian technology of the canoe and the portage. This had been supplemented in a few strategic places by modern canals by the 1830s, and by the new industrial technology of the railway age by the 1850s. What was needed for the late 19th century, and the 20th century that lay ahead, was a fully-developed transcontinental Canadian railway system.

Francis Hincks's old scheme of an Intercolonial Railroad linking Atlantic and Central Canada was completed in 1876. In the other direction, when British Columbia had joined Confederation in 1871, one of its conditions had been that a railway be built from Central Canada to the Pacific coast.

A scandal flowing from Macdonald's early efforts to meet this commitment had played a role in his downfall in 1873. Though there had been some additional modest progress on the project under the new Liberal-Reform government, building a railroad across the rugged Canadian wilderness was a much more arduous and costly undertaking than building a railroad across the wide open American spaces to the south; and (especially during the late 1870s depression) the Canadian Reformers were traditional believers in a lean and limited government that balanced its books.

When he returned to office in 1878, Macdonald picked up the enterprise with new vigour, buoyed by a Canadian Tory tradition that had viewed activist government as an agent of economic progress since the early beginnings of the Canadian Great Lakes canal system in the 1820s, and that had also made the government of Canada a prime mover and even the ultimate owner of the Intercolonial Railroad.

In 1881 a new Canadian Pacific Railway Company was formed by the Montreal financier George Stephen and the Canadian-American businessman James J. Hill. Macdonald pledged $25 million in government aid and other assorted rights and privileges, and gave the company a 10-year deadline to link, in effect, the St. Lawrence River Atlantic seaport of Montreal and the Pacific coast of British Columbia.

Stephen and Hill hired William Cornelius Van Horne, then general manager of the Chicago, Milwaukee & St. Paul Railroad, to mastermind the practical details. Van Horne moved to Winnipeg, and got to work, with Macdonald urging haste from Ottawa. In 1885, well within Macdonald's deadline, the last spike on the main line of the Canadian Pacific Railway was driven at Craigellachie, B.C. It was, according to a late 20th century U.S. guidebook to the history of the world, "the first single company transcontinental railroad in America."

The Tariff Policy of 1879

By the late 1870s the United States had begun to recover from the financial panic and New York stock market crash of 1873. An enormous burst of industrial growth in the Northeast and the Midwest of the Great Lakes began to set the stage for the Gilded Age of U.S. capitalism, that laid the foundations of modern corporate America.

Macdonald's National Policy implied that Canada, blocked from full participation in the wider continental trend, would create its own miniature replica of American prosperity within its own boundaries; and this also implied that the traditional resource economy of the far north would have its own industrial growth.

The new Confederation would not just moan that there were too few foreign markets for its resources. It would use these resources to create its own industrial products. And it would sell these products to the new east-west domestic markets tied together by the Intercolonial Railroad and the Canadian Pacific Railway.

It was not necessary to start the new industrialism in Canada altogether from scratch. Here as elsewhere, in a modest but unambiguous way, what de Tocqueville had called the society of "the Anglo-Americans" had long since spilled over the border into the far north. In particular, the Great Lakes-St. Lawrence corridor from Montreal to the U.S. border at Detroit formed the northern edge of what the early 20th century Swedish geographer, Sten de Geer, would somewhat later celebrate as the "Manufacturing Belt" of the North American New World.

By the mid-19th century, along with many Montreal merchants who had diversified out of furs and into lumber and wheat, there were some who had diversified into textile manufacturing. In Southern Ontario the Massey and Harris families were manufacturing agricultural implements. Various more localized consumer goods industries were falling into place in both Central and Atlantic Canada.

Though Central Canada had no coal of its own, Pennsylvania coal could be economically imported to Hamilton, Ontario via the old Great Lakes canals, to start a Canadian steel industry. In 1874 the telephone was invented in Brantford, Ontario. An early southwestern Ontario oil boom during the late 1850s gave birth to what would become Imperial Oil under the framework of Macdonald's National Policy in the later 19th century.

The key to the framework in this context was a frank emulation of U.S. industrial development policy, which had its roots in Henry Clay's American System of the earlier 19th century. The infant Canadian industrial sector would be allowed to incubate and grow behind a high wall of protective tariffs on imports of manufactured goods.

Even in Canada there were at least hints of earlier precedents for this protectionist approach to industrial development. In the late 1850s Alexander Tilloch Galt, finance minister for an earlier Cartier-Macdonald government in the old United Province, had experimented with a mild tariff on imports of manufactured goods. He had argued that it was a mere "revenue" not a "protective" tariff. But after the Civil War it had provided some grist for the mill of U.S. politicians determined to abrogate the 1854 Reciprocity Treaty.

The new draft reciprocity treaty that the Grit Reformer George Brown had reached with the U.S. administration in 1874 had in fact extended free trade in resource products to a wide range of manufactured goods. (As a sign that protected industrial growth was not strictly a Central Canadian interest, this had been strongly protested by The Manufacturers Association of Nova Scotia). Yet when it became clear that even the Canadian Reformers could not get a new free trade treaty with the United States, it became difficult to argue against a protective industrial tariff in Canada — unless the new country was prepared to do without a manufacturing sector at all.

When John A. Macdonald was re-elected prime minister of the Canadian Confederation in 1878, the ground for what would become this particular feature of a broader National Policy had been well turned. In March 1879 a new Liberal-Conservative government introduced a schedule of tariffs from 15% to as high as 35% on such things as woollen clothing, various iron products, agricultural implements, bricks, carriages, wagons, and railway cars, and refined sugar.

Macdonald stressed that the new tariffs were meant to be permanent. "There is the danger," he explained, "that capitalists who are now with some degree of trembling and hesitancy investing their capital in new enterprise...will be turned aside from their purpose if they find us tampering with the integrity of the National Policy."

The Branch Plant Industrial Economy

In this last respect, John A. Macdonald's creative intentions did leave deep marks on the future of the Canadian Confederation.

With one major, brief, and abortive exception (and with many refinements, and major degrees of moderation and scaling down during the course of the 20th century), the tariff structure of the National Policy would remain at least an implicit ingredient in the program of virtually every Canadian federal administration down to the Progressive Conservative government of Brian Mulroney in the late 1980s.

To no small extent, it did eventually help to create an indigenous, domestic industrial economy producing a notably wide variety of manufactured products for "the Canadian market."

If Canada had been a country like what would become its fellow British dominion of Australia in 1901, this may have been all the National Policy would help to create. But Canada was not a country like Australia. It shared what would later be called "the world's longest undefended border" with the rising industrial giant of the United States of America.

Whatever government policies might be in either place, capitalists, workers, inventors, and entrepreneurs could without much difficulty move back and forth across the border, in response to varying calculations of economic advantage. As the construction of the Canadian Pacific Railway had shown, even Canadian Tory governments were not at all averse to employing American capital and expertise in the Canadian national interest. In 1879 it was even said that Macdonald's government had hired an assistant from the United States Bureau of Statistics, to help with the design of the new Canadian tariff.

Thus the National Policy did not in any sense shut American industry out of the Canadian market (and parallel protective tariffs in the United States did not altogether shut Canadian industry out of the dynamic expansion to the

However it might be criticized from the standpoint of economics, John A. Macdonald's National Policy was a great political success. This commemorative cartoon of the Old Chieftain by Hunter, a progressive voice of at least the new Central Canadian urban common man, suggests some of the breadth of the Policy's appeal.

south). It merely meant that American manufacturers who wanted to sell in Canada found it easiest to avoid high tariffs by establishing branch operations (and hence manufacturing jobs) in Canadian territory (or vice-versa).

There can be little doubt that Macdonald himself understood this particular aspect of the National Policy's impact. In 1879 alone 13 U.S.-based manufacturers established branch plants in Canada, and an additional 24 plants had been established by 1887. (On the other side of the coin, between 1885 and 1890 half a dozen Canadian manufacturers established branch plants in the United States.)

As critics have urged ever since, there are strict limits on the extent to which this kind of activity by itself can be said to have built up indigenous Canadian industrial capacity. At a minimum, however, it did provide industrial jobs for Canadian voters, that, given all the practical circumstances, would probably have otherwise been located in the United States. Beneath his old loyal Tory veneer, John A. Macdonald was a democratic party politician, professionally sensitive to the worth of even such modest advantages.

"Nationalism" in Canada has always been an unusually complicated phenomenon. Not the least of the legacies of the National Policy is that it helped make the new Canadian Confederation something of a proving ground in the early development of the American multinational corporation.

Chapter 6

IMPERIAL PREFERENCE

For at least a short while in the early 1880s it seemed as if the National Policy might actually bring the new Canadian Confederation out of the late 1870s depression. The initial new prosperity, however, was not deeply rooted, and it did not last long.

The policy would play an important role in the growth of liveable, industrial-age Canadian cities. Though Montreal would long remain at the top of a small heap, in the 1880s the population in Toronto doubled and in Winnipeg it more than tripled. Yet even in 1901 only 35% of Canada's population lived in urban places, up from somewhat less than 25% in 1881. And throughout the late 19th century the rate of population growth in Canada at large dropped steadily.

The absolute number of people in the country continued to rise, very modestly. But, relatively, in the early 1870s the Canadian population had amounted to some 9.6% of the population in the United States; by the early 1880s this figure had already fallen to 8.6%, and it continued its downward path: to 7.7% in the early 1890s, and only 7.0% at the turn of the century.

Part of this could be laid at the door of new financial trouble in Europe during the 1880s. The Canadian economy itself was not immobile. The construction of the C.P.R. helped firm up the early beginnings of a new mining sector in the northern resource base. Canada was the site of pioneering work in the application of the new technology of hydroelectricity to the production of wood pulp and paper.

Yet by the later 1880s it was obvious enough that the the Dominion of Canada was missing a great North American urban industrial economic boom. In response, it has been estimated that during the last decades of the 19th century as many as a million Canadians moved to the United States. The most optimistic early boosters of Confederation had predicted a population of as many as 10 million people by the start of the 20th century. By 1901 the total population of Canada was in fact somewhat less than 5.4 million.

Strictly speaking, the National Policy itself (or the high-tariff regime in the United States that had inspired it) could not take all the blame. Deeper forces were at work.

Canada's experience during the generation after the Civil War, for instance, was in some respects similar to that of the defeated Confederacy in the American South, which also found itself sitting most of the Great Barbecue out. From the early 1880s to the turn of the century, the population of Quebec increased at about the same rate as that of Virginia. In a broader North American regional context, Nova Scotia actually grew somewhat faster than Vermont (though neither place grew very much, and some in Nova Scotia blamed Confederation).

All the same, it became increasingly clear that even if the National Policy in Canada was not quite a crashing failure, it was far from a roaring success.

At bottom, the country simply did not enjoy the critical mass in population size required to make its domestic markets any great engine for industrial growth. Despite some significant industrialization, Canada remained predominantly a resource economy, that looked to outside markets.

Unrestricted Reciprocity & Commercial Union

The soft spots the National Policy was showing by the late 1880s revitalized those among the Canadian Reformers (and elsewhere) who had never felt that Macdonald's protective tariffs were an acceptable alternative to a new Reciprocity Treaty with the United States. By this point the memory of George Brown's ultimate failure to achieve a second Canada-U.S. free trade agreement in 1874 was also far enough away to raise fresh hopes.

In some quarters, protests against Macdonald's trade policy were linked with protests against his highly centralized view of the new federal system in the Dominion of Canada. The first Interprovincial Conference of provincial premiers was held at Quebec City in 1887. Five of the seven provinces of the day attended (all except Prince Edward Island and British Columbia). The Conference passed a resolution calling for "unrestricted reciprocal trade relations between the Dominion and the United States."

The resolution had been drafted by Oliver Mowat's "Great Reform Government of Ontario," which had already challenged Macdonald's centralist views of the Confederation in the highest courts of the British Empire. It had also made clear its preference for unrestricted reciprocity (or "u.r.", as the press of the day often abbreviated it) as an alternative to the National Policy (or "N.P.").

On a broad caricature, industry was for tariffs, while agriculture and resources were for reciprocity. Despite Toronto's rapid growth in the 1880s, the dominant social force in late 19th century Ontario was still the family farm. Between 1881 and 1901 Ontario at large grew more slowly than Quebec, and its recovery in the early 20th century would have at least as much to do with its forestry and mining resource sectors, as with its growing strength in manufacturing.

Moreover, Mowat's Great Reform provincial government, along with Honoré Mercier in Quebec and other like-minded provincial regimes, was helping to set the stage for a resurgent federal Liberal-Reform party. It would be led by the French Canadian Wilfrid Laurier, who had begun his professional career in Quebec as a lawyer working for the family of the old Rouge leader Antoine-Aimé Dorion, and who professed a political philosophy of "sunny ways."

This rising star in the federal political firmament would turn its back on George Brown's anti-Catholic legacies (and win new support, or at least acquiescence, among the Quebec clergy). Yet it would also remain faithful to Brown and Dorion's old Canadian Reform enthusiasm for free trade with the United States.

"Unrestricted reciprocity" meant free trade in both resource and manufactured products — as opposed to "restricted reciprocity," or free trade in resource products alone, as in the old treaty of 1854. In the spring and summer of 1887 what would become, for a time, a quite popular campaign for the still more radical proposal of a "commercial union" between Canada and the United States was launched in Ontario, with the special urging and support of the Canadian-born New Yorker, Erastus Wiman.

Unrestricted reciprocity implied free trade between Canada and the United States, but with each country maintaining its own separate tariff barriers with respect to other countries. Commercial union meant that for all countries Canada and the United States would have the same tariffs.

It would soon enough become clear that the great political difficulty with commercial union was its all too obvious potential as a first step toward the American annexation of Canada, on the old model of Benjamin Franklin. (A few years later, it could also be pointed out that an 1876 free trade treaty between the post-Civil-War United States and the former British colony of Hawaii was followed by the American annexation of Hawaii in 1893.)

There were some pockets of annexationist sentiment in late 19th century Canada. But no democratic Canadian politician saw American annexation as anything that remotely approached a winning national issue. In 1888 Laurier and the federal Liberal-Reform caucus at Ottawa took pains to make it clear that their support was for unrestricted reciprocity, not commercial union.

The great political difficulty with unrestricted reciprocity, however, was that there was not really any particular or even general indication that the United States was any more interested in the kind of trade deal it would involve than it had been in 1874 or 1866.

Despite the difficulties, the broad issue was focused in a very direct way during the spring and summer of 1890. A new McKinley Tariff bill, which promised to raise the American tariff wall still higher, began to make its way through the Congress in Washington.

Whatever else, this increased the force of Laurier's opposition arguments that something must be done about Canada's trade relations with the United States. By the start of 1891, with his last federal election campaign in the air, even the founder of the National Policy, John A. Macdonald, was at least pretending to agree.

This Sam Hunter cartoon suggests a characteristic theme in Canadian discussions of Canada-U.S. reciprocity or free trade down to the present. Its original title is "Reassuring Little Infant Industry," and it has the late 19th century premier of "Old Ontario," Oliver Mowat (on the left with hat in hand), saying: "You needn't be afraid of him my dear — you see we keep him confined within narrow limits."

The 1891 Election

In February 1887, just before the campaign for unrestricted reciprocity had begun to gather momentum (and just before Laurier had assumed the leadership of the federal Liberal-Reform party), Macdonald had adroitly managed to win another federal election, with a considerably reduced majority. But the "Old Chieftain," as he was increasingly celebrated in some quarters, correctly anticipated that the election he called for March 5, 1891 would be a major challenge, requiring the full range of his mature political skills.

To start with, in an effort to put Laurier off balance on the practical question of the McKinley Tariff, Macdonald made rather more than a strict respect for the truth would have allowed out of some discussions on Canada-U.S. trade between British officials in Washington and the American Secretary of State James G. Blaine.

The Toronto *Empire*, a leading Conservative paper, reported that these discussions had resulted in American overtures to develop trade relations with Canada. Subsequently, Blaine told a Congressman in Washington that he knew of no plans for negotiating reciprocity with Canada. But the incident took some wind out of Laurier's sails.

Then Macdonald took the position that Laurier's particular Liberal-Reform ideas for improving trade relations with the United States would at the very least almost certainly result in the annexation of Canada by the United States.

In response, the new Liberal-Reformers (or "Laurier Liberals" as some would later say) could argue that their concept of unrestricted reciprocity was quite different from the concept of commercial union, both economically and in its implications for the political future of the Canadian Confederation. They believed as much as Macdonald in the national development of Canada. The final, workable proposal for Confederation itself had been made by the old Grit Reformer George Brown.

Distinctions of this sort, however, were rather subtle for 19th century elections in Canada. Besides, as practical events would soon enough demonstrate yet again, the post-Civil-War government of the United States was still not prepared to give the British Dominion of Canada the kind of free trade deal that the Liberal-Reform party had in mind.

Finally, in a staunch defence of his government's hard-earned record, Macdonald relentlessly talked up the practical achievements and economic interests that flowed from the National Policy he had begun in earnest a dozen years before.

In some respects, the strategy reflected the assumptions of William Caniff and other early Canadian nationalists, who had gathered around a modest and short-lived intellectual movement known as "Canada First" in the mid-1870s. But, with some qualifications in the case of the ill-fated Edward Blake (Laurier's immediate predecessor as leader of the federal Liberal-Reformers), no practical Canadian politician in the post-Confederation era was a serious nationalist in William Caniff's sense, and John A. Macdonald was certainly no exception. As the Grit Reformer George Brown's *Globe* had replied to the original urgings of the Canada First movement: "nations, institutions and sentiments grow, and grow slowly. They cannot be called into existence...Canada is *not* a nation."

P.B. Waite, the modern Canadian historian of the late 19th century, has summarized the underlying argument: Canada "did not yet have the strength to stand alone. If she did, she would at once be captured by the United States. To propose Canadian independence of Great Britain was equivalent to treason." Even when the Reform-dominated Interprovincial Conference of 1887 had called for reciprocal trade relations with the United States, it had set beside its plea a pledge of "fervent loyalty to Her Majesty the Queen."

Macdonald himself, by upbringing and instinct, spoke for that side of the Confederation that especially looked to the heritage of the British Empire — the side that reflected the Tory legacies of the American Loyalists of the late 18th century, whose fundamental and sometimes genuinely noble conservatism had now made common cause with the conservatism of the French Catholic clergy. For the Reformers in the federal election of 1891 Macdonald's nobility was less apparent. They viewed his strategy as an update of an old Tory political practice known as the "Loyalty campaign", whose history stretched back to the struggle for colonial democracy in the 1820s, 1830s, and 1840s.

Macdonald's campaign slogan was "The Old Man, the Old Flag, and the Old Policy." He himself was the old man. The old policy was the National Policy. And the old flag was the Union Jack of the British Empire. In the end, his Liberal-Conservatives won almost exactly 51% of the popular vote, bringing 121 seats in the Canadian House of Commons at Ottawa, compared with only 94 seats for Laurier's Liberal-Reformers. The Old Chieftain had won his last campaign, and he would die with his boots on.

Yet privately he had also come to believe that the National Policy by itself would not be enough to ensure the prosperity of the Confederation. A few months after the election, and not long before his death, he was writing to his old colleague Alexander Tilloch Galt, now Canadian High Commissioner in the United Kingdom, about a tariff scheme he had already pondered in the mid-1870s, known as "Imperial preference."

The World on Which the Sun Never Sets

Ironically, on the haphazard path of Canadian history, it would take Wilfrid Laurier to finally implement this ultimate ingredient in John A. Macdonald's legacy to Canadian economic policy. Yet, more broadly, the creation of preferential rates for the British Empire in the tariff structure of the National Policy was only the culmination of a trend that had been evolving since virtually the start of the 1867 Canadian Confederation, or even the American Civil War.

The economic logic was straightforward. No exclusively national development policy could give Canada the kind of economy it wanted. Its domestic markets were not large enough to sustain rapidly growing resource or even manufacturing industries: it needed outside markets as well. If the post-Civil-War United States was not prepared to accept a Dominion of Canada that both operated its own national development policy and enjoyed special access to American markets (in return for special U.S. access to Canadian markets), perhaps what was still the Canadian political mother country, the United Kingdom, would be more sympathetic.

This implied a return of sorts to the world before the adoption of imperial free trade in the late 1840s. One problem was that the Empire still embraced free trade principles. As the late 20th century recognizes under the rubric "non-tariff barriers," however, tariffs are not the only government policies that help to shape the global flow of wealth. And they were not in the 19th century either.

After the depression of the 1870s the British Empire had also begun to lose economic ground to the U.S., Germany, and even (though few were prepared to see it at the time) Japan. By the late 1880s there were some British statesmen happy enough to contemplate a new special economic relationship with the British Dominion of Canada, as part of wider policies to stiffen the fabric of the Empire.

British capital was still quite active in late 19th century Canada (as in the United States, for that matter). Even more important, British markets were picking up a good part of those Canadian exports that high tariff walls (for both manufactured and resource products) were keeping out of the markets of the United States.

By the late 1880s the lion's share of Canada's agricultural surplus was going to the United Kingdom. After some struggles in the U.S., even the growing farm machinery manufacturing enterprise of the Massey family had begun to expand into the markets of Western Europe and the British Empire.

At bottom, like the Reciprocity Treaty of 1854, the Imperial or British preference effectively introduced into the Canadian tariff in 1897 did not create a trend, but merely recognized and tried to secure a trend that was already established. In 1870 51% of Canadian exports had gone to the United States, and only 38% to the United Kingdom. In 1896 57% of Canadian exports went to the United Kingdom, and only 34% to the United States.

Had the late 19th century American Republic been prepared to give the British Dominion of Canada the kind of free trade treaty it needed to pursue its own national development, Canada might have grown away from the British Empire much more quickly than it did. As things happened, with the 20th century clearly in sight, Canada moved to reassert its ties to the greatest empire since Rome, in a world on which "the sun never sets."

The Compromise on Imperial Preference

The move was not exactly what everyone, even in the party of the Empire, thought most desirable. The Conservative successors of John A. Macdonald, who held together an interregnum between Macdonald's death in 1891 and Laurier's federal election victory in 1896, would make one last pass at the elusive ideal of a new Reciprocity Treaty with the United States.

Neither John Abbott nor John Thompson, the first two of the four somewhat reluctant prime ministers who managed the transitional regime, had been

*The character kneading preferential tariff dough is called "Baker Joe" —
Hunter's Canadian idea of a typical Englishman, complete with monocle. Joe
is saying (in an accent perhaps not quite like that of any actual Englishman
who wore a monocle): "With these 'ere materials, I shall be hable to supply
bread for the ole blooming hempire."*

persuaded by Macdonald's musings about Imperial preference. After their party had just won an election by arguing that Laurier's kind of reciprocity would lead to American annexation, they decided to press a case of their own with American Secretary of State James Blaine.

Contrary to Blaine's own earlier pronouncements, this did lead to discussions between Thompson and Blaine about prospects for a new Reciprocity Treaty, at Washington in February 1892. Blaine made it clear, however, that even "unrestricted reciprocity" on the model of Laurier's Liberals was at best an impossible ideal.

In the language of the late 19th century Canadian debate, the U.S. would not even discuss anything less than commercial union, with its pronounced annexationist overtones. Not only would Canada have to discriminate against the United Kingdom in favour of the United States (which Thompson, like George Brown in 1874, was reluctantly prepared to do), but, as Blaine put it, the Canadian "tariff must be practically the tariff of the United States of America."

Thompson should not have been surprised. Several months before Blaine had clarified his views about Canadian-American trade relations in public: "Beyond the frontier, across the river, our neighbours chose another Government, another allegiance... . They do exactly as they have a right to do... . But I am opposed, totally opposed, to giving the Canadians the sentimental satisfaction of waving the British flag...and enjoying the actual cash renumeration of American markets. They cannot have both at the same time. If they come to us they can have what we have, but... . So far as I can help it, I do not mean that they shall be Canadians and Americans at the same time."

By the end of Thompson's trip to Washington in 1892, Macdonald's Conservative successors were convinced that the Old Chieftain was right: a new Reciprocity Treaty with the United States that would not threaten Canadian national development was impossible.

Meanwhile, Laurier's Liberals held Canada's first federal political party convention in Ottawa during the summer of 1893. While the delegates continued to denounce Macdonald's protective tariff, they did urge more modest revenue tariffs, qualified by support in principle for reciprocity with the United States in resource products, and a modest selected list of manufactured goods.

When his Liberals at last won power in Ottawa in 1896, Laurier sent John Charlton, a well-known old Ontario free trade enthusiast, to Washington — to at least go through the motions of inquiring one very last time about the prospects for such a deal. But by 1897 the U.S. had passed the Dingley Tariff: the highest in the history of the Republic. Charlton's soundings were not remotely promising. In despair, he wrote back to Laurier from Washington: "We may as well tell a Yankee to go to Hades and we will go to England."

Laurier himself wrote to the old commercial union advocate, Erastus Wiman: "Since our American neighbours will not trade with us, we have come to the conclusion that we will have to do without it and I think we can do without it very successfully."

At last, in April 1897 W.S. Fielding, Laurier's new minster of finance (and the former Premier of Nova Scotia), introduced a new Liberal version of the tariff structure in the old Conservative National Policy.

The Canadian tariff would now have two tiers. The first would apply the existing rates for all countries whose tariff was protectionist against Canada (in fact chiefly the United States). A second tier would provide an ultimate reduction of 25% to any country that admitted Canadian goods at a rate equal to the minimum Canadian tariff (in fact chiefly the free-trading United Kingdom and British Empire).

Though the tariff itself did not mention specific countries, Fielding made clear that its effect was to introduce a British or Imperial preference into Canadian trade policy. As they had promised, the old Liberal-Reformers had reduced the tariff, but in a way that reflected the politically adroit traditions of their old Liberal-Conservative rivals.

The Canadian imperial enthusiast, Colonel George T. Denison, wrote to Lord Salisbury in the mother country across the ocean. The Laurier Liberals, the Colonel advised, led by the Confederation's first French Canadian Prime Minister, had "come out straight in favour of the Imperial idea, and have wrapped themselves in the old flag to the satisfaction of all parties except the extreme partisans in the Conservative ranks."

The Compromise on the French Fact

For those who did not share Colonel Denison's enthusiasms, the new Imperial preference, like the old Reciprocity with the United States, also held out dangers for Canadian national development. Reciprocity raised the danger of U. S. annexation. Imperial preference raised the danger of "imperial federation" — a scheme for the political integration of the British Empire, launched in the 1880s by supporters in both the United Kingdom and in a growing list of self-governing British colonies.

Though Laurier was a French Canadian who admired British liberalism, his admiration did not extend to the British Empire as a permanent home for the Canadian state. He would set Canada more firmly on the path that led, as the English Canadian historian Arthur Lower would put it a half century later, from *Colony to Nation*.

Just as the Reciprocity Treaty of 1854 had led to some increase in American cultural influence on Canada, Imperial preference and economic movement toward the British Empire in the 1890s did lead to some increase in British cultural influence. Yet Canada already had an essentially British rather than American form of democratic government. Moreover, in a geographic setting dominated by the increasingly colossal national civilization of the post-Civil-War United States of America, British influence was in some respects an incubator for the slow but steady growth of a Canadian political nation.

In turning once again to the Empire, however, Canada resolved some problems in its national development at the expense of hiding others under the rug. Even allowing for Cartier's unique role during the first half dozen years of the new dominion, Laurier was the first French Canadian Prime Minister of the 1867 Confederation. Yet to consolidate his support among some sections of the

This Hunter cartoon of the day suggests just how well Wilfrid Laurier mastered the Canadian tradition of compromise in the Manitoba School Question. His "Laurier Liberals" somehow united the French Catholic Israel Tarte and the English Protestant Joseph Martin. The signs that the Tarte and Martin marionettes are waving also suggest just how much Canada was once animated by religious wars now largely confined to Northern Ireland.

highly diverse and slowly maturing colonial democracy, he had to turn his back on others, to which he was by both language and religion more closely attached.

The crucial test of his skill in this context came even before the announcement of Imperial preference in 1897. It involved longstanding thorny problems surrounding the public education system in the Province of Manitoba.

The practical question was whether the federal government at Ottawa must ensure that Manitoba operate tax-supported Catholic and French language schools, as both the British North America Act of 1867 and the legislation establishing Manitoba in 1870 certainly seemed to imply. The broader issue was the future of the ancient French, Métis, and even Indian heritage in the old Northwest, and by extension in the country at large.

Laurier's answer was to negotiate a settlement with Thomas Greenway, the Premier of Manitoba (and, more subtly, with the Quebec clergy and even the Vatican in Rome). In effect it declared that there did not have to be Catholic and French schools in Manitoba, but it would be nice if there were at least some tax-supported Catholic and French (or even other non-English language) instruction, where numbers warranted.

Though Manitoba had made noises about a somewhat more generous settlement with the British Canadian Conservatives whom Laurier defeated in 1896, this was perhaps the best settlement that any practical French Canadian politician of the day could have negotiated; and it held out enough of a future for Pierre Trudeau's contributions to Canadian national development more than 70 years later.

On the other hand, it confirmed limits to the expansion of the culture of the old French Catholic Canada in the wider Confederation, that had been quietly evolving since the original establishment of Manitoba in 1870. It could also be said to have confirmed earlier insensitivities to Louis Riel's 1870 and 1885 Métis Rebellions in the old Northwest — and (in a somewhat ironic and complicated but nonetheless genuine sense) to the earliest expressions of the regional aspirations of modern Western Canada.

Canada's turn toward the British Empire in the late 19th century did strengthen the ties of the Atlantic provinces to the Confederation; here the old American Loyalism and the old British connection struck still deeper chords than in Ontario. In an imperfect world, it can even be said that, by incubating the modern Canadian evolution from colony to nation, the new Imperial preference, broadly construed, also helped even the oldest Canada of the French and the Indians somehow survive the enormous challenges that lay ahead.

Yet economic movement toward the Empire was also a means by which Canada participated in a great wider burst of Anglo-Saxon Protestant cultural assertion that, in somewhat different ways, poured forth from both the United Kingdom and the United States in the early 20th century. In this sense at least, Reciprocity with the United States would have produced the same result as Imperial preference with the United Kingdom. In either case there would have been trouble ahead for what Joseph Howe in the 1860s had called the French and English "catamaran of a Confederacy."

PART ONE:
THE LONG ROAD
BEHIND US

B. The Twentieth Century

Chapter 7

"OUR LADY OF THE SNOWS."

By the start of the 20th century the path of Canadian history that ultimately leads to the Canada-U.S. Free Trade Agreement of the late 1980s was moving in both national and imperial directions at once, with at least much more success than in the generation immediately after the Confederation of 1867. Almost in recognition of the new success (or so it seems in retrospect), by the start of the second decade of the new century warmer continental breezes had begun to beckon.

Yet, though it was still a mere British dominion, the Canada of the early 20th century was a considerably more developed political and economic enterprise than the embryonic Canada of the mid 19th century. It would ultimately respond to the beckoning continental breezes, but in its own particular way, and with a concern for its own particular future.

At the bottom of the new success was a new economic boom, driven by the suddenly rapid development of what is now Western Canada. In the late 19th century the region had held no more than 350,000 people, many of whom were Indians or Métis. In 1891 Indians alone accounted for more than a third of the population of British Columbia. In 1885 they had accounted for more than 40% of the population in what are now Alberta and Saskatchewan.

Only a few decades later, in 1911, a new Western Canada had more than 1.7 million people, with the overwhelming majority of European descent. Wilfrid Laurier's Canadian federal government at Ottawa had created the provinces of Saskatchewan and Alberta in 1905. And the booming wheat economy of mid-19th century Southern Ontario had moved to the early 20th century Canadian West. The Hudson's Bay Company was shifting from retail merchandising to Indians for furs, to retail merchandising to new prairie farmers for Canadian dollars. By the end of the First World War two new transcontinental railways were competing with the C.P.R. for east-west freight and passenger traffic.

In 1893 (the year Governor-General Lord Stanley donated the Stanley Cup to the emerging Canadian mass spectator sport of ice hockey) there had been another stock market crash in New York. By Laurier's election victory of 1896, however, an international economic recovery was underway. It was helped along by the discovery of gold in the Klondike area of the Canadian Yukon in 1896; this time Canada would play a full part in the new burst of prosperity. The British Empire burst into a brilliant sunset, and Canada was part of that too.

In its impact on rates of population growth, the Canadian boom of the early 20th century was at least the equal of the boom of the 1850s that had helped pave the way for the 1867 Confederation. As a percentage of the U.S. population, the number of people in Canada still fell rather short of the 9.6% of the early 1870s. But it would rise from 7.0% at the turn of the century to 8.2% in the early 1920s.

The New Culture of the Canadian West

The rapid growth of what had become "the last best west" in English-speaking North America was far from the only element in the new boom, but it was the single most crucial force. Immigration was the great movement behind the force, as Clifford Sifton, Laurier's Minister of the Interior (and the former Attorney-General of Manitoba) developed vigorous programs to populate Western Canada.

Manitoba's growth had been particularly driven by immigration from Ontario and the United Kingdom. Alberta and Saskatchewan had some similar migrants. British Columbia, on the other side of the mountains, was a unique case, especially influenced by British and by Canada's earliest modern wave of Asian immigration.

Still more important, the Canadian cultural mosaic on the western prairie was enriched by a great wave of migrants from the plains of Eastern Europe, promoted by Clifford Sifton and the federal government. Moreover, as in the earlier development of Nova Scotia, Ontario, and Manitoba, the last best west attracted a new wave of neutral Yankees on the nostalgic sunset of the Anglo-American agricultural settlement frontier.

Western Canada went through the modern North American stages of growth with striking speed. Yet, though there had been some violent conflict and Indian protest in the Riel Rebellions of the late 19th century, the process at large unfolded in good order. The Northwest Mounted Police, first established in 1873 (and renamed "Royal," in one among many symbolic gestures toward the new imperial enthusiasm, in 1904), played a different role in the western development of Canada than the U.S. cavalry had played in the western development of the United States.

Part of this flowed from what the American literary critic, Edmund Wilson, would much later describe as the preservation of "a British tradition of good order and capable handling" in Canada. Of greater consequence was the long prior history of the French and Indian fur trade, the North-west Company, and the Hudson's Bay Company — very gradually acclimatizing (if not exactly reconciling) the Indians of Canada to the influence of Europe.

By the early 20th century the American West was largely filled up, and the time had come for the "last best west" in Canada. Like many Canadians of the day Sam Hunter enjoyed the thought that finally, in at least some senses, struggling young Canada was booming and the giant U.S. was not. The original caption for the cartoon has Uncle Sam saying: "Waal, this ain't exactly my busy day."

Even the Riel Rebellions of 1870 and 1885 had been more than noble but futile Indian protests. They had involved or won support from French Catholics, Métis, and even some Anglo-Saxon frontier settlers as well as Indians. In subtle ways they struck blows for the spread of democracy in Western Canada — broadly comparable to the blows struck by the Central Canadian Rebellions of 1837. The last best west of North America would develop its own variation on the Canadian tradition of moderation and compromise.

The New Regionalism in the West & the East

In the federal election of 1891 John A. Macdonald and his National Policy had actually lost seats in Central Canada. The free-trading Toronto *Globe* complained that the old man, the old flag, and the old policy had in fact won the day only "in the new territories where the voters look to the government for daily bread, in Manitoba where the C.P.R. crushed and strangled public sentiment, and in Nova Scotia and New Brunswick where a hungry people succumbed to...hoarse and blatant prodigality."

By the early 20th century, when Wilfrid Laurier had at last managed to make Macdonald's legacy in economic policy show solid results (or so, after the manner of party politicians, he could claim), regional sentiments in Canada had begun to shift in new directions.

In the United States, the post-Civil-War high tariff regime had helped secure the interests of a new big business industrial plutocracy — dominated by, in the words of Theodore Roosevelt, "heejous monsters." By the early 20th century, a still newer "progressive impulse" had arisen to assert the contrary interests and ideals of an older agrarian democracy (that had also begun to spill over into the ethos of new urban industrial middle and working classes). Even the New England historian Samuel Eliot Morison would later report that "the monopoly-securing features" of the 1897 Dingley Tariff were so "blatant" as to threaten the future of the Republican party.

The ultimate success of Imperial preference and the National Policy would finally create miniaturized versions of the same patterns in Canada. Immigrants were sent to the West to grow wheat (or, ideally, start cattle ranches in the most western parts of Alberta). They struggled in a challenging environment and, if they were lucky, prospered in modest ways.

Meanwhile, railways headquartered in Montreal, mercantile enterprises like the T. Eaton Company in Toronto, assorted banks and insurance companies, and protected manufacturers in Ontario and Quebec grew rich back east. There were precedents for the syndrome in what John Bartlet Brebner, the Canadian-American historian of the *North Atlantic Triangle,* would later describe as the "American cartoonist's cow that stood on a map of the United States, eating corn in Kansas and being milked in Wall Street."

Circumstances in Atlantic Canada were more ambiguous. Newfoundland's continuing refusal to join Confederation, despite periodic attempts at persuasion from Ottawa, in some ways symbolized a continuing broader scepticism about the Canadian enterprise in the old Maritime provinces. The combined population of Nova Scotia, New Brunswick, and Prince Edward Island rose from some 880,000 people in 1891 to just under 940,000 in 1911. But P.E.I. (the smallest province in the Confederation), actually lost some 15,000 people during the same two decades.

Along with the Atlantic fisheries, Nova Scotia had coal and New Brunswick had lumbering, and (like P.E.I.) both places had mixed farming. Halifax was a historic metropolitan centre with some financial strength and industrial aspirations, and a long tradition of looking east across the Atlantic Ocean to the United Kingdom, and even south to the British West Indies.

Even with protective tariffs to help boost the domestic market for Nova Scotia coal, however, for the northern edge of the North American manufacturing belt in Southern Ontario it was a shorter trip to Pennsylvania. Halifax's metropolitan and industrial aspirations were squeezed between the much larger centres of Boston and Montreal.

In 1901 the Merchants' Bank of Halifax had moved to Montreal, and changed its name to the Royal Bank of Canada. By 1911 even Calgary, Alberta could almost match Halifax's population of some 58,000 people. Winnipeg (mid-point of the Canadian transcontinental rail network and the country's third-largest city for the first few decades of the 20th century), Vancouver, Quebec City, and even Hamilton, Ontario were much larger.

Yet the Bank of Nova Scotia, even though it had a substantial share of its operations in Toronto by the early 1900s, remained formally headquartered in Halifax, and it profited significantly from the early 20th century Canadian economic boom. There were also some continuing legacies of the 19th century transatlantic shipping magnate, Samuel Cunard, who had been born in Halifax and died in London, England just before Confederation.

Moreover, the Dominion of Canada's new turn toward the British Empire in the late 19th century helped offer Atlantic Canada's most ambitious sons alternative outlets for their energies. Max Aitken from New Brunswick (Lord Beaverbrook after 1917), following some early hi-jinks in Montreal, went on to become a leading press baron in the United Kingdom. In the early 1920s Bonar Law, also from New Brunswick, would briefly serve as Prime Minister of the United Kingdom — achieving a success much greater than anything that could be offered by Canada (or even, on noble imperial views of the matter, by the United States).

Montreal & "La Belle Province"

The great metropolitan centre of the booming early 20th century Canadian economy was Montreal. Frank Underhill — a "Presbyterian Grit" from rural Ontario and a 20th century northern North American "agrarian socialist," would later write that by 1911 "Canadian capitalism" could celebrate "its coming of age. The dream of the Montreal merchants of one hundred years before had at last come true. The northern commercial state was a reality. Slowly, in spite of many discouragements and setbacks, it had been built up, and now its trade flowed in and out by the St. Lawrence, 'the River of Canada.'"

This was an ideologue's exaggeration, but it captured a real trend. To no small extent, the C.P.R. and the Bank of Montreal had at last managed to revive the east-west transcontinental romance of the fur trading Northwest Company in the age of industry. In 1911 Montreal's population of some 616,000 people put it well ahead of Toronto's 478,000 or Winnipeg's 157,000. In varying degrees both of the new large urban centres paid homage to what Underhill, in a Canadian radical's deference to the old British sense of hierarchy, would somewhat quaintly call "the senior metropolis."

Yet the good fortune of the British merchants of Montreal did not spread uniformly throughout the province of Quebec. The Banque D'Hochelaga (La Banque Canadienne Nationale after 1925) reflected a very modest French financial presence in the new Central Canadian prosperity. And there was some French Canadian westward migration to the new mining and forestry frontier of Northern Ontario (which, like Southern Ontario, had a somewhat attenuated tax-supported Catholic Separate School system, dating from the time of the old United Province). But the resolution of the Manitoba Schools Question, among other things, helped restrict French Canadian participation in the growth of Western Canada. In Ontario partisans of a more Anglo-Saxon Protestant dominion tried to thwart the further development of Catholic schools and French language education.

Unlike another old survivor of the ancient French American empire in the U.S. state of Louisiana, Quebec itself remained predominantly French-speaking. Particularly to English-speaking Canadians, it also seemed to remain something of a peasant-like European agricultural society, profoundly influenced by the Roman Catholic Church — and looking more to the Vatican in Rome for outside inspiration than to the cultural capital of the western world in Paris, France.

There was, English-speaking Canadians sometimes forgot, a side to "la belle province" that equally bore some marks of the old North American agrarian democratic culture, and increasingly even of the new industrialism. Wilfrid Laurier himself spoke for this side of his native region. "I am," he wrote to an American correspondent in 1900 (with some genuine feeling as well as diplomacy), "a great admirer of your nation and of its history."

Still another side of French Canada remembered the old cosmopolitan wilderness romance before the British Conquest, and the old dream of a French nation in the New World. It was not cowed by new empire-minded Canadians who liked to point out that the French Canadians were, after all, a conquered people. And it was increasingly unhappy with the fate of its heritage in the Confederation of 1867.

By 1911 Henri Bourassa, a kind of intellectual and emotional blend of both René Lévesque and Pierre Trudeau some two generations later, had strayed from Laurier's path, to speak with a separate voice for a different kind of Canadian nation, with clearer and more assertive French connections.

The New American Cousins

From one standpoint, it was highly ironic that the Laurier Liberals should preside over the ultimate fruition of John A. Macdonald's National Policy, as amended by his final thoughts on Imperial preference. From another, anchored in the increasing depths of the Canadian tradition of compromise, it made perfect sense.

In any case, prosperous times have advantages for the governments that preside over them. After the election of 1896 Laurier's Liberals handily won federal elections in 1900, 1904, and 1908. They regularly took at least a bare majority of the popular vote, and close to two-thirds of the seats in the House of Commons at Ottawa. They had depth of support in all parts of the country, and were particularly strong in Nova Scotia, Quebec, and the two new western provinces of Alberta and Saskatchewan.

Where he could afford to be, Laurier was also something of an idealist, faithful to the heritage and principles of his party. The Canadian Reformers had traditionally opposed John A. Macdonald's highly centralized vision of the new federal system. Laurier's first cabinet included W.S. Fielding, the former Premier of Nova Scotia, and the former Premier of Ontario (now the 76-year-old "Uncle Oliver" Mowat, who had argued unsuccessfully for an elected federal Senate during the Confederation debates of the 1860s).

Laurier himself was a French Canadian politician who understood that the provincial government of Quebec was a strong arm for the survival of French Canada. He was sensitive to the provincial rights won by Ontario's struggles in the highest courts of the British Empire during the late 19th century. While he was at least as fervent an apostle of Canadian national development as Macdonald had been, he never quite lost the principled enthusiasm for closer trade relations with the United States, announced at the first Interprovincial Conference in 1887.

As it happened, from the dispute over the boundary between Canada and Alaska in the late 1890s, down to the 1908 election of President William Howard Taft (hand-picked successor of the "progressive Republican" Theodore Roosevelt), there were various causes for discussion between the governments of the United States and Canada.

In 1907 the Laurier Liberals, in an effort to broaden the principles of Imperial preference and seek still wider markets for Canadian exports, introduced a third tier into the Canadian tariff. This provided for an intermediate set of rates, in between the highest or general rates and the lowest (or so-called "British preferential") rates, to be applied to countries prepared to offer reciprocal concessions to Canada. Limited international agreements for applying the intermediate preference were then successfully negotiated with France and (in an even more limited way) Japan, and Italy.

In effect, this meant that Canadian trade policy was now discriminating against the United States not just in favour of the colonial mother country of the United Kingdom, but in favour of other non-British countries as well (including the much earlier Canadian mother country of France). Though the United States itself was discriminating against Canada with general tariff rates as high as 40%, some more chauvinistic currents of American opinion felt that Canada should either apply its intermediate tariff to the U.S.A. as well, or face additional penalties for unfair discrimination against the Republic.

Other currents of American opinion, however, were moving in other directions. As in Canada, progressive (and especially more westerly) U.S. farmers, and some of their urban allies, had long railed against protective tariffs that served to enrich monopoly manufacturing interests at the expense of the common man. By the early 20th century the progressive impulse had acquired real political muscle, and even the Republican Party had concluded that it must take notice. In 1908 the avowedly progressive Republican William Howard Taft was elected president on a campaign that stressed tariff reduction.

Through the vicissitudes of domestic politics, after he came to office in 1909 Taft had found himself supporting a Congressional tariff bill that had virtually nothing to do with tariff reduction. Though a historic general moderation of U.S. tariffs was in fact in the wind (and Washington would sign a historic trade treaty with Japan in 1911), by 1910 President Taft needed an issue to get the wind blowing in the right direction.

The question of what to do about the 1907 intermediate Canadian tariff was on the U.S. federal agenda. The President himself had a summer place in Canada. Despite high tariffs, a new mass-circulation newspaper industry in the U.S. Northeast and Midwest had become increasingly dependent on pulp-and-paper newsprint made from the forests of Canada: it would be happy to see American tariffs on Canadian forest products disappear.

It was now close to a half century since the end of the Civil War, which had entrenched the protectionist trade regime of the American System, and brought U.S. anti-British sentiment to a peak. At the bottom of its heart, the U.S.A., with a growing empire of its own in Hawaii, the Philippines, and even the Caribbean, could sense that in the early 20th century it was at the very least on the verge of supplanting the British Empire as an international economic force.

In the late 1890s Laurier had announced that Canada would be making "no more pilgrimages" to Washington in futile pursuit of a new free trade deal with the United States. In 1910, for the first time since the establishment of the Republic in the late 18th century, the government of the United States itself approached the government of Canada, with proposals for tariff reduction and a new Reciprocity Treaty that would at last renew the long-lapsed Treaty of 1854.

The 1911 Canada-U.S. Treaty

The initial spirit of the proposals that the Taft administration brought to Laurier's Liberals was quite different from the pronouncements of James Blaine in the 1890s. A U.S.A. more confident of its future in the world than it had ever been before was now prepared to extend its northern cousins a generous offer (or so at least it seemed).

*In this cartoon of the day a pensive Uncle Sam reflects: "Say, whenever I look
at that plugged-up tunnel and that thar di—verted stream — I just want to
set up nights and kick myself." To some Canadians his ultimate answer was
the Reciprocity Treaty of 1911, the ultimate result of the first and only
occasion on which Washington approached Ottawa (as opposed to the many
occasions on which Ottawa approached Washington) about a Canada-U.S.
free trade agreement. The original title to the cartoon is: "He Did It With His
Little Congress."*

Generosity aside, at the time the U.S. had a very favourable balance of trade with Canada. In 1910 Canada sent the United States only 37% of its exports, but 59% of its imports came from south of the undefended border. Even with Imperial preference only 26% of Canadian imports came from the United Kingdom (which was absorbing some 50% of Canadian exports).

In absolute numbers U.S. exports to Canada totalled some $242 million, while Canadian exports to the U.S. amounted to only $97 million. Moreover, as the *New York Times* would later explain, Taft had already watched a successful reciprocity agreement in action when he had served Theodore Roosevelt as governor of the new U.S. colony in the Philipine Islands.

Stirred by the success of their fellow partisan cousins across the border, progressive Canadian farmers (especially from Ontario and Western Canada) had demonstrated for the old ideal of Canada-U.S. reciprocity in Ottawa in 1910. Yet, even with such pressure, Laurier's government was much less anxious about the issue than Canadian governments had been in the past.

The Taft administration had approached Canada: the Canadians were no longer humble supplicants. They would consider nothing that smacked of the old annexationist commercial union. Fielding, still Laurier's finance minister, initially indicated that Canada was only prepared to consider free trade in resource products, not manufactured goods. In the end a deal was struck that did provide for practically free trade in resource products, with only some modest reciprocal tariff reductions on a few minor classes of manufactured products.

Negotiations were concluded amicably, and with surprising speed, by late January 1911. At Canada's request, to avoid muddying the waters through the diplomatic channels of the British Empire, the new Reciprocity Treaty was to be implemented by simple concurrent legislation in the American Congress and the Canadian Parliament.

As unanticipated as it all had been only a short decade before, Laurier quickly convinced himself that he had at last managed to achieve the heretofore impossible ideal of a new reciprocity treaty with the United States, that would not threaten Canadian national development.

At first he was far from alone in this conviction. When the details of the agreement were announced, even the courtly Robert Borden from Nova Scotia, now the federal leader of a Canadian Conservative Party that had been lost in a political wilderness since 1896, gloomily confided to his diary that it no doubt meant Laurier would win yet another election.

Less than a month later, however, the issue had begun to grow contentious in Canada, even more quickly than the original agreement had been negotiated. As the contention mounted, Laurier felt it prudent to call an election.

The Conservatives, suddenly invigorated by unanticipated new support and potent new resources, forged an increasingly aggressive attack against the new free trade deal with the United States, taking cues from the strategies of John A. Macdonald 20 years before, in the election of 1891. Though Laurier remained confident to the end that this time reciprocity would win, when the election finally took place on September 21, 1911, he was decisively defeated, by a much less gloomy Robert Borden.

The 1911 Canadian Election

In one of its several aspects the Canadian federal election of 1911 was a culmination for the popular British North American imperial sentiment that had begun with the Loyalists in the late 18th century, and then been pushed to new strategic heights by the Old Chieftain, John A. Macdonald, in his last election Campaign.

This is how the event appeared to more than a few Canadians of the day, especially in English-speaking Atlantic and Central Canada. It is also how it often seems to appear to American historians. As related by the New Englander Samuel Eliot Morison (still perhaps carrying a small sentimental torch for a version of loyalism that never left the Republic): in Canada in 1911 "the 'King and Country' argument was freely employed, and one of Rudyard Kipling's worst poems, 'Our Lady of the Snows,' was widely circulated to rebuke the impudent Yankees."

Despite Laurier's protests to the contrary, as in 1891 significant numbers of Canadians were persuaded that any free trade agreement with the United States could too easily lead to an ultimate American annexation of Canada, which had increasingly distinctive habits and a national future of its own. To many English-speaking and even some French-speaking Canadians of the day, standing up for Canada and Canadian sovereignty still meant, above all else, standing up for the British Empire.

At the same time, it would be misleading to exaggerate the importance of imperial sentiment in this context — just as it is misleading to exaggerate the importance of the Loyalist strain in Canadian history at large. For many other Canadians standing up for Canada simply meant standing up for Canada.

Writing on the 1911 election some two decades later, J.W.Dafoe, celebrated Laurier Liberal and reciprocity supporter of the day, and noble editor of the *Winnipeg Free Press,* suggested: "Perhaps the determining factor with the man in the street was the conviction that at last he was sufficiently prosperous to be able to sacrifice further gain for himself — or for his neighbours — in order to show his resentment of long years of United States hostility and condescension."

Moreover, like almost everything else in the highly diverse and increasingly decentralized British Dominion of Canada, the 1911 federal election result also had strong regional overtones. And the provincial variations in support for free-trading Laurier Liberals and loyal protectionist Conservatives were notably different than they had been in 1891.

The Pacific lotus land of British Columbia was the only chunk of the vast Canadian geography to behave with complete consistency in both elections. It gave less support to Laurier and free trade with the United States than any other province in 1911, and it had done the same in 1891 (though in the earlier election the territory of the Northwest, whose most populous parts would not become the provinces of Alberta and Saskatchewan until 1905, had given even less).

Part of the logic was that B.C. had been the original proponent of the Canadian Pacific Railway, and still had strong interests in the east-west transcontinental world of Canada that it sustained. Another part, perhaps, was an increasingly deeply rooted history of immigration from the United Kingdom. Yet another was protectionist farming interests in the lotus land's southern tender fruit belt.

All the other provinces tended to move in opposite directions between 1891 and 1911. From the standpoint of winning seats in the House of Commons, the most significant shift took place in Ontario, which even in 1911 was home to some 35% of Canada's total population. In 1891 Laurier and unrestricted reciprocity had won more support from Ontario than from any other province except Prince Edward Island. In 1911 Ontario gave Robert Borden's anti-reciprocity Conservatives 73 of its 86 seats at Ottawa, and clinched Laurier's defeat.

Percent of Popular Vote for Liberals & Reciprocity

1891		1911	
P.E.I.	52	Saskatchewan	59
Ontario	49	Alberta	53
Quebec	48	Nova Scotia	51
Manitoba	47	New Brunswick	51
Nova Scotia	46	Quebec	50
New Brunswick	40	P.E.I.	49
British Columbia	28	Manitoba	45
Northwest (Sask. &	19	Ontario	43
Alta. after 1905.)		British Columbia	38
ALL CANADA	47	ALL CANADA	48

Ontario & the Toronto Eighteen

There is more than one explanation of Ontario's role in the 1911 election. To begin with, 61% of the Ontario population had still been living in rural areas in 1891. This figure had fallen to 47% by 1911, and a majority of Canada's most populous province now lived in urban places. Then, to strengthen native imperial sentiments, in the early 20th century, as in British Columbia, Ontario's new urban labour force had been bolstered by a new wave of immigration from the old urban centres of the United Kingdom. Finally, changes had been taking place in the Toronto business elite — and these prompted some of the most strategic bursts of support for Borden's Conservatives.

Especially since the 1850s, Toronto capitalism had developed strong ties with high finance in New York City, in contrast to the financial ties with London, England that still predominated in Montreal. The Canadian Bank of Commerce, flagship of Toronto's aspirations as a regional financial centre in North America, had been traditionally oriented toward New York. For all the talk of "Tory Toronto," dating back to the early 19th century reign of the Upper Canadian oligarchs, since even before Confederation the cream of Toronto capitalism had supported the cause of Liberal-Reform.

Yet, as Frank Underhill would later point out, by the early 20th century "Toronto capitalists, who at times had shown some inclination to challenge the position of the senior metropolis" in Montreal "were now working hand in hand with it." The unremitting escalation of the U.S. protectionist regime after the Civil War had made it increasingly difficult for Toronto to play New York off against Montreal. As the combination of the National Policy and Imperial preference began to show solid results in the new Canadian economic boom, Toronto's ties with Montreal and the imperial metropolis in London, England became, for the moment at least, more advantageous than its continental ties with New York.

Less than a month after Laurier's new Reciprocity agreement had been reached with the United States, Edmund Walker, President of the Canadian Bank of Commerce, told a special meeting of the Toronto Board of Trade that it threatened Canada's all-important connection with the British Empire.

Four days later, eighteen prominent Toronto Liberals (including, on Underhill's calculations, Walker himself, "two other financiers prominent in the Commerce group, three men high in the directorates of other banks...two managers of great insurance companies," and "the head of the largest department store in Canada") broke with Laurier, and declared his new Reciprocity Treaty, as a later commentator would put it, "the worst blow ever to threaten Canadian nationality." This support from the junior metropolis helped prompt William Van Horne, former president of the C.P.R. in Montreal (and a Canadian businessman who had begun life as an American citizen born in Joliet, Illinois), to declare that he was "out to bust the damned thing."

Among the less eminent but ultimately sovereign democratic electorate, there was as well a more strictly patriotic and emotional dimension in Ontario's reaction. For imperialist and nationalist alike, in all the Confederation it was the place where the English-speaking population had been calling itself "Canadian" the longest. It was the place that had borne all the brunt of the American invasion in the War of 1812, almost exactly a century before.

When it heard President Taft in the United States repeat that "Canada is at a parting of the ways," it wondered. And it wondered some more when Champ Clark, Speaker of the U.S. House of Representatives, urged support for the new Reciprocity Treaty in Congress by declaring: "I hope to see the day when the American flag will float over every square foot of the British North American possessions, clear to the North Pole... . That is the way things are tending now."

"The noble Bird of Freedom is said to be again hatching." When U.S. Speaker of the House of Representatives Champ Clark declared: "I hope to see the day when the American flag will float over every square foot of the British North American possessions, clear to the North Pole," he helped to seal the defeat of the one U.S.-initiated Canadian-American Reciprocity Treaty in the Canadian Reciprocity Election of 1911.

"History has many cunning passages."

Ontario's large population made it crucial to Laurier's defeat. Yet, along with British Columbia, Manitoba and Prince Edward Island also gave a majority of their votes to Borden and the Conservatives.

Along with the "Toronto Eighteen," Clifford Sifton, Laurier's Minister of the Interior and the one-time Attorney-General of Manitoba, also broke ranks with his party in the 1911 election. He had devoted his national political career to building up the east-west transcontinental economy in Canada, and like William Van Horne of the C.P.R. he saw free trade with the United States as a threat to its profitability.

Even Laurier's home province of Quebec did not give its native French Canadian son quite the kind of support that might have been expected. The fly in the ointment here was Henri Bourassa—early 20th century herald of a new French Canadian nationalism. In Bourassa's view reciprocity was far from a crucial issue for French Canada. Like many French-speaking Quebec Conservatives, he was profoundly opposed to Borden's strong postures on behalf of the British Empire, and their reflection in his plans for a Canadian contribution to the Imperial Navy. Borden's naval policy was another ingredient in his appeal to the English-speaking imperial sentiment that was traditionally opposed to national sentiment in French Canada.

For much of the 1911 campaign Henri Bourassa was full of hesitation. Yet in the end he came down against Laurier and reciprocity, and for Borden and the Conservatives—in a strange alliance between radical French nationalism and conservative British Toryism that had earlier precedents in Canadian history, and would echo in the future as well. As a result Laurier, who could count on a steady 56% of the Quebec popular vote in 1900, 1904, and 1908, managed only a bare 50% in 1911.

From the standpoint of the popular vote in Canada at large, the final result of the 1911 election was far from lopsided. Borden's Conservatives took 51% and Laurier's Liberals took 48%, with the balance going to various independent and early Labour and Socialist candidates. Yet the 1911 election would put the formal question of comprehensive free trade between Canada and the United States on the back burners of Canadian federal politics for more than two generations.

One among several ironies was that the Reciprocity Treaty the Laurier Liberals had actually negotiated with Washington came at least extremely close to the kind of agreement Canadian governments had virtually gone begging for since the U.S. abrogation of the Reciprocity Treaty of 1854 in the wake of the Civil War. From this standpoint, there is a final explanation of what happened.

In an increasingly shrinking world economy, Canadian-American Reciprocity in 1911 was only a straw in the wind for the future of U.S. trade policy in the 20th century. In the mid-term American elections of 1910 the free-trading U.S. Democrats had gained control of the House of Representatives in Washington. By 1910 it was clear from the American press that the long regime of high tariffs in the great Republic was, for a while at least, about to change. And by 1913 the U.S. Congress had indeed passed the Underwood Bill — "America's first low tariff since before the Civil War."

In a recent revisionist flourish of historical writing on the subject, Tom Velk and A.R. Riggs, Co-Directors of North American Studies at Montreal's McGill University in the late 1980s, have suggested: "aside from fears of annexation and encroachment on her cultural sovereignty, Canada was placed in a classic 'no lose' situation by the American elections of 1910. The United States had telegraphed its intent before the battle was even joined. Canada could accept an agreement advantageous to her, or wait until Democrats lowered the tariff, unilaterally, with even greater concessions. In the eyes of many Americans she chose to wait for a better deal."

Whatever the complete truth may be, the haphazard path of Canadian history was once again about to confound the best intentions of those who would too narrowly define its course. In commenting on other features of the new 20th century, T.S. Eliot (the American poet who moved to England and became a "Royalist in politics") would soon enough explain that any kind of history "has many cunning pasasages."

By the end of the First World War, despite the Canadian Reciprocity Election of 1911, economic relations between Canada and the United States had begun to grow somewhat warmer. By the Second World War they would be very warm indeed. As the University of Toronto professor Alexander Brady would try to make clear for those who might be confused, Canada was "in the British Commonwealth." But it was also "in North America," and the "profound and interacting implications of both facts explain the nature of Canadian nationality."

Chapter 8

THE INCREDIBLE CANADIAN

The First World War, it is often said, was a great crucible in the evolution of Canadian nationality. In fact, on the 29th of December 1900 a 26-year-old Winston Churchill had already assured an upper crust crowd in Toronto that in the Boer War in southern Africa "Canada had drawn her maiden sword, in an honourable way and in a righteous cause." By sending more than 7,000 fighting men to the bottom of the "Dark Continent" (89 of whom would die in battle) the first British dominion won "a dignity and standing which many years of commercial progress and advancement in the arts of peace might not have gained for her."

If this were true, Canada gained enormously from the more than 625,000 fighting men she sent to Europe between 1914 and 1918 (more than 68,000 of whom would die in battle). During the course of the First World War it was established that Canadian armed forces were Canadian armed forces, not armed forces of the British Empire. At the end, Canada's national contribution to making the world safe for democracy won her a separate seat in the new League of Nations; and by this time the Confederation's status as a self-governing British dominion was no longer unique: it was shared by the Commonwealth of Australia, the Dominion of New Zealand, and — on an odd twist of "self-governing", the Union of South Africa.

The League of Nations was the dream of the U.S. president, Woodrow Wilson. The American Senate, however, would decide that the United States itself could not be a part of the dream. Isolationist currents in the middle American heartland (along with more scattered sentiment for "Asia First"— the concept that the U.S. future was not in the Atlantic, but in the Pacific) had also kept the American Republic aloof from the war in Europe until April 1917.

In the same year Borden introduced "conscription" of civilians for military service in Canada. It was violently opposed in Quebec, and (less violently) by English-speaking farmers and farm organizations in other parts of the country.

John Bull congratulates Jack Canuck on a fine showing in the Boer War. Somewhat more than a decade later, official records indicate that some 68,300 Canadians were "killed" in the First World War, compared with 53,513 American "battle deaths" and 63,195 "other deaths" — at a time when Canada's population was only some 8% of the population of the United States. Canada's sacrifice did much to mobilize new national sentiments.

But the urge for New World isolation from the problems of the Old World was never quite the same potent political force in Canada that it was in the United States.

In one sense, even for French Canadians it was part of the emerging Canadian nationality that the most northern part of North America also belonged to a larger world on which the sun never set (though for French Canada the world was headquartered in Rome, not London, England). On the other hand, when the war was over even the son of Empire Robert Borden stood up staunchly for Canada's newly won rights in what some at least imagined might be a new, more law-abiding, democratic world of nations, at the 1919 Peace of Versailles.

The Progressive "Normalcy" in Canada

As in the United States, the First World War helped shape domestic politics in Canada. The Confederation in the north, however, would follow a somewhat different path out of the war, and through the 1920s to the start of the 1930s Great Depression.

In the U.S. the progressive impulse had peaked in 1912, when Theodore Roosevelt ran as an unsuccessful presidential candidate for a new Progressive Party, and Woodrow Wilson won the White House for the Democrats. Canada had elected Robert Borden's Conservatives in 1911. Even some Liberals would support what became Borden's wartime coalition government, which did not face the electorate again until December 1917. Yet by the end of the war a fundamentally conservative party was still in power.

In 1920 Borden resigned as party leader, for reasons of health. He was replaced by Arthur Meighen, an Ontario Conservative in a high-minded imperialist mold. For many Canadians Meighen would personify the postwar British connection. Yet while blessed with great ability and intelligence, he had only minimal popular instincts — in a mass democracy that (like the United States and many other places) had just given adult women as well as adult men a place among the sovereign electorate.

With Meighen at its head, the government that had brought Canada through the First World War went to consult the electorate for its last time in early December 1921. It was at this point — a year after Americans had elected the Republican President Warren G. Harding — that the North American progressive impulse peaked in Canada. As in both the United States and the United Kingdom, the end of the war had brought a surge of political radicalism, most dramatically reflected in the Winnipeg General Strike of 1919. But the "normalcy" that Warren Harding brought back to the U.S. in 1920 returned to Canada more slowly, and in a different way.

In the election of 1921 a new federal Progressive Party at last made a bid for power at Ottawa. It did not have a broad enough base of support to win the election Yet, just as the American Progressives had taken enough votes away from Republicans to elect Woodrow Wilson and the Democrats in 1912, in 1921 the Canadian Progressives took enough votes away from Conservatives to elect a resurgent collection of old Laurier Liberals, now under the unique leadership of William Lyon Mackenzie King, aptly described by his early biographer Bruce Hutchison as *The Incredible Canadian.*

Mackenzie King, who could only form a minority government in 1921, was kept in power by an informal arrangement with the Progressives, whom he wisely chose to regard as mere 'Liberals in a hurry.' Yet this was enough to lay the ground-work for a new Canadian Liberal Party. It would enjoy what Hutchison, a leading Ottawa political journalist of the era (with roots in British Columbia), would finally describe as "a longer term of office under one leader than any party had ever known in any English-speaking state."

The Firebrand's Grandson

It is hard to know just which of Mackenzie King's many incredible sides is worth stressing in a short space. To start with, he was the maternal grandson of William Lyon Mackenzie, leader of the old Upper Canadian Rebellion of 1837. For balance, he was descended on his father's side from old American Loyalists, who had subsequently apostatized to the Canadian party of Reform.

He himself grew up comfortably in a family that belonged to the modest social and economic elite of late 19th century Berlin, Ontario (which would prudently change its name to Kitchener during the First World War). But his mother seared the memory of her father's controversial political career on her son's youthful soul. When Mackenzie King won the Liberal leadership in 1919, he told the convention delegates: "I can never forget, and I hope you will permit me to mention it on this occasion, that my grandfather...and Papineau in Lower Canada were seeking to bring about...change."

The modern edge of change was not the struggle for colonial democracy, but the conflict between labour and capital induced by the new industrialism. And Mackenzie King's earliest career was as an expert in the problems of managing this conflict. He had been Laurier's Minister of Labour, and had spent much time helping to resolve early labour disputes in various parts of the country.

After Laurier's government was defeated in 1911, Mackenzie King spent several years doing similar work for the Rockefeller family (or, as he himself liked to insist, "The Rockefeller Foundation") in the United States. Drawing on all his experience, he wrote a ponderous book entitled *Industry and Humanity,* a few themes from which he used in his 1919 leadership campaign: "Human personality is more important than any consideration of property... . Industry exists for the sake of humanity, not humanity for the sake of industry."

On the surface he was a dull, small, and rather odd-looking man — a penny-pinching, lifelong bachelor who, as Hutchinson has put it, "coddled his health, watched his diet, rationed his exertions, and lived as regularly as a grandfather clock." His habits of physical movement were peculiar, and when he appeared in newsreels in the new age of motion pictures, Canadian voters would sometimes laugh out loud.

At the same time, he was a man of great intuitive political intelligence, who had been contemplating the problems of the Canadian Confederation since childhood. He was also a shrewd, devious, and (in his own roundabout way) resolute political operator, who freely confessed: "I've always found you can control people better if you don't see too much of them."

In public, his manners were proper and even obsequious, in the worst traditions of late 19th century gentility: as Hutchison put it, he was "prostrate before the Divinity and the electorate." In the privacy of his office, "his eyes sparkled with a cynical wit, he gaily lampooned his colleagues and discussed the sworn secrets of Cabinet with the wildest abandon."

He also turned the ever deepening Canadian tradition of compromise into a minor art form. During both the 1911 reciprocity election and a subsequent party crisis over conscription in 1917, he had remained a loyal Laurier Liberal. From Laurier he learned what his Conservative opponents, with both Cartier and Macdonald long gone, never quite seemed able to remember — that you cannot govern Canada without strong support in French-speaking Quebec.

King himself was too much of a southern Ontario Anglo-Protestant to understand the soul of French Catholic Canada. In effect, he appointed Ernest Lapointe from Quebec as what the press of the day termed his "French Canadian lieutenant." Lapointe was a tall man with an impressive physique that contrasted intriguingly with Mackenzie King's diminutive flab. He had only learned to speak English when first elected to the federal Parliament in the early 1900s; but he alone among Mackenzie King's mature colleagues would call the prime minister by his boyhood nickname of "Rex."

During King's first term in office, his dependence on support from the Progressives, who had particularly deep roots in Western Canada, made both him and his Liberal Party sensitive to the regional aspirations of the newest parts of the country. From the former Premier of Nova Scotia W.S. Fielding, Laurier's old finance minister (and, in effect, Laurier's "English Canadian lieutenant"), Mackenzie King had inherited a Liberal party that was already very conscious of just how important it is to keep your fences well-mended in Atlantic Canada.

Finally, to compensate for his dullness in ordinary life, he had deep mystic interests, a well-developed faith in the world beyond this one, and recurrently consulted mediums and psychics in connection with his personal and sometimes even public affairs.

In all contexts, as Hutchison has put it, he "believed implicitly in luck and propitiated it with comic zeal. The numeral seven, he said, was favourable to his enterprises. He liked to launch them on the seventh day of the month or in the seventh month of the year. If possible, he would take no decisive step until the hands of the clock were directly opposite each other in a straight line."

"Of the people, for the people..."

Despite the 1911 election, trade policy remained an irritant in Canadian federal politics during the election of 1921, particularly for the Progressive Party. Mackenzie King, however, declared: "The real issue is not protection or free trade. It is whether...we shall have a Liberal policy of government of the people, for the people, and by the people or its alternative of continued autocracy, or government for and by a class."

Decoded, this meant that for the new federal Liberal party Canadian prosperity still implied increasing continental integration of the North American economy. But especially since the low U.S. Underwood Tariff of 1913, continental integration was increasing anyway. There was no point in going over the old reciprocity debate again: that had done no good in 1891, and it had actually lost Mackenzie King his seat in parliament in 1911.

Moreover, there was another side to Canada's trading future in the 20th century. Fielding and the Laurier Liberals had foreshadowed it with the intermediate preference in the tariff of 1907. Mackenzie King himself had discussed the matter in *Industry and Humanity*, when he wrote about a new international economic system "which has substituted world for local markets and interdependence for self-sufficiency in Industry and Trade."

Hard times right after the First World War had actually prompted some increases in U.S. tariffs, and this helped prolong the hard times in Canada well into the early 1920s. Yet, as a gesture of Canadian support for the North American economy (and in deference to their Progressive supporters), Mackenzie King's Liberals made modest annual reductions in Canadian tariffs.

Of more consequence, in both its resource and industrial sectors, the Canadian economy had developed new depth and diversity in the great boom before the First World War. Politics notwithstanding, by 1923 Canada was joining in on the short, giddy North American economic boom of the Roaring Twenties. And the pattern of Canadian exports began to assume an increasingly more complex shape.

The Changing Resource Base

The historic fur trade was now at the extreme margins of Canadian economic life (though still vital for some Indians and crusty white trappers on the most northern frontiers). The wider resource economy, however, remained the greatest engine of growth.

Fishing was still crucial on the Atlantic, and even the Pacific coasts. Wheat was now the great staple of Western Canada. Forestry was vital in parts of Atlantic Canada, in Central Canada, and in British Columbia. Pulp and paper, produced in conjunction with new hydroelectric projects, was especially important in Central Canada — and particularly in Ontario, whose new Conservative provincial government had established the world's first publicly-owned hydroelectric power corporation in 1906.

Mining was the great new resource sector. It had some significance in some parts of virtually every region of the country, and it was the underlying engine of growth for the rugged Canadian Shield frontier of northern Quebec and especially Northern Ontario. More than anything else, mining in Northern Ontario would give Toronto the kind of financial muscle that made possible its ultimately successful challenge to Montreal's historic status as Canada's "senior metropolis," after the Second World War.

Before the First World War "Laurier's Tariff Mixture," as this Hunter cartoon puts it, had diversified, broadened, and even moderated John A. Macdonald's National Policy. In the 1920's, William Lyon Mackenzie King — an aggressively loyal Laurier Liberal, carried on with his old leader's vision.

American capital played a key role in the development of Canadian mining, as elsewhere in the northern resource economy. The first three years of the First World War, when the United States remained neutral, had created some difficulties in this context; and these difficulties had prompted successful government-inspired pressures for more "Canadianization" in such enterprises as the International Nickel Company.

Particularly after the war, American markets became increasingly important consumers of all manner of Canadian resource products. Some large metropolitan newspapers in the U.S. found it prudent to operate their own pulp and paper mills north of the border.

British capital and British markets were declining in importance, but they remained significant. Even in 1930 British markets took more than a quarter of all Canadian exports.

Harold Innis at the University of Toronto summarized the broad thrust of change when his *The Fur Trade in Canada: An Introduction to Canadian Economic History* was first published in 1930. In the conclusion to his pioneering study of the romantic wilderness commerce that had pioneered the Canadian resource economy, he noted that Canada "has continued...chiefly as a producer of staples for the industrial centres of the United States even more than of Great Britain making her own contribution to the Industrial Revolution of North America and Europe."

At the same time, perhaps because the trend was still quite new, Innis did not stress that, as he wrote, Canada's fastest-growing external markets were in neither the United States nor the United Kingdom (or even the British Empire).

Several years after *The Fur Trade* first appeared, Frank Scott, a rebel socialist intellectual from an old Montreal British establishment family, declared: "It is clear that Japan, like Great Britain, looks to Canada as a source of supply of raw materials." Moreover, by this time Canadian business had interests as well as markets in various parts of the world. As Scott also reported, "Canadians own large utilities in places as remote as Mexico and Brazil and have mining interests as far away as Rhodesia."

Changing Destination of Canadian Exports, 1910-1930

To	% 1910	% 1930	Change
United Kingdom	50	27	- 23
Other Preferential	6	8	+ 2
United States	37	45	+ 8
Other Countries	7	20	+ 13

Industrial Development in Various Directions

The boom before the First World War did more than energize and deepen the traditional resource base of the Canadian economy. It also promoted the dominion's somewhat eccentric particular version of the new industrialism — in some eyes the most favoured child of the Canadian national development policies that had begun to evolve in the awkward times of the late 19th century.

By the mid-1920s, for instance, there were significant domestic manufacturing and service sectors, particularly concentrated in Central Canada, and generating goods and services for a protected east-west Canadian market. Textile producers in Ontario and Quebec, the unusually centralized (in comparison with the U.S.A.) Canadian financial system, dominated by a few large banks and insurance companies, the Canadian Pacific Railway headquartered in Montreal, and retail chains like the T. Eaton Company headquartered in Toronto, were key figures in this corner of the picture.

Yet by the end of the First World War it was once again clear that even with the early 20th century boom, and the development of Western Canada, there were limits on the industrial growth-generating capacities of the east-west domestic economy. The two new transcontinental railways that had been built to compete with the C.P.R. — the Canadian Northern and the Grand Trunk Pacific — plunged into financial difficulties as the end of the war approached. Under Arthur Meighen's last gasp of Borden's regime, the Canadian federal government took them over, following the honourable old Canadian Tory tradition of government intervention in the interests of national development. A few years later they were joined with the old Intercolonial Railroad, to form the modern government-owned Canadian National Railways.

As in the resource sector, other elements in Canada's version of the new industrialism sought wider markets elsewhere. What had become the Massey-Harris agricultural machinery enterprise (one of the few big-league industrial success stories in the first two generations of the Confederation) had long been following the path of Imperial preference into the markets of the British Empire.

By the 1920s Massey-Harris was also well established in international markets beyond the Empire. Even some highly centralized Canadian banks would open branches in the British West Indies, on the exotic North American islands of the Caribbean Sea.

Both Massey-Harris and the banks had begun to expand into the United States as well. Moreover, even in the hard times of the late 19th century, a few other dynamic Canadian industrial enterprises, like the Moore Corporation, had begun to make inroads on the American market.

In 1879 (the year that John A. Macdonald's National Policy was born) S.J. Moore had started a small printing shop in Toronto that began to specialize in producing business forms, using the raw materials of the early Canadian pulp and paper industry. This proved to be an unexploited niche that, suitably organized, could penetrate even high U.S. tariff walls. By the late 1880s Moore had a branch operation in Buffalo. In the great boom of the early 20th century his American interests expanded dramatically. By the late 1920s the Moore

Corporation was operating four business form and related manufacturing facilities in Canada, and 11 in the United States —all headquartered in Toronto.

American Multinationals & the Imperial Idea

In a final corner of the picture all the strands in Canada's somewhat eccentric national industrial development patterns came together, to form a polyglot Canadian-American-Imperial structure—whose highest expression was the early Canadian automobile industry.

Initially, a few strictly Canadian automobiles (the Russell and the Iroquois, for instance) were produced by small firms in Southern Ontario. But, like smaller firms in the United States, they were swallowed by the rapid, large-scale corporate growth of the continental industry, even with high 35% levels of tariff protection.

The most practicable wave of the future had been signalled quite early in the 20th century, when a group of Canadian businessmen in Windsor, Ontario (across the river from the old French Canadian wilderness fur trade metropolis at Detroit) made arrangements with Henry Ford to manufacture his automobiles in Canada, and sell them to both the domestic Canadian and British Empire markets, as Ford of Canada.

At the end of the First World War General Motors of Canada was created, when the McLaughlin Motor Company of Oshawa, Ontario merged with Chevrolet Motor Company of Canada, under the presidency of the Oshawa entrepreneur Sam McLaughlin. Chrysler, Studebaker, and other American firms soon acquired comparable Canadian corporate extensions.

The east-west Canadian market absorbed a large enough share of this production of "Canadian-made, U.S.-type motor vehicles." Canada joined the United States in ushering in what the U.S. historian John Lukacs would much later call "The Automobile Century"—*a mari usque ad mare.* Yet by the mid-1920s almost half of all Canadian automobile production was being exported overseas, particularly to such places as Australia, the United Kingdom, British India, New Zealand, and the Argentine Republic. Thanks to international markets, in 1929 Canada produced more automobiles than any country in the world except the United States.

This linkage between the American multinational corporation and Canada's special access to Empire and other international markets, in return for the Imperial and intermediate preferential rates in its tariff structure, was not strictly confined to the automobile industry. In 1916 the American business press reported that the Goodyear Tire and Rubber Company had organized its Canadian subsidiary "to handle Canadian and such other foreign business as can be shipped advantageously from Canada owing to tariff conditions."

In broad perspective, the importance of Imperial preference for Canada's trading patterns declined between 1910 and 1930: the United Kingdom's share of Canadian exports fell from 50% to 27%. Yet even after almost a decade of Mackenzie King's early continentalist rumblings, the international tilt that

Empire trade had helped give the Canadian economy remained an ingredient in Canada's continental economic role. A pioneering study of the 1930s (by a trio of economists known as Marshall, Southard, and Taylor) would report that, as an "indication of the importance of Empire trade in the calculations of the American company considering Canada as a producing point...about 40 per cent of the companies questioned replied that they were serving foreign — chiefly Empire — markets from Canadian plants."

In 1930 Harold Innis had also summarized this side of Canadian economic development in his conclusion to *The Fur Trade:* "Canada has participated in the industrial growth of the United States, becoming the gateway of that country to the markets of the British Empire."

Even as Innis's book began to reach its first small audience, however, for all parts of the Canadian economy, a new round of hard times, creative destruction, and world war loomed ahead. Out of all this, and after a brief period when Canadian trade policy would once again veer more strongly toward the British Empire, a still more obviously North American and more prosperous Canadian Confederation would greet the second half of the 20th century.

Chapter 9

CONTINENTAL STRUGGLES

A s a mark of the American Republic's rising importance in an expanding international industrial economy, the Great Crash of October 1929 on Wall Street in New York led to the Great Depression of the 1930s in many different parts of the world.

In the United States itself, it also sparked a return to the high tariff regime of the 19th century — helping to set the stage for a global movement toward trade protectionism which, it is now widely agreed, deepened the Depression virtually everywhere. In Canada, among many other things, the Canadian-American automobile industry would not return to its 1929 production levels until the late 1940s.

Still more profoundly, as the 1930s progressed, drought on the Canadian prairie combined ecological with economic crisis for the 20th century wheat economy. This wreaked particular havoc on Saskatchewan, which had become Western Canada's most populous province by 1921. Saskatchewan's population started to fall absolutely in the 1930s, and would not return to its 1931 level of somewhat less than a million people until 1961. Manitoba and (until after the Second World War) Alberta did not fare all that much better.

Even in the West, however, the depression in Canada was not a uniform disaster. The population of British Columbia actually increased by some 18% between 1931 and 1941. The opening of the Panama Canal at the start of the First World War, and the early beginnings of Canadian trade with Japan and other parts of Asia, had already helped Vancouver supplant Winnipeg as Canada's third largest city by 1931.

Atlantic Canada continued to have the lowest per capita incomes in the country, and unemployment shot up to as high as a national average of 19.3% in 1933. Yet in the 1930s Prince Edward Island actually gained population, for the first time since the 1890s. The population in both Nova Scotia and New

Brunswick increased by some 12%, compared with only 6% in the American state of New Hampshire, and no growth at all in Vermont.

Absolutely, the historic concentration of Canada's population in the central provinces of Ontario and Quebec, which had so many more people than the others to begin with, increased slightly between 1931 and 1941 (from just under 61% to just under 62%). But, relatively, Quebec, with a population increase of about 15%, grew somewhat more slowly than B.C. And Ontario's population increased about 10% — somewhat less than in either Nova Scotia or New Brunswick.

The population of Canada at large increased just under 11%, compared with just over 7% in the United States. By 1931 Canada at last had the more than 10 million people predicted by the most optimistic boosters of the early Confederation. In 1941 its population amounted to 8.7% of the population in the United States, up from 8.2% in 1921. By 1931 more than half the Canadian population was living in urban areas, compared with only 18% just after Confederation in the early 1870s. By 1941 the figure had increased to 56%.

As elsewhere, the Great Depression led into the Second World War. As in the First World War, unlike the United States Canada was a party to the conflict from its beginnings in 1939. Moreover, for better or for worse, the domestic war effort finally pulled Canada out of the Depression. To the surprise of some, when the war ended a new wave of growth and prosperity almost immediately took hold. By the early 1950s the Confederation was in the midst of a new economic boom, that would prove a worthy successor indeed to its historic great booms of the 1850s and the early 20th century.

Imperial Preference Revisited

The first political impact of the Depression in Canada was to put Mackenzie King and the Liberals out of office for some four years and two and a half months — in an election called for July 28, 1930.

By this point Mackenzie King had managed to absorb the leading Progressives of the early 1920s into Liberal ranks. In the wake of the Wall Street crash, however, even this would prove insufficient to prevent defeat at the hands of a resurgent Conservative Party, under the new leadership of Richard Bedford Bennett.

Bennett, a native of Hopewell, New Brunswick who had migrated to Calgary, Alberta in the late 1890s, was in most respects an unlikely popular candidate for hard times. He was less unappealingly serious and high-minded than Meighen, but an anonymous journalist would later describe him as "a well-groomed prosperous-looking millionaire, who has an autocratic habit of speech."

Just before the election, in June of 1930, President Herbert Hoover had signed a new "Smoot-Hawley" high U.S. tariff bill into law. This was a genuine blow to Mackenzie King's quiet Canadian Liberal development strategy of creeping continentalism, gradually moderating (but not abandoning) the old

National Policy and Imperial preference, while looking to new international markets via the intermediate preference of 1907.

King had in fact decided on the late July Canadian election several months before, with other things than trade policy on his mind (including some advice from one Mrs. Bleaney, a Kingston, Ontario psychic). Nonetheless the Smoot-Hawley tariff played into the hands of Bennett's contention that the only realistic response to the Depression for Canada was a much more rigorous emphasis on John A. Macdonald's old protectionist trade policies, Imperial preference, and the British connection.

In his election campaign Bennett had told a Winnipeg audience: "I will use tariffs to blast a way into the markets that have been closed to you." Mackenzie King ridiculed the concept, but even he made noises to the effect that, once again, with access to the markets of the United States newly blocked, Canada ought to be doing more than it had done in the past decade to strengthen its ties with the markets of the British Empire.

By this time the United Kingdom itself was ready to abandon the revolutionary policy of imperial free trade that it had boldly embarked on almost three generations before. In February 1932 it too would at long last return to a policy of protective tariffs. Within the context of this new British mood, Bennett was actually quite successful in negotiating new imperial trade arrangements that, for a time, would bring Canada real benefits. By 1937 some 38% of all Canadian exports were going to the United Kingdom, compared with only 27% in 1930.

Yet these benefits were far from enough to bring Canada or any other part of the British Empire out of the Great Depression. And efforts to forge a major new Empire trading bloc, at an Imperial Conference held in Ottawa during the summer of 1932, were much less than successful. The English historian A.J.P. Taylor would later report that the Ottawa Conference brought "no great charter of empire, only twelve individual agreements over details of preference between Great Britain and the Dominions, and between the Dominions themselves." It "was merely a symbolic gesture towards the idea of a closed empire; a repudiation of Free Trade principles in theory, though not in practice."

As the Depression grew deeper down to 1934, Bennett himself started to loose faith in his original strategy. As the time for calling a fresh election drew nearer, he began to think that perhaps a Canadian version of Franklin Roosevelt's New Deal in the United States, along with some new Canada-U.S. trade agreement, would make more sense.

He now moved in this direction, but it only blurred his image in the election that finally took place on October 14, 1935. In his home region of Western Canada old automobiles pulled by horses for want of money to buy gas had been christened "Bennett Buggies." Bennett defended his record before the electorate by proclaiming: "We have not only done what we said we would do. We have done far more than we have even told you of."

Mackenzie King told the electorate that Bennett foolishly regarded trade as an act of war rather than exchange. The Liberals would both continue working to clear imperial trade channels, and seek a broad reciprocal trade agreement with the United States. What Canada needed most of all was a return to "the

When the 1930's Depression sparked the high U.S. Smoot-Hawley Tariff, which once again blocked Canadian access to American markets, Canada once again looked to the markets of the Empire. The original title of this cartoon, showing R.B.Bennett trying to lead John Bull's 80 odd years of free trade toward a protected Imperial trading bloc, poses the question: "Can he lead the bull?" In the end the answer was yes, but it didn't do either Canada or the British Empire at all as much good as Bennett had hoped.

sympathetic physician's touch." Meanwhile, Liberal Party advertising declared: "Bennett let us down. Drive him out," and "It's King or Chaos."

When the ballots were counted, the Liberals had won 173 seats at Ottawa, and the Conservatives only 40. The incredible Canadian was back in the saddle, and he would stay there until his retirement in 1948.

Nation Building in the 1920s & 1930s

Because the relationship between the dominions and Great Britain had begun as one of metropolitan mother country and overseas colonies, the underlying problem with a strengthened British Empire trading bloc was that it only made real sense for the United Kingdom if Canada and its fellow self-governing Commonwealth democracies were prepared to take serious steps down the road to imperial federation. A.J.P. Taylor would later write that Bennett himself "thought only of Canada's troubles, not of the Imperial cause."

Laurier had already resisted imperial federation in the late 19th and early 20th centuries. Canada had moved further along the road from colony to nation during the First World War. Mackenzie King had continued the journey in the early 1920s, and brought the issue to a head domestically in 1926 — when he at last won a majority in parliament by challenging the rights of the British-appointed Governor-General to intervene in the workings of Canadian democracy.

At Imperial Conferences in 1926 and 1930, this led to clear statements that only the symbolism of the British Crown, not any practical workings of the government of the United Kingdom, now linked Canada and the other autonomous, self-governing dominions to the old mother country. Canada, Australia, New Zealand, South Africa, and (for the moment) the Irish Free State and Newfoundland, were no longer parts of the British Empire, but parts of a new association to be known as the British Commonwealth of Nations. All this was given legal force through the Statute of Westminster, passed by the parliament of the United Kingdom in 1931.

For Canada it would be another half century before the journey was finished altogether. Canadian Governor-Generals would now be appointed by the British Crown only on the advice of the Government of Canada (in effect, the Canadian Prime Minister). But British aristocrats would continue to fill the position for another two decades. The first Canadian Governor-General born in Canada would not be appointed until 1952. And the highest court in the Canadian legal system would remain in the United Kingdom until 1949.

More decisively, the power to amend the Canadian Constitution, embodied in "the British North America Acts, 1867 to 1930," remained with the parliament of the United Kingdom until 1982. This did not flow from any wish of the mother country, but from still unresolved conflicts within the highly diverse Canadian Confederation itself, over the relative balance between the powers of the federal government at Ottawa and the rights of the provinces.

On John A. Macdonald's view, it made sense to say that the Canadian Constitution could be amended by the federal parliament alone. But this view had been far from universally accepted, even in the Confederation era. And much had happened since the high tide of Macdonald's career.

The provincial government of Quebec had increasingly come to see itself as the only real strong arm for the protection of French Canadian culture. In the late 19th century a series of constitutional cases argued by Ontario in the highest court of the British Empire (known as the Judicial Committee of the Privy Council) had given new prominence to provincial rights more generally.

Laurier's early 20th century regime confirmed the tilt in the Confederation toward the decentralized model of federalism that had nurtured de Tocqueville's democracy in America before the Civil War. By the late 1920s Ontario, Quebec, Saskatchewan, and British Columbia (the four most populous provinces of the day) would not agree to any method of amending the Canadian Constitution that did not include some form of provincial consent.

For the moment, no one could agree on just what the form should be, and under section 7 of the Statute of Westminster the power to amend the Constitution was left in British hands. The issue of a suitable Canadian amending formula would be decided at a later date. Yet, as this agenda for the future itself implied, the course of the Confederation remained unalterably set on the road from colony to nation.

In increasingly subtle ways, the heritage of the British Empire (and its modern successor, the Commonwealth of Nations) has remained influential in many parts of Canada down to the present. John Diefenbaker's final bow in the direction of Imperial preference would not come until the late 1950s. By the Second World War, however, the concept of imperial federation had slipped from whatever part of the mainstream of Canadian national politics it may have occupied a generation before.

Making Peace with the American Dream

Before the electorate turned him out, Bennett had actually begun discussions with the United States about new trade arrangements. In this as in other respects Franklin Roosevelt (elected in 1932) had proved a somewhat different president than Herbert Hoover, with a somewhat different Congress. Roosevelt's Secretary of State, Cordell Hull, believed the Smoot-Hawley Tariff had been a great mistake. By 1934 a new Hull Act was offering up to 50% cuts in U.S. tariffs in return for reciprocity pacts with major American trading partners.

It was Mackenzie King's good fortune that by the time he returned to office in 1935, the U.S. political climate was ripe for a return to the continental priorities that remained at the top of his list of Canadian Liberal development policies. He quickly picked up the threads of Bennett's earlier discussions, and negotiated two of some 20 agreements that the United States would sign with various countries under the framework of the Hull Act.

The first of these was struck late in 1935, very soon after King had returned to power, to take effect on January 1, 1936. It had nothing like the broad free trade elements in the rejected Reciprocity Treaty of 1911, but it did substantially reduce levels of tariff protection in both countries.

As a general matter, Canada applied its intermediate preference to the United States, and still further reduced its tariffs on 88 specific American products. The United States significantly reduced tariffs on 60 Canadian products. The Canadian-American historian John Bartlet Brebner would later write that the main effects "were to make easier American sales to Canada of farm implements, automobiles, electrical apparatus, gasoline, and machinery; and Canadian sales to the United States of lumber, cattle, dairy products, fresh and frozen fish, whisky, and potatoes."

The second agreement was signed in 1938, to bring the new mid-1930s trading arrangements between Canada and the United States into some more sensible relationship with the protectionist agreements between Canada and the United Kingdom signed in the early 1930s. It was preceded by a new more liberal trade treaty between Canada and the United Kingdom in 1937, and accompanied by a new trade treaty between the United Kingdom and the United States in 1938.

The United Kingdom, other parts of the British Empire, and the world at large would remain significant markets for Canadian production, taking more than a third of all Canada's exports even in the early 1950s. By the late 1930s, however, the trend toward continental integration with the economy of the United States was making its deepest inroads since the old Reciprocity Treaty of the mid 19th century.

There were other signs of Mackenzie King's economic and even political commitment to the life of the North American continent. The Second World War led to the creation of a Joint Defence Board for Canada and the United States in 1940, and defence production sharing arrangements were negotiated under the Hyde Park Declaration of 1941. In 1944, following trends that had begun with the U.S. Underwood Tariff in 1913, Canada and the United States removed all tariffs on each other's agricultural machinery.

Yet in the early new boom atmosphere that followed the war King would show that his particular continental vision had its limits. In 1947 he acceded to advice that the time was ripe for at last renegotiating a new version of the rejected Reciprocity Treaty of 1911. Very quiet discussions with Washington proved very promising. But in 1948, not long before he settled into his brief retirement, King called the project off.

No doubt, he remembered what had happened to his party in the 1911 election. The Canadian economy was doing well enough. He had recently returned from the Royal Wedding of Princess Elizabeth and Prince Phillip in London. The March 15, 1948 issue of Life magazine in the U.S. had talked about a customs union between Canada and the United States — on the model of Erastus Wiman's old commercial union proposal. And perhaps, as Bruce Hutchison has suggested, in the now deeply rooted tradition of compromise, the prime minister who stood for economic continentalism in North America had also become an "unquenchable Canadian nationalist."

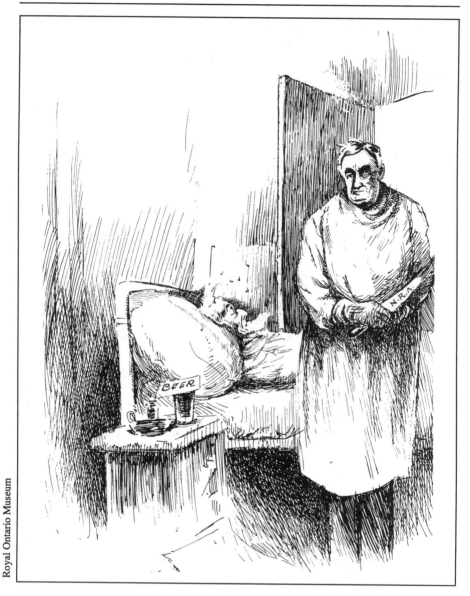

As part of its efforts to revive an ailing Uncle Sam, the new Roosevelt administration in Washington managed to change directions on the Smoot-Hawley Tariff. When Mackenzie King returned to office he took advantage of the changed American mood, and negotiated new Canada-U.S. trade deals in the mid and late 1930s. These were tariff-reduction rather than free trade agreements, but they did strengthen the North American continental dimensions of the Canadian economy. Roosevelt, who probably never looked as glum about anything as Sam Hunter has him pictured here, liked to refer to Mackenzie King simply as "Mackenzie" - the surname of the Canadian prime minister's rebel grandfather in the first half of the 19th century.

Changing Destinations of Canadian Exports, 1930-1950

To	% 1930	% 1950	Change
United Kingdom	27	15	- 12
Other Countries	20	14	- 6
Other Preferential	8	6	- 2
United States	45	65	+ 20

Conscription & the Early Federal Welfare State

Like the First World War, the Second World War was another crucible in the evolution of Canadian nationality. Canada declared war on Germany on September 10, 1939 — seven days after the United Kingdom (to clearly assert Canadian sovereignty in such crucial matters). More than a million Canadians would serve in the country's armed forces between 1939 and 1945, and more than 46,000 would die in battle. Canada was a founding member of the United Nations organization that was established at the end of the war.

Leading a party that depended fundamentally on support from Quebec, which had violently opposed conscription for military service in 1917, Mackenzie King began the war effort cautiously. After the Fall of France in June 1940, he stepped up Canada's contribution: it was in high gear by the time the Americans joined in 1942. Conscription, supported by all provinces but Quebec in a plebiscite held the same year, prompted King's most celebrated policy statement: "conscription if necessary, but not necessarily conscription." Ultimately, he managed to put off even very limited compulsory overseas service until the autumn of 1944.

Domestically, the war facilitated plots for a more socially interventionist federal government, hatched during the 1930s Depression.

The modern Canadian welfare state had its earliest beginnings at the provincial level of government in the late 19th century, and this is where much of it would remain. But, following Mackenzie King's background as a labour expert with an interest in social issues in the 1920s, the demands of the 1930s, and Bennett's experiments with a Canadian New Deal, a new national unemployment insurance program, begun in 1941, finally mobilized a more effectively muscular federal role in social policy.

Disproportionately severe impacts of the Depression in Atlantic and especially Western Canada had also raised pressures for new federal financial grants that would "equalize" the capacity of all provincial governments to provide a standard national level of public services. The "Rowell-Sirois" report on Dominion-provincial relations of 1940 formulated the concept. Some of the larger provinces (especially Ontario and Quebec) resisted, and it would not be seriously implemented until the 1950s.

Along with a stronger role in social policy, however, the centralizing effects of the war effort would eventually help the federal government take a stronger role in offsetting "regional disparities" generated by the private sector of the economy (or, as the matter was recurrently viewed outside Central Canada, by John A. Macdonald's old National Policy).

Early Varieties of Canadian Culture

Among much of the fledgling native intelligentsia that began to set down its first serious roots in Canada between the two world wars, the great problem with Mackenzie King was that he deliberately seemed to avoid projecting any coherent underlying vision for the evolving Canadian nationality.

Frank Scott of Montreal summed the point up in a poem: "He blunted us./ We had no shape/Because he never took sides,/And no sides/Because he never allowed them to take shape." In the idiom of the late 20th century, creeping continentalism thwarted the development of a strong Canadian national culture: Canada was simply exchanging one imperial allegiance for another, even though it stopped short of formal annexation to the United States.

Yet, however one might see it, there was more than one side to the story. By the 1940s, for instance, the National Hockey League that had been established in Canada in 1917 had teams representing six cities — Montreal, Toronto, New York, Boston, Detroit, and Chicago. This was either a telling illustration of how Americans took over Canadian institutions when the business of mass spectator sport went continental, or the most successful case yet of Canadian cultural imperialism in the United States.

Canadians who wanted to succeed in the entertainment industry (like Mary Pickford, Walter Huston, Raymond Massey, or Guy Lombardo) went to New York or Hollywood (sometimes, as in Raymond Massey's case, after an apprenticeship on the London stage). On the other hand, Bennett's regime had established the Canadian Broadcasting Corporation (with at least half an eye on the model of the British Broadcasting Corporation in the imperial metropolis), to bring a Canadian voice to the new radio airwaves of North America.

Raymond Massey's brother, Vincent, had worked at establishing the beginnings of a Canadian theatre. Lawren Harris (like both the Masseys, a legatee of the Massey-Harris agricultural machinery enterprise) had helped establish a Canadian style of northern wilderness art. Morley Callaghan and Hugh MacLennan had developed literary careers based in Canada, as had such different earlier writers as Stephen Leacock, Lucy Maude Montgomery, and Mazo de la Roche.

Though much of the strictly literary and artistic energy had a more easterly focus, Lawren Harris began his career in Toronto and ended it in British Columbia. The West was the home of the RCMP (which even made it into Hollywood movies), and the best hockey players. It could take credit as well for innovations in Canadian political culture, as the Depression gave birth to two new political parties, in the cradle of the drought-ravaged Western wheat economy.

The Co-operative Commonwealth Federation (CCF) combined left-wing British socialism with North American agrarian populism. A more industrial labour-oriented faction set down roots in Ontario as well as Western Canada, and though federal success proved elusive, in 1944 a CCF provincial government took power in Saskatchewan. The other new party, Social Credit, combined North American agrarian populism with the doctrines of a popular right-wing British political theorist known as Major Douglas. It would set down its deepest roots in the provincial governments of Alberta and British Columbia, but would later have surprising success as a federal political party in Quebec.

There were innovations in French Canadian political culture as well, reflected in the rise of Maurice Duplessis's Union Nationale party in Quebec provincial politics (which had given la belle province its own "national" flag by 1948). In 1945 Brebner reported that "the most extreme form" of "French Canadian particularism" was "now a demand for secession from the Dominion and for the creation of the separate state of 'Laurentia'."

As the middle of the 20th century approached, the new English-speaking intelligentsia itself did not have any real vision of how to go about bridging what Hugh MacLennan had called the "two solitudes" of the evolving Canadian nationality. Yet through the good offices of Ernest Lapointe (and then Louis St. Laurent) — and even through his own strategy of remaining particularly prostrate before the Quebec wing of the Canadian electorate — Mackenzie King at least coped with the issue practically, in a way that left options for the future.

At least one leading figure among the new English-speaking intelligentsia did ultimately come to believe that the incredible Canadian knew what he was doing rather better than many of his critics. In the late 1940s Frank Underhill, one of the authors of the CCF's "Regina Manifesto" in the early 1930s, felt compelled to confess: "Evidently Mr. King meets the needs of the Canadian people much more satisfactorily than we and other critics have been willing in the past to admit."

On King's retirement in 1948, Underhill went on to summarize the case for his virtues as a democratic politician: "His statesmanship has been a more subtly accurate, a more flexibly adjustable Gallup poll of Canadian public opinion than statisticians will ever be able to devise. He has been the representative Canadian, the typical Canadian, the essential Canadian, the ideal Canadian, the Canadian as he exists in the mind of God."

Sam Hunter's impression of the incredible Canadian — reviled continentalist to some, "unquenchable Canadian nationalist" to others, and supreme master of the tradition of compromise to everyone. Hunter himself was in his early 60s when Mackenzie King first became prime minister of Canada. When Hunter died in his early 80s in 1939, King still had almost another decade in power ahead of him.

Chapter 10

THE POLITICAL NATION

A t the end of the Second World War the seismographic Mackenzie King had detected new currents of popular feeling for a Canada that was at last neither an essentially Anglo-American place destined to be annexed by the United States, nor a fundamentally British North American place which would always remain a political appendage of the United Kingdom. Soon enough, he promised the electorate in his last federal election in 1945, parliament would be asked to approve a distinctive Canadian national flag.

Following the haphazard path of the tradition of compromise, his Canadian Liberal Party would fulfil the promise. But it would take almost 20 years: parliament would not finally vote on the matter until late in 1964. By this time King had long since departed for the world beyond this one. (Though on his own assumptions about what that world is like, he no doubt somehow witnessed parliament's final action with a sense of accomplishment.)

In fact, in the mid-1940s the living Mackenzie King had discovered that the evolving Canadian nationality was still not quite ready to express itself with a distinctive national flag. The highly diverse Canadian Confederation could not be the same kind of nation as the traditional, ethnically defined nations of Europe. And the French and English catamaran of a Confederacy could not adopt the aggressively unifying melting-pot strategy of the U.S.A. after the Civil War.

In 1865 George-Etienne Cartier had proposed "a political nationality with which neither the national origin nor the religion of any individual would interfere." In 1967 the English-speaking political scientist Donald Smiley revived the proposal in a book on *The Canadian Political Nationality*. Yet it would take time, patience, and even a kind of courage to mobilize the concept — in a world where the British Empire had only begun to disappear and French Canadian ethnic nationalism was growing: where the United States had taken on a new global role that reminded some of the old British Empire, and where deadly nuclear weapons and a new Cold War with the Soviet Union in Russia sometimes seemed to have etched a deep chasm across the path of human history itself.

Nonetheless, beginnings were made in the late 1940s. In 1947, a year before Mackenzie King's retirement, the federal parliament at Ottawa created the status of "Canadian citizen" (as opposed to "British subject," which is all that inhabitants of the country had technically been up to this point). King also presided over the negotiations that would at last bring Newfoundland into the Confederation in 1949. In the same year the Supreme Court of Canada became the final court of appeal in the Canadian legal system. Early in 1952, just over a year and a half after King's death, Vincent Massey became the first Canadian-born Governor-General of Canada.

The gradually emerging Canadian political nation was stepping into a new post-1945 world of nations in the company of some old imperial colleagues. India, "jewel of the Empire," gained its independence in 1947, along with Pakistan, and followed by Ceylon (later Sri Lanka) and Burma in 1948. All but Burma chose to remain in a still newer Commonwealth of Nations. In 1949, however, India also wished to become a republic which did not recognize the British Crown as formal head of state. Louis St. Laurent, Mackenzie King's successor as Prime Minister of Canada (and leader of the Canadian Liberal Party), helped out by suggesting an amendment to the symbolic precedents of the old Empire that made this possible.

Two years later St. Laurent's government itself quietly raised the issue of Canada's own New World Indian history, with its own ancient roots in Asia. In 1951 the federal Indian Act received its first major revision since the early Confederation era of the late 19th century. Ultimately, the rights of the Canadian Indians — and of the far northern Inuit, and the Métis descendants of Canada's earliest multiculturalism — would become the most historic ingredients in a political nationality that was at last beginning to contemplate its many complications and complexities.

The Economic Boom & the New Migrations

The new postwar economic boom helped keep the unresolved contradictions of the emerging political nation under control. The boom stalled somewhat at various points. But by any comparative standard virtually the entire period from 1949 to 1968 was an age of milk and honey. The average Canada-wide unemployment rate for the 20 years was 4.6% (though with lower rates of labour force participation than earlier or later).

The resource sector remained an engine of growth. The Western wheat economy climbed back on its feet. Mining and forestry continued to grow in other parts of the country, and the Canadian-American St. Lawrence Seaway completed in 1959 brought new hydro-electric projects on stream.

The biggest new boost came from the discovery of continentally significant oil and gas resources in Western Canada in the late 1940s, especially in the province of Alberta. For Canada at large, what wheat in the West had been in the early 20th century, oil and gas in the West would be in the late 20th century — in more ways than one.

"A Cold Dip" is the original title of this Hunter cartoon, showing an aggrieved Miss West with a brazen foot in the Western Wheat Pool. Western Canadian concern over wheat prices in the first half of the 20th Century would be matched by Western Canadian concern over oil prices in the second half of the 20th century. (At a finer regional grain, wheat had been the particular pride of Saskatchewan, and oil would be concentrated in Alberta: British Columbia, in many ways a region in its own right, would sometimes complain that even when Central Canadians like Sam Hunter looked west, they couldn't see beyond the Rocky Mountains.)

Both the resource and industrial sectors of the Canadian economy profited from the destruction that the Second World War had brought on Europe and Japan. For a brief period, while the vanquished nations of the war were rebuilding, Canada could exploit something of an international vacuum.

Put another way, Canada was now to no small extent a national region of the North American economy, with a trade and development policy pointing outward to the world at large. It was also a place where American capital and the American multinational corporation played an increasingly important role, and it joined in on the postwar economic expansion of the United States. Through to the mid-1960s Canadian exports to the United Kingdom held their modest 1950 levels; and the relative share of exports to the United States fell in favour of exports to other parts of the world.

Changing Destinations of Canadian Exports, 1950-1965

To	% 1950	% 1965	Change
United States	65	57	- 8
United Kingdom	15	14	- 1
Other Preferential	6	6	0
Other Countries	14	23	+ 9

Beyond resources and manufacturing, Canada joined the United States in what seemed to be the newest era of economic history as well. By 1850 the United Kingdom had become the world's first industrial nation, with more than half its work force employed outside agriculture and other resource sectors. Around 1950 the United States became, as the economist V.R. Fuchs would put it, "the world's first 'service economy'," with more than half its work force employed outside agriculture, other resource, and even industrial manufacturing sectors.

Canada followed the trend. In 1951 just over 51% of its labour force worked in agriculture, other resource industries, manufacturing, and construction, with just under 49% in transportation, trade, and and a growing assortment of other services. By 1971 only 37% of the labour force was producing goods of any sort, and 63% was producing services. Following a parallel trend, more than 76% of the country's population was living in urban areas.

The economic boom also fuelled a dramatic surge of population growth in Canada. In the early 1960s a U.S. year-book reported that the "population of the world as a whole is increasing at the rate of 1.7 percent a year. The growth rate of individual areas, however, ranges from a low of .7 percent in Europe to 2.8 percent annually in Canada and China."

The U.S. itself, at this point, was growing at the global average rate of 1.7 % a year. By the early 1950s Canada's population amounted to 9.3% of the population in the United States, up from 8.7 % in the early 1940s. The figure had risen to 10.6% by the early 1970s.

Part of Canada's dramatic population growth flowed from increased birth rates, as in the United States. But the telling factor was a major new wave of immigration. As before, there were sizeable contingents from the United Kingdom. The main thrust, however, was an expansion of the trend toward much more cosmopolitan migrations that had begun in the early 20th century.

In the 1950s southern and eastern Europeans were dominant. After 1960 immigration from Asia and the Caribbean, and virtually every other region of the globe, grew increasingly more important. By the 1970s the Canadian cultural mingling that had begun with the French and the Indians in the 17th century was taking a new lease on life. And the new mosaic that had developed in Canada after the American War of Independence in the late 18th and early 19th centuries was growing still richer and more complex, as the end of the 20th century drew within sight.

Politics & Economics in Transition

Neither the benefits of the economic boom, nor the new migrations, were spread exactly evenly across the political nation. Ontario, Quebec, British Columbia, and Alberta (the four most populous provinces by 1951) profited most. But population and employment increased significantly everywhere, and by the late 1950s the federal system of equalization grants planned for in the 1940s was in full operation.

In federal politics Mackenzie King's Liberal regime was carried on by Louis St. Laurent, who had succeeded Ernest Lapointe as King's French Canadian lieutenant. In 1957, and then massively in 1958, the Liberals were defeated by resurgent Conservatives (or "Progressive Conservatives," as they had been renamed in 1942) under John Diefenbaker. The new prime minister was a Saskatchewan populist, later dubbed the *Renegade in Power* by the Ottawa political journalist Peter Newman ("renegade" being an epithet for troublesome individuals in a traditional lexicon of the Central Canadian establishment).

In 1963 Diefenbaker's Conservatives were defeated by somewhat resurgent Liberals under Lester Pearson, a former federal civil servant from Ontario, who had earlier been St. Laurent's English Canadian lieutenant, and still earlier a favoured bureaucrat under Mackenzie King himself. The CCF transformed itself into the New Democratic Party in 1961. It prospered moderately in the radicalism of the 1960s, and would be running provincial governments in Manitoba, Saskatchewan, and British Columbia in the early 1970s. But even in the late 1960s and early 1970s it could not come close to forming a federal government at Ottawa.

Social Credit had even less success federally, despite the brief rise of its Créditiste Quebec wing in the 1960s. Moreover, by the 1970s it had been replaced by Peter Lougheed's more stylish Progressive Conservatives in Alberta provincial politics. At least in name, it would survive in British Columbia, which expressed its cherished Pacific exoticism by operating a unique two-party provincial political system that put Social Credit at one extreme and the New Democrats at the other. (For contrast and variety, at the most easterly end of the Confederation, traditionalist Atlantic Canada would have nothing but the Liberal and Conservative "old-line parties.").

Canada-U.S. trade issues were somewhat muted ingredients in Canadian federal politics during the 1950s and 1960s. As in other parts of the world, however, tariff levels in both countries gradually declined under the multilateral framework of the General Agreement on Tariffs and Trade.

"GATT" had been organized at the end of the Second World War, along with such bodies as the United Nations and the International Monetary Fund, to help resolve some of the problems of the new international economic system that, as Mackenzie King noted at the end of the First World War, had "substituted world for local markets." It began in 1948 with 23 member nations (including Canada), and a staff headquartered in Geneva, Switzerland. Down to the 1980s (by which point it had some 95 member nations) it would sponsor seven successive rounds of multilateral negotiations, resulting in a significant liberalization of international trade.

In the 1950s GATT became another point of reference for a Canadian trade and development policy that looked to the world at large. Yet it could do little to soothe more profound anxieties over the relationship between Canada and the United States, that became increasingly influential in various quarters as the 1950s wore on.

St. Laurent continued with Mackenzie King's creeping continentalism. Bilaterally, the concept of a formal free trade treaty had been abandoned in 1948, and the old tripartite framework of National Policy, Imperial preference, and intermediate preference remained intact. But there was much attenuation and downward moderation in tariff rates. The highest rates of the old National Policy would become inoperative for all but a few countries like Albania, which remained virtually sealed off to an emerging global village. And the post Second War Canadian Liberal Party was full of enthusiasm and encouragement for American capital and U.S. direct investment.

At the same time, St. Laurent's regime continued to work hard at Canadian national economic development. In effect, the Canadian economy increasingly had both east-west and north-south priorities (not altogether unlike the pre-Confederation modern Canadian embryo in the 1840s and 1850s, or even the Canadian fur trade before the American War of Independence — legacies which were, even after 1776 and 1866, never really lost). As in the past, there were difficult questions and thorny disagreements about the appropriate balance.

The government's handling of the Trans Canada Pipeline, designed to bring Western Canadian natural gas not just to eastern Canada, but to parts of the American Midwest as well, stirred a controversy that helped lead to the Liberal downfall in 1957. St. Laurent himself compared the Pipeline to the Canadian Pacific Railway in the late 19th century. There were similarities, but also differences: John A. Macdonald's image of Confederation was giving way to George Brown's. And while this helped some parts of the emerging political nation, it did not seem to do much for others.

The Protest Against Continentalism

In this and in other respects Diefenbaker's renegade regime reflected a diffuse, vague, and unfocussed protest against creeping continentalism and all the "Liberal nationalist" assumptions that were thought to sustain it. "The Chief" talked about developing "the north" in a way that captured the enthusiasm of the Canadian electorate, and in 1958 gave him the largest electoral victory of any prime minister of Canada, before or since.

He won at least support in principle from Ontario representatives of a postwar (politically if not quite economically) conservative intelligentsia — like Donald Creighton, who had written a two-volume biography of John A. Macdonald in the 1950s, and George Grant, who would write *Lament for a Nation: The Defeat of Canadian Nationalism* in the 1960s.

Their complaints about the wonders Mackenzie King had wrought were essentially cultural. They flowed from the old noble Toryism of the likes of John Beverley Robinson in the 19th century. At their most convincing, they were critiques of postwar commercialized North American mass culture, not unlike critiques produced in Europe and (more significantly) the United States itself. (Grant's book, for instance, appeared at about the same time as the New York literary critic Edmund Wilson's *O Canada: An American's Notes on Canadian Culture;* and in a North American continental context both books were about what Wilson called "The Struggle Against Centralization," or what Grant termed "particularity" and "universalism".)

Not long before its defeat in 1957, the St. Laurent regime had dabbled at the issue with the creation of the Canada Council, which offered government financial support to a wide range of more traditional cultural activities. But this had been recommended as long ago as 1951, in the report of the Massey Commission on "National Development in the Arts, Letters, and Sciences." For many among the aspiring intelligentsia at least, the delay in implementation seemed to reflect what was going wrong.

Of much greater consequence for practical politics, Diefenbaker won support in Atlantic Canada and Western Canada, whose regional cultural and economic aspirations seemed to be ignored in Liberal national development strategy. Creeping continentalism was helping Toronto gain ground on Montreal. But, to some at least, it also seemed to keep the centre of Canadian business and the fledgling national mass media even more in Central Canada than before.

On yet another front of the struggle against centralization, in 1958 the Chief even managed to win massive support in Quebec — perhaps because the Quebec electorate thought it prudent to back what looked like a winner, and because Diefenbaker's campaign was supported by Duplessis and the Union Nationale:

but perhaps also because the vague vision of northern development struck some responsive chords among both French and English-speaking Canadians.

Imperial Nostalgia & the Canada-U.S. Auto Pact

Despite a chronic inability to pull much more than vague aspirations together, Diefenbaker's regime did make some substantial contributions to the growth of the emerging political nation.

The only recently begun system of federal equalization grants to qualifying provinces was stiffened. New federal programs that tried to address the thorny problems of regional development in less prosperous parts of the Confederation were established.

Under Davie Fulton, Diefenbaker's justice minister from British Columbia, a constitutional debate that would last for some two decades was set in motion. The debate focused on the problem of achieving federal-provincial consensus over a constitutional amending formula, that would at last allow "patriation" of the Canadian Constitution from the United Kingdom. As time passed it also became a magnet for other constitutional issues, that were more direct and more emotional.

Fundamentally, however, the Chief stumbled over the big questions he had raised so successfully. He guessed that, as George Grant would later suggest, trade and trade policy had something to do with the problem of northern national development. As the first signs of postwar international economic change began to appear, he made some ill-conceived moves to see if yet another tack in the direction of the United Kingdom and the old Imperial preference was a possible solution.

In particular, not long after he came to power in 1957 Diefenbaker announced, as Donald Creighton would later put it, "that his government planned to divert 15 per cent of Canada's imports from the United States to the United Kingdom." As it happened, this proposal was both illegal under the new GATT arrangements, and an embarassment to the United Kingdom, which was now rapidly dismantling the British Empire, and would in the not too distant future join the new European Economic Community.

To show it was still mindful of its old commitments, the British government did propose a Canada-U.K. free trade area as an alternative to Diefenbaker's announced scheme. Yet the heirs of the old imperial officialdom were (to quote Creighton again) "perfectly well aware of the fact that the Canadian government disliked the free-trade plan and could not possibly accept it." In the end the Chief showed sounder instincts about the future of the new Commonwealth of Nations when he led the struggle that resulted in South Africa's resignation over its apartheid racial policies.

Even Diefenbaker had felt some of the economic logic in the continental pull, when his government signed a Defence Production Sharing Agreement with the United States in 1958. At the same time, it was a mark of the political force in even his vague vision of northern development that when the Liberals returned to power under Lester Pearson in 1963, they brought a few new

Another Sam Hunter cartoon on the theme of R.B. Bennett's revival of Imperial preference in the early 1930s. The original title is: "She still sticks to the old-fashioned waltz" (a view that would in fact prove to be wrong). In the late 1950s John Diefenbaker, the next Conservative prime minister after Bennett, would try the last waltz with Canada's old mother country. There could be no real Imperial preference without the Empire itself, however, and this was ending forever.

overtones of more overtly economic nationalist strategies, orchestrated by Walter Gordon, a representative of old 1911 anti-reciprocity factions in the Toronto business and cultural establishment.

Yet it was now clear enough that old empires and establishments alike were ending forever; Canada had some new opportunities in the world at large but it also was starting to have some problems, and business was good in North America. Following the current majority sentiment in Canadian business, in Toronto, Montreal, Vancouver, Halifax, and everywhere else, the mainstream of Pearson's policy picked up the continentalist ambitions of Mackenzie King from where St. Laurent had left them, before the renegade's six-and-a-half-year interlude.

Under Pearson, a new plateau was reached in 1965, when the new Liberal government signed the Canada-U.S. Automotive Trade Agreement, negotiated on the Canadian side by a rising Ottawa bureaucrat named Simon Reisman. The "Auto Pact" brought a regulated form of continental free trade in "road motor vehicles and parts", with guarantees for a "fair share" of vehicle and parts production in Canada.

It was an early sign that both North American automobiles and even the post Second World War version of Canada's historic trade policies were starting to have new trouble in international markets. In other ways as well, it would be a harbinger of the more distant future.

The French Fact & the Vietnam War

The crucial nation-building obsession of Lester Pearson's five short years as Prime Minister of Canada — during a time when the world at large was taking some unusual twists and turns — was the late 20th century reassertion of the French fact in Canada, and the rise of a politically serious independence movement in Quebec, carrying on the separatist rumblings that John Bartlet Brebner had observed in the 1940s.

The dynamic economic boom that followed the Second World War was transforming the traditional society of French Catholic Canada. In 1960 Jean Lesage had begun a "Quiet Revolution" in Quebec provincial politics. René Lévesque would ponder the same trends that disturbed George Grant, observe an English-speaking Canada that seemed increasingly buried in what Henri Bourassa had bemoaned as "l'américanisme saxonisant," and organize for what eventually became known as "sovereignty association," in a new French-speaking nation of "les québécois."

Diefenbaker's failure to successfully grasp this particular challenge was perhaps his, and his party's, greatest failure. Pearson inherited the mantle of St. Laurent and the old master Mackenzie King (a loyal Laurier Liberal, who remembered Lafontaine and Baldwin, and his grandfather and Papineau). "Mike" Pearson himself was no charismatic leader, but he knew what to do.

He assiduously accommodated more moderate reform forces in Quebec, appointed a Royal Commission on "Bilingualism and Biculturalism," and linked the new French fact up with the constitutional amending formula debate that Diefenbaker's regime had begun. Above all else, he recruited into the federal Liberal Party "three wise men", fresh from the struggles inside Quebec: Jean Marchand, Gérard Pelletier, and a wealthy Montreal intellectual named Pierre Elliott Trudeau.

Despite the relative brevity of his regime, Pearson also managed to tie up a number of other loose ends in the legacy of the Firebrand's grandson to the 20th century Confederation. The flag in 1964—based on the maple leaf that Canadian soldiers had worn on their sleeves during the First World War—was one example. Of more practical consequence, Pearson's regime carried on the more muscular federal role in social policy that had crystalized in the early 1940s. Under the Medical Care Act 1966-1967 the federal government committed itself to the financial support of provincially operated health insurance programs that met minimum national standards. In 1967 a Guaranteed Income Supplement was added to the basic federal Old Age Security program established by the St. Laurent government in 1952.

Beyond domestic policy, Pearson had earlier served as St. Laurent's external affairs minister, and won the Nobel Peace Prize for his role in resolving the Suez Crisis of 1956. After the Second World War, the Liberals had been more willing than Diefenbaker's Conservatives to extend support for the adventures of American foreign policy. Some argued, as Harold Innis had quipped in the late 1940s, that in this as in other respects Canada was moving "from colony to nation to colony." Before Pearson's career ended, however, the Confederation had also struck a few gentle blows for a foreign policy of its own.

In the Korean War of the early 1950s Canada fought beside the United States, much as it had fought beside the United Kingdom in the Boer War some half a century before. Though Canada did not enter the conflict until it officially became a United Nations "police action," more than 25,000 Canadians served in Korea, and more than 500 died in battle. Canada was also a founding member of the North Atlantic Treaty Organization (NATO), established in 1949 to express the North American commitment to the defence of Europe in the Cold War. In 1958 it signed the North American Air Defence Agreement (NORAD) with the United States.

After the Korean War, however, Canadian forces confined themselves to United Nations peacekeeping operations, on the model of Pearson's Nobel prize-winning plan for the Middle East. And, unlike Australia (which had much more direct interests), Canada did not fight beside the United States in Vietnam during the 1960s. In 1965 Lester Pearson gave a speech in the U.S. advocating moderation in American policy in Vietnam. This subsequently brought the Prime Minister of Canada a very mild dose of actual physical abuse from Lyndon Johnson, President of the United States; but, within the evolving tradition of moderation and compromise, it showed the new aspirations of a new post-colonial political nation in the most northern part of the North American New World.

Chapter 11

TRUDEAU'S EXPERIMENTS

In December 1967 Lester Pearson announced his intention to resign as leader of the Canadian Liberal Party and Prime Minister of Canada. In April 1968 a Liberal convention, caught up in the somewhat apocalyptic enthusiasms of the late 1960s, found a new leader in Pierre Elliott Trudeau, one of the three wise men whom Pearson had recruited from Quebec in 1965. By the end of June 1968 the Liberals under Trudeau had won their most decisive federal election victory since 1953.

The Confederation of 1867 had now endured for more than 100 years. A wave of what the Canadian mass media called "Trudeaumania" announced that the long colony-to-nation era of Laurier, Borden, Meighen, Mackenzie King, Bennett, St. Laurent, Diefenbaker, and Pearson was over. Trudeau would challenge his country to grow up at last. It would not make everyone happy, but the modern history of Canada had begun.

One implication was that the problems involved in what Trudeau called *Federalism and the French Canadians,* which had been swept under the rug with the swing to Imperial preference in the late 19th century, at last had to be faced squarely—or at least more squarely than before. In 1867 Macdonald and Cartier had occupied adjacent offices in the East Block of the neo-gothic Parliament Buildings in Ottawa. By tradition all subsequent prime ministers had worked out of Macdonald's old office. Trudeau broke the tradition and moved into Cartier's office, giving Ottawa insiders immediate hints about what his more than 15 years in power would be like.

Part of Trudeau's initial strength was that much of English-speaking Canada at first perceived him as a French Canadian who would put the increasingly less than quiet-revolutionary Quebec in its place.

When terrorists on the extremist fringe of the Quebec independence movement kidnapped a British diplomat and murdered a provincial cabinet minister, the new prime minister did show that he had no "weak-kneed" compunctions about proclaiming the War Measures Act, arbitrarily detaining some radical Quebec intellectuals, and putting armoured cars on the streets of Montreal. This incensed civil libertarians in both French and English-speaking Canada, but won much broader support among the federal electorate, and put an end to terrorism in the independence movement.

Trudeau was in fact a profound philosophical opponent of separatism and independence for les Québécois. Yet his countervailing national vision proved to be bad-tasting medicine for many English-speaking Canadians.

On his assumptions, separatism or even "special status" for Quebec would ultimately mean confining French Canadian culture to a reactionary ethnic ghetto on the banks of the lower St. Lawrence River. He wanted to open up room for French expansion in the wider political nation — in effect reversing, or at least renegotiating, the compromises Laurier had felt obliged to make over the Manitoba Schools Question in the 1890s (or even Macdonald's nervous handling of the issues raised by Louis Riel in the 1870s and 1880s).

Among other things, the Quebec revolution itself was ending the traditional political power of the French Roman Catholic clergy. For the rest of Canada, even beginning to live up to Trudeau's ideals did require much more bilingualization in the federal civil service, a new Official Languages Act which significantly increased the status of French in Canadian national life more generally, and the transformation of Ottawa into a gallicly stylish bicultural capital region, that took in both the Quebec and Ontario sides of the Ottawa River.

Trudeau's ambitions in this context had other dimensions, none of which were easy to sell to the English-speaking electorate at large. Yet between 1968 and 1984 both he and the independence movement in Quebec convinced enough Canadians of all sorts that much greater degrees of justice for French Canada were long overdue. Just as Mackenzie King's Liberals had started in the early 1920s, Trudeau's Liberals ended with almost no seats in Western Canada in the mid-1980s. Nonetheless, even in his last election of May 1980 Trudeau won 28% of the popular vote in Manitoba, 24% in Saskatchewan, and 22% in each of Alberta and B.C.

The New Competition

One judgement about Pierre Trudeau's still quite recent performance as prime minister of Canada, during the somewhat turbulent beginnings of the Confederation's modern history, is that he did at least well enough with the constitutional issues that focused on language rights and Quebec, but not well at all on some equally or even increasingly more urgent issues that focused on economic development — for which he lacked the right background.

Whatever grains of truth there may be in this view, it cannot be altogether convincing. Though he was a Montreal intellectual with academic credentials, Trudeau was also the independently wealthy, globe-trotting son of a French Canadian businessman and a Scottish mother, with very direct self-interests in

Another Hunter cartoon on the Manitoba School Question of the late 19th century. The Indian matriarch "Mani-to-ba" is telling Wilfrid Laurier: "The young Liberal chief is cunning but he does not follow a straight trail...." Pierre Trudeau would have been somewhat more to her liking. He himself did not explicitly revive the Manitoba School Question in the 1960s and 1970s; but, among many other things, he set forces in motion that prompted sometimes agonized and always contentious reassessments of French language education and Catholic separate schools in the 1980s — in Ontario, Manitoba, and even Saskatchewan and Alberta.

the success of Canadian capitalism. His personal friends and supporters during his years in power included Robert Campeau, the Northern Ontario French Canadian who would build one of the country's largest real estate development empires, and then start buying up department store conglomerates in the United States.

By the time Trudeau had settled into the first few years of his regime, however, it became clear enough that the economic base of the new political nation was facing a new era of stress, challenge, and change. There had been early warnings late in Diefenbaker's regime, when the Canadian dollar was pegged at $.92 U.S. (continued under Pearson, but not, as of 1970, under Trudeau). The troubles of Canada's northern sector of the North American automobile industry which led to the 1965 Canada-U.S. Auto Pact were another signal — though not altogether read that way at the time.

The bottom line was that the postwar international economy of the late 1940s and 1950s was getting more crowded. The vanquished nations of Japan and West Germany were rebuilding with fresh gusto, and a whole new group of national economies outside Europe and America were struggling onto the world stage.

One implication was that the traditional Canadian resource sector, with a good century and a half of rising depletion behind it, faced new international competition. Another was that North American industrial products found it increasingly hard to compete in world markets, and even in the markets of the United States and Canada themselves.

The upshot was that the trend toward diversification of Canadian export markets during the two decades immediately after the Second World War began to reverse itself. Imperial preference and the British Empire had ended forever. Even the classification of Canada's trading partners had a new look. And increasingly, the most accessible, easiest, and most profitable external markets for Canadian business were the markets of the United States.

Changing Destinations of Canadian Exports, 1965-1985

To	% 1965	% 1985	Change
United Kingdom	14	2	- 12
Other Countries	18	11	- 7
Other Eur.Ec.Com.	7	4	- 3
Japan	4	5	+ 1
United States	57	78	+ 21

International Pressure & Domestic Change.

By the mid-1970s the postwar boom had ended. There had been a major international energy crisis in 1973. The international economic framework organized by the victors at the end of the Second World War was in increasing disarray. A great new wave of inflation had set in. The Canadian economy, like economies elsewhere, was beginning to "restructure" in response to increasingly harsh pressures in its international environment.

Trudeau's regime had to face these challenges in the context of the rising independence movement in Quebec, which became undeniably serious when René Lévesque's "sovereignty-association" Parti Québécois won the Quebec provincial election of 1976 — and of a host of other domestic political pressures with roots in the 1960s. The setting was framed by increasingly diverse waves of immigration from the world on which the sun never set (a kind of final legacy of the old British Empire to the new Confederation that was taking shape in the continuing constitutional debate).

In some ways Trudeau underplayed the old tradition of compromise. He was a combative figure with strongly held and well thought out views on many subjects, often expressed forcefully and sometimes even with style. Yet if he ultimately struck some as an unusual creation of the traditions of even Central Canada, he was also a great traditionalist. The Winnipeg-born Toronto wit Larry Zolf summed up the new prime minister's first few years in office as: "from philosopher king to Mackenzie King."

Just as King had been obliged to lean on the Progressives in the early 1920s (for support in Western Canada among other things), after the federal election of 1972 Trudeau was obliged to lean on a caucus of some 31 New Democrats, until he managed to regain a Liberal majority in a fresh election in 1974. The New Democrats had become ardent spokesmen for economic nationalist concerns over increasing levels of foreign (especially American) investment in the Canadian economy. These found echoes among Liberals who looked to the more business-oriented nationalism of Walter Gordon. And in 1973 the Trudeau regime established a Foreign Investment Review Agency with quite modest objectives.

Trudeau also made efforts to embrace at least some of the national development issues that had helped elect Diefenbaker in the late 1950s. Outside Quebec, perhaps his greatest success was among the English-speaking media and cultural intelligentsia in Central Canada. But he also showed reciprocated concerns for regional development in Atlantic Canada. Reminiscent of Laurier and W.S. Fielding, Allan MacEachen from Nova Scotia would gradually become Trudeau's closest approximation to an English Canadian lieutenant.

The prime minister had much less success with a rapidly changing and developing Toronto business community, particularly after finance minister John Turner left the government in 1975. He had almost no success with a rising Western Canadian business community, in Vancouver and Calgary. A new oil-rich Alberta in particular led a revival of the old Progressive Western wheat economy's protest against Central Canadian economic domination and Montreal-Ottawa-Toronto cultural imperialism.

In Trudeau's native city both the quiet revolution and the independence movement were assaulting the ancient economic inner sanctum of the British merchants of Montreal. French Canadians grew increasingly determined to disprove the English Canadian prejudice that they had no talent for business. Parts of the old English-speaking Montreal business community moved to Toronto, which finally became Canada's largest metropolitan region in the mid-1970s.

The restructuring Canadian economy was opening up fresh opportunities as well as setting new challenges. In 1965 the Ottawa sociologist John Porter had published *The Vertical Mosaic: An Analysis of Social Class and Power in Canada*. Ten years later the Toronto-based journalist Peter Newman took a different path over the same ground in *The Canadian Establishment*. Both books, however, documented a traditional Canadian national elite about to undergo massive restructuring itself.

What had become the Massey-Ferguson agricultural machinery enterprise, whose heirs had done much for Canada in an earlier era, would eventually be restructured to the point of disappearing into a new Varity Corporation. But the Moore Corporation, earlier a Canadian pioneer in the American market, was now the world's largest producer of business forms.

The Alberta-born Torontonian Marshall McLuhan (taking some cues from the post fur-trade preoccupations of Harold Innis) had become a guru on the impact of television and the new electronic communications in the 1960s. By the late 1970s the modern homegrown Canadian multinational Northern Telecom had become a leading international producer of telecommunications systems, with 25 manufacturing plants in Canada, 21 in the United States, two in Ireland, and one each in England, Turkey, Brazil, and Malaysia.

The Reichmann family, which had come to Canada from Eastern Europe by way of North Africa in the 1950s, was on its way to becoming the world's largest real estate developer, with increasingly major holdings in the United States (and then later in the United Kingdom as well). As a sign that the old colonialism really had come to an end, on its 300th anniversary in 1970 the Hudson's Bay Company had moved its headquarters from the United Kingdom to Canada, and reincorporated itself under Canadian law.

The Belzberg interests were rising in British Columbia, Canada's most obvious window on a new "Pacific Rim." Though Hong Kong business was taking an interest in Toronto as well as Vancouver, by the late 1970s growth in both B.C. and especially oil-rich Alberta was outstripping growth in Ontario.

By the 1980s the National Hockey League had teams in Quebec City, Montreal, Toronto, Winnipeg, Calgary, Edmonton, Vancouver, Boston, New York, Washington, Philadelphia, New Jersey, Hartford, Buffalo, Pittsburgh, Detroit, Chicago, St. Louis, Minnesota, and Los Angeles.

Creating Counterweights to U.S. Influence

Canada had more than 24 million people in 1981, and the United States had more than 227 million. Living next door to the U.S., Trudeau once observed, was like sleeping next to an elephant. Despite the disparities in population and market size, by the 1970s the United States was feeling the same international economic pressures as Canada; and when the elephant moved, as in the past it was impossible for Canada not to react.

U.S. difficulties were complicated by the use of the American dollar as a stabilizing unit for the International Monetary Fund system established at the end of the Second World War. Even by 1970 this was creating major difficulties for the U.S. balance of payments. In August 1971 the Nixon administration in Washington took action. The convertibility of the American dollar into gold, which underpinned its use as an international stabilizing unit, was suspended. Of more immediate consequence for Canada, a surcharge of 10% was levied on about half of all U.S. imports.

By this point successive rounds of the General Agreement on Tariffs and Trade (GATT) were making high or even moderate tariff protection an increasingly insignificant barrier to Canada-U.S. trade, on both sides of the border. The 10% surcharge of 1971, which Canada faced like all other U.S. trading partners, was meant to be temporary only. It was clear, however, that Washington was growing more and more sensitive about pressures on the American domestic market. And in the world economy at large "non-tariff barriers" (arguably including a vast assortment of government economic and even social policies) were becoming a key issue in international trade debate.

Moreover, even in the last half of the 1960s the trend toward increasing Canadian dependence on U.S. export markets had become clear. By 1970 some 65% of Canadian exports were going due south, up from 57% in 1965 — and back to the high immediate postwar level of 1950. The figure would rise to 68% in 1971 and 69% in 1972. Under pressure over increasingly high levels of American investment in the Canadian economy as well, the Trudeau regime experimented with new policies to diversify the Canadian export base and provide some alternative to more and more dependence on the economy of the United States.

The bottom line here was an imaginative and perhaps overambitious update of Canada's old policies for dealing with what was by now a very old problem. The Foreign Investment Review Agency (FIRA) of 1973, for instance, was conceived in the spirit of John A. Macdonald's National Policy. Some eight years later, in 1981, Trudeau's last government would stiffen its initial modest objectives somewhat, and introduce a system of oil, gas, and other energy regulation known as the National Energy Policy (NEP). Like its original model, the NEP sometimes seemed even more irritating to Western Canada than to the United States. American policy-makers, however, were also irked by specific new Canadian government measures to promote the domestic print and electronic media industries.

To update Imperial preference in the new post-Empire age of both British and Canadian history, the Trudeau regime invented "the Third Option." This had two main objectives: rehabilitate old trading links with the more economically developed world outside North America, in Europe and Japan; and, with an eye on the longer-term future, forge new trading links with the as yet less developed "Third World."

The mission was very difficult at best. By 1976 Trudeau's government had managed to sign rather vague "framework agreements for economic co-operation" with Japan and the European Economic Community. Ottawa pursued both agreements, but had only limited practical success in improving real access to European and Japanese markets for more Canadian processed and manufactured goods.

On the Third World side of the Third Option, in 1974 the Trudeau regime had added a fourth level to the historic three-level tariff structure, known as The General Preferential Tariff, reflecting, in the words of the *Canada Year Book,* "Canada's international commitment to developing countries under a generalized system of preferences." The benefits to developing countries were blunted by the exclusion of textile products (where low-cost labour gave a particular competitive edge to some Third World economies), but the new preferential tariff was at least a signal of good intentions for the future.

In 1981 Trudeau's last government made a major effort to promote a reduction in the economic gap between the more developed countries of the North and the less developed countries of the South, in the world at large. This was also seen as a way of improving Canada's trading links with Third World economies, and for a brief time in the late 1970s and early 1980s the share of the country's exports going to developing countries did increase slightly.

The New Constitution

Trudeau's undeniable great success in the constitutional debate was not that he managed to resolve many among the growing number of issues involved in what was sometimes termed Canadian "re-confederation." In Western Canada in particular he probably created more problems than he solved. Yet he did manage to patriate the Canadian Constitution left in the United Kingdom more than half a century before, and to begin a workable process of discussion and problem-solving on other issues. And he left the process on a high and noble note that reached back to the earliest beginnings of Canadian history.

After more than a decade of increasingly rancorous domestic debate, his first concrete victory was the "Non" vote in the 1980 Quebec referendum on sovereignty association, organized by René Lévesque's Parti Québécois. Trudeau, who regularly received rather more federal electoral support from Quebec than Lévesque could count on provincially, intervened skillfully in the referendum campaign, and promised immediate federal constitutional changes if the Non forces won. The promise was backed up by strategic English-speaking provinces, and this set the stage for the successful federal-provincial negotiations of 1981.

The negotiations initially pitted the federal government, Ontario, and New Brunswick against Quebec and the seven other provinces (collectively dubbed "the Gang of Eight" by what some saw as the Central Canadian-dominated English media).

Ultimately, however, Trudeau won support from 9 out of 10 provinces (all except Quebec) for a pragmatically crafted package of necessary constitutional innovations. The package included: an amending formula that at last allowed patriation of the Canadian Constitution from the United Kingdom; amendments entrenching French language rights in the Confederation, and explicitly recognizing provincial control of natural resources in Western Canada; and a new, constitutionally entrenched Canadian Charter of Rights and Freedoms (on the model of the American Bill of Rights).

Unexpectedly, in the next stage of the debate not long before his resignation in 1984, Trudeau also subtly gave ground on the principle of recognizing distinctive cultural sovereignties within the new Canadian political nation — not for the culture of the Québécois, but for the revived ancient aspirations of Canada's Indian, Inuit, and Métis peoples. Their demand for constitutionally entrenched rights to self-government could not win support from the seven provinces representing at least 50% of the national population required by the new amending formula. But it was endorsed by four provinces and the federal government.

Though the Indian, Inuit, and Métis constitutional issue was not resolved, Canadian practical politics had at least begun to recognize what Harold Innis had begun to urge a half century before: that "the Indian and his culture" were "fundamental to the growth of Canadian institutions".

The New Economic Development Priorities

On the heels of the last Trudeau government's constitutional successes, the worldwide recession of 1981-82 turned attention once again to economic development issues, with a new sense of urgency. Just before, the election of Margaret Thatcher in the United Kingdom in 1979 and Ronald Reagan in the United States in 1980 had signalled political changes in key parts of the English-speaking world (though for Canada, particularly under a French Canadian Prime Minister, the signals were qualified somewhat in 1981, by the election of the socialist François Mitterand in France).

The U.S. Senate's veto of the recently negotiated Canada-U.S. East Coast Fisheries Treaty in 1981 also confirmed steadily rising American sensitivities over even its largest and most friendly international trading relationship, with Canada. As a result of earlier Canada-U.S. trade agreements and continuing rounds of the GATT, by the mid-1980s some 65% of all U.S. exports to Canada and 80% of all Canadian exports to the U.S. were in fact crossing the border duty free. And the "Tokyo round" of GATT cuts, negotiated between 1973 and 1979, would bring tariffs on an additional 25% of U.S. exports to Canada and 15% of Canadian exports to the U.S. to less than 5% by the end of 1987.

In this (of course somewhat exaggerated) cartoon on the early 20th century Canadian economic boom, Uncle Sam is saying to Jack Canuck: "Say young feller you've got no licence to occupy the hull of the seat, have ye?" Though any Canadian boom of the 1970s was largely confined to the energy-rich West, something of the cartoon's spirit is still apt. In the late 20th century the Canadian population amounted to more than 10% of the U.S. population, up from 7% at the turn of the century. The extent of Canadian investment in the U.S. was growing more like that of the U.S. in Canada. In some resource and even manufacturing sectors the inroads of Canadian business in the North American marketplace were beginning to draw complaints from U.S. domestic interests — at a time when both countries were facing new challenges in the markets of the world at large.

Canada was beginning to face new pressures, however, from non-tariff barriers and so-called U.S. "trade remedy laws," designed to provide special relief for American industries judged to face unfair foreign trading or dumping practices. In 1979, for instance, the U.S. government imposed a countervailing duty on optical sensing equipment made in Canada by the American multinational Honeywell, on the claim that research and development for the product had been unfairly subsidized by the Canadian government. Rather further down the road, shakes and shingles produced by the British Columbia forestry industry would face similar difficulties, with the U.S. claiming that low Canadian stumpage fees constituted an unfair subsidy.

Moreover, by the early 1980s it was clear that whatever the long-term potential of the Trudeau regime's Third Option trade diversification policies might be, over the short to mid term they were simply not working. By 1983 more than 73% of all Canadian exports were going to the United States, up from 69% in 1972.

The National Energy Policy of 1981 and a modest stiffening of FIRA were the Trudeau regime's last efforts to deal with its economic development problems by (in Trudeau's phrase) "creating counterweights" against U.S. influence. Pointing to a new wave of the future, the Canadian dollar had begun to fall significantly on international currency markets in the late 1970s. By 1984 it was below $.80 U.S.

The only obvious policy followed by the Canadian government in this context was to let international market forces determine the value of its dollar, and the decline had much to do with increases in Canadian relative to American industrial wage rates during the early 1970s. Nonetheless it also had the notably positive effect of making Canadian resource and industrial products increasingly competitive in U.S. markets.

Canada's automobile industry, operating under the 1965 Canada-U.S. Auto Pact, especially prospered under these circumstances. By 1983 the Trudeau government had moderated its objectives for FIRA and the NEP, and made approaches to Washington about the possibility of additional "sectoral free trade" agreements modelled on the Auto Pact — for such industries as steel, telecommunications and computers, and urban transportation equipment. Discussions between the governments of Canada and the United States on sectoral free trade began in Washington in December 1983.

To address broader complaints that his government was faltering on economic development issues, Trudeau had also appointed a Royal Commission on Canadian economic prospects, headed by Donald Macdonald, a Toronto corporate lawyer and former Liberal cabinet minister.

Trudeau himself kept faith with his long-term goals. His last few years were marked by crusades for world peace, better international trading terms for developing Third World economies, and extensive travels to promote Canadian trade with the rising Asian economies of the Pacific Rim.

Yet the new economic troubles of the early 1980s had brought even his government to confront the stubborn shorter-term priorities of Canada's ties to the U.S. market. Trudeau had led Canada into a complicated but increasingly successful reassessment of its ancient French and Indian past. Now, by initiating trade discussions with the United States, he had set the stage for another reassessment of the Canadian Confederation's not quite as ancient relationship with the American Republic — that would ultimately prove to have a scope unprecedented since the Reciprocity Election of 1911.

In the late 19th and early 20th centuries, the United States typically urged broader definitions of Canada-U.S. reciprocity or free trade than those proposed by Canada. In the late 20th century as well U.S. officials urged a broader "comprehensive" rather than a narrower "sectoral" free trade agreement. Trudeau's Liberal regime had begun by proposing the sectoral approach; Mulroney's Conservatives ended by accepting the more comprehensive challenge. Were Sam Hunter still alive, his Jack Canuck might still have at least a version of the somewhat sceptical look that he has here.

PART TWO:
THE ISSUE TODAY

Chapter 12

MULRONEY'S
TRADE AGREEMENT

T he final steps on the path of Canadian history that leads to the Canada-U.S. Free Trade Agreement of the late 1980s can be specifically dated to the year of George Orwell's fabled book *1984*. Though Canada is not a place where the more apocalyptic of Orwell's prophesies seem at all compelling, it is nonetheless a part of the late 20th century real world where the actual year can lay claims to some practical significance.

More broadly, the mid-1980s mark at least a modest watershed in modern Canadian political history. To start with, in 1983 the federal Conservatives, Progressive and otherwise, did something unprecedented in the history of their party since the 19th century era of Cartier and Macdonald. They elected a leader from Quebec, who spoke French as well as he spoke English.

Brian Mulroney was not exactly a French Canadian, but he was a Canadian of Irish Catholic extraction who grew up in rural Quebec, and was partly educated at Université Laval in Quebec City. He practised law (and became president of the American multinational, Iron Ore Company of Canada) in the resolutely French-speaking Quebec of the quiet revolution and the independence movement.

Moreover, Mulroney had defeated Joe Clark from Alberta as PC leader. Clark had actually served as a prime minister of a minority government for nine months in 1979 and 1980, until Allan MacEachen, crafty old Liberal warrior from Nova Scotia, adroitly set the stage for Trudeau's last resurrection in an unexpected 1980 federal election.

Despite his very brief sojourn in power, Clark had managed to shape the federal Conservatives into a new voice of Western Canadian aspiration, somewhat in the style of John Diefenbaker from Saskatchewan. And, with Joe Clark's high-minded assistance, Brian Mulroney would do his best to carry torches in Ottawa for both Quebec and Western Canada.

In 1984 Trudeau himself resigned. He was replaced as leader of the federal Liberal Party, and for some two months as prime minister of Canada, by John Turner — the Liberal finance minister who had resigned in 1975 and was often identified with the Toronto business community (though he would successfully seek a parliamentary seat in Vancouver, B.C.).

Despite some hints in early opinion polls that the switch from Trudeau to Turner might just have saved the Liberals from what had seemed certain disaster, in the election Turner called for early September 1984 the disaster proved certain after all. Mulroney's PCs won almost as large a victory as Diefenbaker in 1958, with 74.8% of the seats at Ottawa and 50.2% of the popular vote (compared with 78.5% of the seats and 53.6% of the vote for the Chief just over a quarter-century before).

Meanwhile, changes were taking place in Canadian provincial politics. In 1981 the New Democrat Howard Pawley replaced the Conservative Sterling Lyon as Premier of Manitoba, and the Conservative James Lee replaced the Conservative Angus MacLean in P.E.I. In 1982 the Conservative Grant Devine replaced the New Democrat Allan Blakeney as Premier of Saskatchewan.

In 1985, not long after Mulroney's federal victory, the Liberal David Peterson replaced the Conservative Frank Miller (who had succeeded William Davis) as Premier of Ontario. The Conservative Don Getty replaced the Conservative Peter Lougheed in Alberta. In Quebec the Liberal Robert Bourassa replaced Pierre-Marc Johnson (and just before him René Lévesque) of the Parti Québécois.

In 1986 the Liberal Joe Ghiz replaced the Conservative James Lee in P.E.I., and Social Credit's Bill Vander Zalm replaced Social Credit's Bill Bennett in British Columbia. In 1987 David Peterson, who had come to power in Ontario in 1985 with a minority government dependent on a written Accord with the Ontario New Democrats, won a dramatic Liberal majority. In the same year the New Brunswick Liberals under Frank McKenna defeated Richard Hatfield's Conservatives, winning every seat in the provincial legislative assembly.

With the first era of its modern history now behind it, and its newly patriated Constitution in hand, the electorate of the Canadian Confederation at all levels seemed to have decided that it was time for new faces in power. By electing so many strong new majority governments, the people of Canada also seemed to be calling for some kind of bold new leadership.

At the same time, the provincial election results suggested continuing fealty to the old tradition of compromise and moderation — or even some characteristic primal urge toward balance and equilibrium. Within some three years of Mulroney's massive federal majority at Ottawa, elections had been held in all 10 provinces. Four went to the Progressive Conservatives, four went to the Liberals, one went to the New Democrats, and one to Social Credit.

146

"A healthy, strong relation with the U.S...."

There has been some tendency to see Brian Mulroney's 1984 federal election victory as a case of modern Canada's at last falling into line with the broader political trends established by Ronald Reagan's 1980 election in the United States, or Margaret Thatcher's 1979 victory in the United Kingdom. There is a side to the Mulroney government's policy that, making due allowances for particular Canadian circumstances, fits this characterization not all that badly. Yet there are other sides that have simply carried on with the legacies of Trudeau, for whom Mulroney himself has sometimes displayed a significant unrequited admiration.

On the haphazard path of Canadian history, it is also true that in his 1983 campaign for the federal PC leadership Mulroney opposed any late 20th century comprehensive free trade agreement between Canada and the United States — with a paraphrase of Trudeau's elephant metaphor. It is true as well that Mulroney made no mention of a free trade agreement with the United States in the 1984 federal election campaign.

From the start, however, he did distinguish himself from Trudeau on the broader question of relations between Canada and the United States. Trudeau and the Liberals (the story went) had stirred up too much antagonism with Canada's American cousins, just as they had stirred up too much antagonism between Canada's own provinces and regions. Mulroney and the Conservatives would restore old friendships along the world's longest undefended border. Only three weeks after his September 1984 election victory, the new prime minister was in Washington, declaring that "a healthy, strong relation with the U.S. in no way presupposes any degree of subservience on our part."

In an increasingly cold and troubled global village, this appealed to some genuine sentiments of North American cousinhood in English and even French-speaking Canada, that Trudeau had tended to overlook and perhaps underestimate. It also appealed to the common-sense perception that, whatever the long-term future might hold, given the increasing short-term significance of American markets for Canadian exports, it was only elementary wisdom to work at improving relations between the governments of Canada and the United States.

Moreover, when Mulroney came into office he inherited the sectoral free trade discussions that the Trudeau regime itself had begun with the United States late in 1983. Not much more than a month after his 1984 election victory, and in support of the ongoing discussions, the U.S. Congress had passed a trade bill authorizing the negotiation of new trade agreements with Israel and Canada.

As in the 1850s, 1870s, 1890s, and 1940s, these new Canada-U.S. trade discussions of the 1980s had been initiated (formally at least) by Canada, not the United States. As they progressed, it became clear that the Reagan administration in Washington had scant enthusiasm for additional "sectoral free trade" agreements between the two countries, on the model of the 1965 Auto-Pact. It would be much more interested, however, in a broader "comprehensive free trade" agreement.

By early 1985 it seemed that the prospects for any successful sectoral agreements with the United States were extremely limited. By this time, even the Canadian research and consulting apparatus set up to study the matter was beginning to wonder whether sectoral free trade was what Canada wanted in any case. In late February 1985 Donald Macdonald, the former Liberal cabinet minister whom Trudeau had appointed to report on "the Economic Union and the Development Prospects for Canada," told an interviewer: "we need a global agreement with the U.S. to control non-tariff barriers."

Late in 1984 Mulroney had already tried to show his new government's sensitivity to American and other international concerns about Canada's image "as a reliable trading partner and as a good place to invest." He announced plans to abolish Trudeau's National Energy Policy (also welcome news for the oil and gas industry in Western Canada), and to convert the Foreign Investment Review Agency into more of a vehicle for economic boosterism, to be known as Investment Canada.

By October 1985 Mulroney had written to Ronald Reagan proposing trade negotiations focused on the "broadest possible reductions in barriers to trade in goods and services," and the President of the United States had agreed. In November Simon Reisman, the Ottawa bureaucrat who had successfully negotiated the Auto Pact in 1965, was appointed to organize a Canadian negotiating team.

By late April 1986 the U.S. Senate Finance Committee had narrowly granted "fast-track" authority to the negotiations (limiting the approval role of Congress to a simple yes or no majority vote on a final document rather than a detailed clause-by-clause debate and vote). Simon Reisman's discussions with U.S. negotiator Peter Murphy began in Ottawa a month later, and formal negotiations began in Washington in the middle of June 1986.

Sectoral & Comprehensive Free Trade

Pierre Trudeau's ultimately successful drive for a new constitution prompted Canada to reconsider the modern implications of its early French and ultimately even Indian history. Brian Mulroney's trade agreement, which came out of the process begun in Washington in June 1986, prompts us to reconsider the modern implications of the late 19th century Canada-U.S. trade debates that preoccupied the early history of the Canadian Confederation.

The language of the debate today is different: in ordinary life as well we have long ago, even in Canada, left the vocabulary of the late 19th century behind. But some of the underlying concepts are quite similar.

"Sectoral free trade", for instance, broadly signifies what "restricted reciprocity" signified in the late 19th century (and in the Reciprocity Treaty of 1854), allowing for subsequent major changes in the economic structures of both countries.

A century ago the concept implied restricting Canada-U.S. free trade to resource products, and excluding manufactured goods. Today it implies restricting free trade to several specific sectors of the economy, on the model of the 1965 Auto Pact (which also includes potential tariff safeguards to ensure a "fair share" of automobile production in Canada). Similarly, "unrestricted reciprocity" in the late 19th century is broadly equivalent to "comprehensive free trade" in the late 20th century.

Such terms of democratic political debate, of course, are not meant to be taken altogether literally. No one seriously discussing the issue in either Canada or the United States today has imagined that there is any even remote prospect of removing all barriers to trade in all parts of both national economies.

For the United States (pioneer of the modern service economy), a key point about "comprehensive" free trade has been that late 20th century trade agreements should have some impact across all major sectors of the contemporary industrially developed economic base: resource products, manufactured goods, and (especially 'higher-order' or more sophisticated) services. The U.S. has taken this position in the continuing multilateral trade negotiations under the GATT framework, as well as in its negotiations with Canada.

For Canada "comprehensive" free trade in its most ambitious sense has meant the aspiration to secure what Donald Macdonald referred to as "global" protection from the arbitrary invocation of U.S. trade remedy laws — as in the case of Honeywell's optical sensing equipment in the late 1970s, and shakes and shingles (and then softwood lumber, crude oil, and other products) in the 1980s.

In an effort to stake out another crucial concern in the Canadian definition, before formal negotiations with the U.S. began in June 1986 Brian Mulroney, Joe Clark, and other federal cabinet ministers tried to set some particular limits to comprehensive Canada-U.S. free trade.

In December 1985 Mulroney informed a Chicago audience that "our political sovereignty, our system of social programs, our commitment to fight regional disparities, our unique cultural identity, our special linguistic character...are not at issue in these negotiations." (In theory the United States did not have explicit subjects that it wanted "left off the table," though in practice it proved notably sensitive to issues impinging on what it saw as its own sovereignty and national security.)

From another Canadian standpoint, it is arguably a mark of progress in Canada-U.S. relations over the past 100 years that the final option, and key stumbling block, in the late 19th century debate — "commercial union" — has not been seriously discussed in the debate of the late 20th century.

The contemporary term for the concept is "customs union," but it still implies an agreement under which the two countries would have the same tariff or even other trade barriers against all other countries, as well as bilateral free trade. *Life* magazine in the U.S. published an article supporting a future of this sort for Canada and the United States as recently as the late 1940s. Yet as Quebec Premier Robert Bourassa urged late in 1987, whatever the comprehensive free trade agreement that the governments of Brian Mulroney and Ronald Reagan finally endorsed may or may not involve, it does clearly seem to fall short of a customs union between the two countries.

On the other hand, it is true enough that the Canada-U.S. Free Trade Agreement which was formally signed by both governments early in January

1988 is considerably broader than the ancient Reciprocity Treaty of 1854. And it is notably more comprehensive than the one U.S.-initiated reciprocity agreement turned down by the Canadian electorate in 1911. An American business magazine has described it as "quite simply, the most ambitious regional trade venture since the EC (or European Economic Community) was formed in 1957."

The Political Process

A lively enough question for nativist discussions of Canadian political trends is whether Brian Mulroney will finally prove to be an heir of the long-lived incredible Canadian, Mackenzie King, or the more short-lived renegade in power, John Diefenbaker.

The dispatch (or, from another point of view, haste) with which Mulroney has handled the Canada-U.S. trade issue since coming into office in the late summer of 1984 — particularly considering that it was not an issue in the 1984 election — could be evidence for the side that argues he cannot possibly be a political reincarnation of King.

In 1987, for instance, Canada's gross domestic product grew faster than that of the United States (3.9% compared to 2.9%), or of virtually any other industrially developed country except Margaret Thatcher's at last boldly reviving United Kingdom. By early 1988 it seemed that a falling American dollar might at last be improving terms of trade in world markets for both the United States and Canada.

Rather more of the incredible Canadian's famed creeping gradualism may have been in order. Such speculations are impossible to prove or disprove, but Canada might have been able to negotiate a better trade agreement with the United States in the early 1990s than in the late 1980s.

On the other hand, there were pragmatic reasons for haste. Despite their massive majority of seats at Ottawa, by early 1987 opinion polls were recurrently suggesting that Brian Mulroney and his party only had the support of somewhat more than one-quarter of the Canadian federal electorate. Increasingly the federal Progressive Conservatives needed some major concrete achievements they could present to the electorate in the next election, to justify the magnitude of their victory in 1984.

Mulroney had made a valiant but ultimately unsuccessful effort to secure provincial agreement on the constitutional issue of Indian and Inuit self-government that had eluded Trudeau during his last months in office. In the late spring of 1987 he did manage to secure unanimous provincial agreement on Quebec's place in the new 1982 Constitution (which Trudeau had also left dangling), in the Meech Lake Accord. Along with recognizing Quebec as a "distinct society," however, the Accord made provisions for all provinces that struck some as a mindless and overly expedient decentralization of Canadian federalism. The agreement was contingent as well on approval in all provincial legislatures over a three-year period, and could not quite be regarded as all wrapped up.

In this early 20th century Hunter cartoon, Jack Canuck (right) is saying of Wilfrid Laurier (centre): "He may have a good card up his sleeve and fool Uncle Sam but it seems to me he is a heap too humble." In the late 1980s even such Canadian supporters of the new Canada-U.S. Free Trade Agreement as the Montreal novelist Mordecai Richler would offer similar observations about Brian Mulroney. Note that in this particular cartoon Jack (or Jacques) Canuck appears in his French Canadian persona, dressed in the Quebec habitant's traditional toque and sash.

Once formal trade negotiations with the United States had begun in June 1986, there were the pressures of tight deadlines linked to the U.S. fast-track process for Congressional approval of international agreements.

There was as well a growing Canadian sense of urgency over the increasing use of U.S. trade remedy laws to protect American markets. In October 1986 U.S. trade remedy actions against Canadian lumber and foreign crude oil generally created both some economic problems for Canadian business and even more political problems for the Mulroney government.

Randall Wigle, a University of Western Ontario economist inclined not to overestimate the strictly economic potential of any agreement, put the point this way: "even though the benefits associated with Canada-U.S. free trade are likely to be modest, the alternative of a retaliatory trade war with the U.S. is extremely unattractive for Canada, even though the U.S. would be virtually indifferent between free trade and a retaliatory trade war with Canada."

Put another way, though Canada (not Japan or West Germany) is the U.S.A.'s largest trading partner, Canada depends much more on its exports to the U.S. than the U.S. depends on its exports to Canada. Throughout the 1980s the U.S. has depended on Canadian markets to dispose of only some 20% of its exports; Canada has depended on American markets to dispose of well over 70% of its exports — and, by the late 1980s, to earn as much as 25% of its national income. Wigle is no doubt exaggerating somewhat when he says the U.S. would be "virtually indifferent" to either alternative — free trade or a trade war with Canada; but, in any relative assessment, it does not have at all as much at stake.

Only a dozen days before the agreement in principle of October 4, 1987, Simon Reisman walked away from the bargaining table, and negotiations seemed to have broken down. They resumed at the political level, headed by Canada's Finance Minister Michael Wilson and U.S. Treasury Secretary James Baker. In Canada at least, rumours about the significance of these events have abounded — the truths and falsehoods of which must be left to future historians, with access to sources and perspectives not available now.

The practical point is that a preliminary agreement was reached early in October. The text of a final agreement was published in December, and signed by both Brian Mulroney and Ronald Reagan, in separate, low-key ceremonies in each country, on January 2, 1988 — on schedule for Congressional approval via the U.S. fast-track process later in 1988 (and parliamentary approval by Mulroney's massive majority in Canada), and thus more than likely in time for final implementation on January 1, 1989.

The December 1987 Document

Just what is in the agreement? This is the still somewhat mysterious question that preoccupies the remainder of this book.

Any agreement on paper, of course, only comes alive in practice — and the agreement on paper and the agreement in practice do not always relate to each other in direct and unambiguous ways. Moreover, because of its breadth and somewhat innovative quality (or the extent to which it addresses some inherently difficult issues), the Canada-U.S. Free Trade Agreement of the late 1980s has some notable ambiguities even on paper.

Some crucial elements do little more than establish processes for continuing to discuss still largely unresolved issues. The U.S.-based *Business Week*, in an unfortunate metaphor from a Canadian standpoint, has suggested that the agreement "will work something like a trial marriage." At any point after the agreement takes effect, it can be cancelled or abrogated by either party on six months notice. (By way of historical comparison, the ancient Reciprocity Treaty of 1854 was set for an initial 10-year period, after which it could be abrogated by either party on one year's notice.)

All this having been said, a brief overview of the final text of December 1987, is a logical point of departure. The document includes a one-page Preamble, followed by eight separate parts of varying length. The Preamble lists nine broad goals of the agreement, including: **"TO REDUCE** government-created trade distortions while preserving the Parties' flexibility to safeguard the public welfare;" and **"TO CONTRIBUTE** to the harmonious development and expansion of world trade and to provide a catalyst to broader international cooperation."

The eight more detailed parts then set out the particular provisions of the agreement:

Part One: Objectives and Scope.
This establishes a "free-trade area" in Canada and the United States consistent with the General Agreement on Tariffs and Trade, and itemizes some broad objectives and definitions.

Part Two: Trade in Goods.
By far the longest of the eight parts (it is divided into nine chapters), this sets out rules for trade in resource products and manufactured goods. Broadly, it prescribes the gradual phasing-out of existing tariffs between the two countries over a 10-year period, subject to a number of exceptions (such as "Beer and Malt Containing Beverages"). It includes as well specific provisions regarding agriculture, wine and distilled spirits, energy, and automotive goods and the 1965 Auto Pact.

Part Three: Government Procurement.
This somewhat liberalizes specific bilateral rules for government purchasing, while broadly continuing to permit governments in both countries to discriminate in favour of their own nationals when procuring goods or services.

Part Four: Services, Investment and Temporary Entry.
Parts Four and Five are among the more innovative sections of the agreement.
Part four liberalizes trading arrangements for a selected group of professional
and related services, makes provisions regarding "Temporary Entry for Business Persons" from one country to the other to facilitate the delivery of these
services, and significantly liberalizes rules for U.S. investment in Canada and
Canadian investment in the United States.

Part Five: Financial Services.
U.S. nationals are exempted from Canadian restrictions on the foreign ownership and operation of banks and other financial institutions. Though Canadian
nationals cannot be granted directly equivalent status in U.S. financial markets
as a result of restrictions on even U.S. nationals under the Glass-Steagall Act,
future changes in the U.S. system for U.S. nationals will be extended to
Canadian nationals as well.

Part Six: Institutional Provisions.
This establishes machinery to administer the details of the agreement, and a
binding binational dispute-settling mechanism for complaints about trade
remedy laws in either country. For the time being, the criteria for settling
disputes will be the domestic law of the country whose trade remedy action is
at issue. But a five to seven year process for at least trying to agree on common
binational criteria is established.

Part Seven: Other Provisions.
Part Seven collects together a number of somewhat random items that, it is said,
did not seem to fit elsewhere in the agreement. It includes the exemption of
"cultural industries" (Article 2005, paragraph 1), with some qualifications, and
hedged by a paragraph 2 providing that "a Party may take measures of
equivalent commercial effect in response to actions that would have been
inconsistent with this Agreement but for paragraph 1."

Part Eight: Final Provisions. The penultimate page and a half of the agreement
contains short items regarding the statistical requirements for administration
and enforcement, publication of administrative documents, amendments, entry
into force, and duration and termination.

The very final page of the document, the official form of which bears Brian
Mulroney's and Ronald Reagan's signatures, declares that the agreement is
"DONE in duplicate, in the English and French languages...FAIT en double
exemplaire, dans les langues anglaise et française."

Chapter 13

THE REAL WORLD OF ECONOMICS

As in 1911, when "Mulroney's trade agreement" with the United States was announced late in 1987 it prompted immediate opposition in Canada. The nature of the opposition, however, suggested how the country had changed in the intervening years.

Among what pollsters and market researchers call "opinion leaders," confirmed opponents of the principle itself had begun to mobilize when discussion about re-opening the old question of Canada-U.S. free trade began in earnest earlier in the decade. Mel Hurtig, an untypical Alberta publisher, inspired the most visible national protest group. The events of late 1987 compelled mainstream political actors to take more or less firm positions — no longer on abstract concepts, but on the specific document that the Mulroney and Reagan governments had negotiated.

Both the federal opposition Liberals and New Democrats came out opposed (though in varying degrees both also implied that they would have supported a narrower sectoral trade agreement, but not the quite broad and comprehensive treaty that the federal government in fact signed).

Opposition from Ed Broadbent's New Democrats, accompanied by opposition from organized labour (in both Canada and the United States, as it would turn out), was no surprise. Yet, just as Brian Mulroney had earlier made noises against the concept of Canada-U.S. free trade, federal Liberal leader John Turner had earlier made noises in support of it. And Donald Macdonald's Royal Commission report, which had also proposed a new Canada-U.S. trade agreement, would arguably have been Turner's preferred Canadian Liberal Party wisdom on the subject, were he not, like Mulroney himself, caught on the horns of so many practical political dilemmas.

The two Liberal and one New Democratic premiers of three of Canada's 10 present provinces opposed the agreement. The opposing provinces (P.E.I., Manitoba, and Ontario) collectively represented just over 40% of the total Canadian population, and included both the country's least and most populous provincial jurisdictions. None of them, however, gave any strong hints of resolute determination to obstruct the progress of Mulroney's trade agreement.

P.E.I. made clear that it would not entertain any legal challenges to the agreement in the courts. Ontario— traditionally reputed "fat cat" of the Confederation — showed concern not to unduly stir up predictable antagonisms from the seven premiers who supported the deal that Canada had managed to make. In March 1988 Howard Pawley's New Democratic government in Manitoba was unexpectedly defeated in the provincial legislative assembly by the vote of a wayward New Democrat, precipitating an April provincial election that brought a Conservative minority government to power.

Perhaps the most striking difference between 1911 and 1987 (or 1910-11 and 1987-88) is the lack of anything in the late 1980s that remotely compares with the very quick and potent Central Canadian big business opposition to the 1911 agreement. There has been no group among Mulroney's Conservatives at all like the "Toronto Eighteen" who broke with Laurier's Liberals over reciprocity. No modern figure of William Van Horne's stature in early 20th century Montreal has expressed any determination to "bust the damn thing."

There has been a degree of specific business discontent. The Bank of Nova Scotia, for instance, has lodged a polite protest about Part Five of the agreement on financial services. Some business leaders in economic sectors widely expected to be hurt by the agreement — such as electrical products or wine— have voiced predictable complaints.

Yet generally the modern big business heirs of William Van Horne, Edmund Walker, and early corporate Canada have shown strong support for Mulroney's trade agreement. Polling data has also suggested that the concept of Canada-U.S. free trade is rather warmly endorsed by much of Canadian small business enterprise — which, in both Canada and the United States, has lately been providing far more jobs than big business, and is in at least this important sense the real engine of new economic growth in the late 20th century.

Businessmen & Economists: Then & Now

On the face of things, the generality of Canadian business support for the U.S. free trade deal of the late 1980s is evidence for the argument that it will be good for Canadian business (and thus, it might be suggested, for the shorter to mid-term economic prospects of the Canadian Confederation). This assessment has been broadly endorsed by the mainstream of professional economists, who also tend to argue that the general longer-term impact should be to raise incomes and lower prices in both countries.

After some two generations of creeping continentalism in various forms, tariff barriers themselves have not been dramatic impediments to Canada-U.S. trade for a considerable time now. (Average recent levels in Canada have been

This late 19th century Hunter cartoon shows the Central Canadian C.P.R. business magnate William Van Horne (born in Joliet, Illinois) about to catch one of his trains. Oliver Mowat, former Ontario premier and new federal minister in Laurier's first cabinet, is carrying the great man's bags. Some might argue that in one sense things have not changed much in the intervening generations. Yet in the late 1980s no Canadian businessmen of William Van Horne's stature — from Central Canada or anywhere else — has voiced anything like the utterly resolute objections to Canada-U.S. free trade that Van Horne expressed in the national controversy which led to the Canadian Reciprocity election of 1911.

about 4%, and even less in the United States; as noted earlier, some 65% of U.S. exports to Canada and 80% of Canadian exports to the United States were already crossing the border duty free by the mid-1980s.)

Yet Paul Wonnacott, a leading American specialist on Canada-U.S. free trade, has urged that the kind of gradual elimination of bilateral tariffs prescribed in Part Two of the new agreement still has significant potential for increasing exports and stimulating growth in both the United States and Canada. And he has pointed to the quite potent impact of the 1965 Auto Pact over the past 20 years as evidence of the possibilities held out by the much broader removal of even rather low tariffs in the agreement of 1987.

From at least a short to mid term economic standpoint, the specific energy provisions of the 1987 agreement hold out new opportunities, particularly for Canadian producers of oil, gas, uranium (though U.S. domestic politics after the agreement was signed raised some questions here), and hydroelectricity. The investment provisions should help bring new capital into the country, and make life easier for the increasing number of Canadian investors who are looking at opportunities in what is still the late 20th century world's largest consumer market.

In the midst of such healthy present-day optimism, there does remain an intriguing historical question. Much of the general logic was also advanced on behalf on the agreement of 1911. What happened to the early 20th century Canadian big business opposition to free trade with the United States, that helped finance Wilfrid Laurier's defeat on the reciprocity issue more than three quarters of a century ago?

The New Industrial Machismo

The fundamental answer, it would seem, lies in economic changes in both Canada and the United States that have taken place during the past 75 years.

(These changes, it is also worth noting, are reflected in changes in the partisan political colourings of the historic trade debates in both countries. Traditionally, Conservatives in Canada and Republicans in the United States have leaned toward protection, while Liberals in Canada and Democrats in the United States have leaned toward free trade. There are factions in all four parties which still honour the old ways; but, John Turner's and Brian Mulroney's sometimes hypothesized true preferences in Canada notwithstanding, in both countries the old two-party partisans to the debate have broadly switched sides.)

Particularly in the more recent past, Canada's economic structure has been moving progressively away from the historic resource economy that began with the French and Indian fur trade some 400 years ago. The Canadian resource economy is still important, but no longer quite at the centre of things in the way it was once. According to Donald Macdonald, "Canadians' notion of themselves as 'hewers of wood and drawers of water' is not borne out by the figures anymore. If we want to grow, we have to grow in manufacturing."

Canada's manufacturing base, still concentrated (though far from exclusively) in Quebec and especially in Ontario, has some of its earliest origins in

As this late 19th century Hunter cartoon makes clear, the Liberals in Canada have been the traditional proponents of Canada-U.S. free trade. The rink manager is Richard Cartwright, an Ontario federal Liberal of the day particularly noted for his free trade advocacy and North American continental enthusiasms. In the late 20th century the Liberals have switched sides on the issue, as have the Conservative inventors of the protectionist National Policy.

the old National Policy and Imperial preference. It was affected by the subsequent creeping continentalism of the 20th century, and, it seems clear enough, strongly stimulated by the 1965 Auto Pact.

Most recently, it has been notably energized by the rather steep fall in the value of the Canadian dollar, relative to the U.S. dollar, that began in the late 1970s. By the mid-1980s manufactured products accounted for a major share of Canada's export base (and especially the more than three-quarters of it currently destined for the markets of the U.S.A.).

The automobile industry in Canada (but not the allied auto parts industry) is thoroughly multinational — though it now includes representatives of Asian and European as well as American-headquartered corporations.

Canada's modern manufacturing machismo, however, can also boast such home-grown multi-billion dollar enterprises as Seagram's, Moore Corp., Stelco Inc., and Northern Telecom. Through its American branch operations headquartered in Tennessee, Northern Telecom made the current telephone switching system in the White House at Washington.

Canada's Exports of Goods to all Countries, 1986

Major commodity grouping	% Total exports
Automotive products	28.5
Industrial goods & materials (incl. metal ores, metals & alloys)	19.0
Machinery & equipment	15.6
Forestry products	14.6
Energy products	9.4
Agricultural & fishing products	9.1
Other consumer goods	2.0
Other	1.8
TOTAL EXPORTS	100.0

Another, longer-term change in the structure of the trading relationship between Canada and the United States dramatically sets off the circumstances of the late 1980s from those of 1911. In 1910, for instance, the value of U.S. exports to Canada was some two-and-a-half times greater than the value of Canadian exports to the U.S.

In 1985 Canada exported (according to Canadian statisticians) goods worth $93.2 billion (in Canadian dollars) to the United States, or (according to American statisticians, and still in Canadian dollars) $94.2 billion. On Canadian calculations, the U.S. exported goods worth C$74.6 billion to Canada, or on American calculations C$64.5 billion.

It says something about the state of Canada-U.S. trade relations in the mid 1980s that for some considerable time the two countries had been indulging in minor statistical wars over just what the magnitude of their bilateral exchange of goods was. As background to the 1986-87 negotiations, meetings between the opposing national statisticians were held. In Canadian dollars, "reconciled data" indicate that Canadian exports to the U.S. amounted to some $95.0 billion in 1986, while U.S. exports to Canada amounted to some $73.5 billion.

No matter which set of figures is used, it is indisputable that in the mid 1980s Canada was exporting considerably more to the United States than the United States was exporting to Canada.

Restructuring Costs

Even the most optimistic forecasters of the strictly economic impact of the 1987-88 agreement do not deny that it will also bring some transitional economic hardship to particular parts of both national economies — and to specific individuals and even groups in both countries.

From the economist's standpoint, the great attraction of the tariff elimination elements is that they will prompt a more efficient organization of resource and manufacturing industries on both sides of the border, as individual firms and businesses restructure to take advantage of the new economies of larger markets.

Yet in the course of this restructuring, some firms will go out of business and some individuals will lose jobs. Ultimately, an even larger number of new firms and new jobs should be created, but this in itself will do nothing to relieve transitional hardships. This kind of analysis is at the bottom of the quite logical and even binational opposition of organized labour, which necessarily speaks loudest for the jobs that already exist.

Moreover, of particular consequence for the smaller party to the agreement, the relative population weights of the Canadian and American economies alone would suggest that restructuring impacts will be greater in Canada.

Similarly, though average tariff levels in both countries are now quite low, they are rather higher in Canada. And, for all its modern machismo, Canadian manufacturing, economists have been telling us for at least a generation, has some notable historic inefficiencies, especially as a result of the way both domestic industry and the American multinational corporation have mixed and mingled with the old National Policy and Imperial preference.

Safeguards Against Restructuring Costs

Supporters of the 1987-88 trade agreement in Canada have a number of plausible enough answers to such essentially economic criticisms of the deal that seems to have been struck.

First and foremost, the time has come for us to, as it were, bite the restructuring bullet (or as Donald Macdonald has put it, make a "leap of faith"). For both Canada and the United States there are tougher bullets ahead in the colder world outside the warmth of North America. There are both challenges and opportunities down the road: if we don't make the challenges we won't be able to take the opportunities.

Beyond such inspirational (and perhaps apt enough) economic development rhetoric, the 1987-88 agreement itself takes some account of hardship issues. The remaining tariffs between the two countries, for instance, are not being suddenly ended but only phased out gradually over 10 years, to allow time for required economic adjustments. Broadly, tariffs for industrial sectors likely to face the greatest restructuring difficulties will be phased out last, and various special arrangements for specific industries in both countries have been "grandfathered" into the agreement. Brewing industries have been exempted.

The agriculture chapter in Part Two allows both Canada and the United States to continue with many of the kinds of government programs that have been used to shield the historically embattled North American family farmer and his successors (and those elsewhere in the world as well) from the sometimes excessive rigours of the agricultural marketplace. According to the Canadian federal government's commentary, "nothing in the Agreement will in any way affect the right of the federal government and the provinces to introduce and maintain programs to protect and stabilize farm incomes."

The chapter on trade in automotive products largely preserves the safeguards for a Canadian fair share of North American production in the 1965 Auto Pact, which in effect becomes part of the new agreement. It does set limits on the extent to which Canada can continue to attract European and Asian auto investment in the North American market, through waivers of Canadian customs duties against countries other than the United States. Yet only an America that saw itself in a much stronger way (and Canada in a weaker way — like the America of the 1950s and 1960s) would be prepared to tolerate many more extensions of this particular arrangement, with or without a free trade agreement.

For some industries certain to face unusual hardships not allowed for in the agreement, the Mulroney government in Canada has also indicated intentions to take remedial measures. The most obvious cases are textiles and clothing, which unlike most industries, still have unusually high levels of tariff protection in both countries (23.7% for clothing in Canada and 18.4% in the U.S.).

Finally, one of the most convincing shields Canada has against the disproportionate restructuring burden it is taking on in Mulroney's trade agreement is the low value the Canadian dollar has displayed relative to the U.S. dollar, since the beginnings of its current free-market decline in the late 1970s. The value of the Canadian dollar will no doubt continue to be a matter of great strategic economic significance for the Confederation of the late 20th and early 21st centuries, as and if the agreement is gradually implemented.

Predictions About Employment Impact

Considerations of this sort draw attention to the debate over the magnitude of the economic impacts that the 1987-88 agreement will likely have for Canadian employment markets.

Early in 1988 the Economic Council of Canada helped set the most recent tone for assessments of the agreement itself, as opposed to various earlier abstract concepts of Canada-U.S. free trade. And the tone is rather modest. The ultimate number of new jobs created in Canada, the Council suggested in April 1988, will probably not be dramatic. Its projections for the actual agreement indicate some 250,000 new jobs over a 10-year period — considerably below the 350,000 jobs projected earlier on the basis of more theoretical assumptions, and quite modest in a wider setting where the Canadian economy has recently been creating some 250,000 to 300,000 jobs every year, without free trade.

In a similar spirit, the Canadian federal government's estimates of job losses brought on by the agreement have been modest as well: implying a need for not too much more remedial action than what is provided by the government's existing unemployment insurance and manpower training programs. Late in January 1988 federal cabinet minister Barbara McDougall suggested that as few as 160,000 jobs could be lost over a 10-year period.

If estimates of this sort are correct (and there have been others), part of the explanation may be that the Mulroney trade agreement is not quite as comprehensive as some earlier scenarios envisioned. Or, as the Economic Council has explained, its initial studies made "assumptions about the contents of the deal that were not borne out by the final agreement."

Another part of the explanation is that the kind of restructuring the final agreement will promote is nothing new. For some considerable time now, the economies of both Canada and the United States have been restructuring in response to a host of new realities in the international economy. As Canadian General Electric Chairman William Blundell has put it, Canada in particular has already dealt with "massive restructuring."

With some reason, critics have pointed to free trade's potential unhappy consequences for the American multinational corporation branch plant structure that marks much of Canada's manufacturing base. On the other hand, the character of multinational enterprise in the world economy at large is not the same today as it was in the late 19th or even the mid 20th-century.

In the early 1970s IBM became one of the first multinationals to adopt global-product rather than national-market strategies for its branches and subsidiaries around the world. Since then IBM Canada has been gradually restructuring, from an operation producing a range of IBM products for the Canadian market, to a specialist in software development, which now has a world product mandate to produce all software for mid-range IBM computers.

In a more narrowly North American variation on the theme (and on the pattern of the 1965 Auto Pact), a Canadian General Electric plant in Oakville, Ontario now produces all GE 40-watt lightbulbs for both Canada and the United States. And, as the recent development of the North American auto industry itself suggests, Canadian locations (with social programs that help ease some restructuring burdens, and a low dollar) can be quite efficient producers for continental markets.

Put another way, in the late 20th century the crux of the economic issue for Canada in Canada-U.S. free trade cannot really be: can Canadian enterprise compete in U.S. markets? Both the increasing share of Canadian exports headed due south, and Canada's growing trade surplus with the U.S., imply that Canadian enterprise is already competing effectively enough, in a continental economy that already has a quite long history behind it.

The Very Bottom Line

Fundamentally, like the ancient Reciprocity Treaty of 1854 and the Imperial preference of 1897, from Canada's standpoint the Canada-U.S. Free Trade Agreement of 1987-88 is not so much an innovation that will create new trends, as an institutional arrangement to stabilize and manage trends that have already established themselves.

The economic line of last resort for proponents of the agreement is not so much that it will open new American markets for Canadian resource and manufacturing industries, as that it is better than no defence at all against the latest wave of a historic protectionist impulse in America — no longer expressed through high tariffs, but through assorted non-tariff barriers and *ad hoc* trade remedy laws. The crucial minimum objective is to protect the access to U.S. markets that Canadian industry already has.

Thus shortly after the preliminary agreement was initialed in October 1987, former Alberta Premier Peter Lougheed argued that the alternative to it was not the status quo, but a still more robustly protectionist American trade regime. At the time it was true enough that an "Omnibus Trade Bill" with unseen implications for Canada was wending its way through Congress. By the spring of 1988 the most stridently protectionist features of the bill in its initial form had disappeared. Yet John Hein of the influential U.S. Conference Board was suggesting that even the more benign version of the Omnibus Trade Bill "puts our major trading partners on notice that we are concerned with the trade deficit; that we will keep no restrictions on trade here if others open their markets to us."

The crux of Canadian objectives from this angle is to institutionalize some protection from unpredictable attacks on the share of U.S. markets that Canadian business already enjoys, through American non-tariff barriers and trade remedy laws. Thus Judith Maxwell of the Economic Council has argued: "job-creation should not be the major criterion for assessing the agreement; secure access to U.S. markets is more important."

On this criterion, the key element in the agreement is Part Six on "Institutional Provisions," which includes a binational mechanism to settle *ad hoc* trade disputes between Canada and the United States. Briefly, what Canada has achieved so far here is a panel of two Canadians, two Americans, and sometimes one more Canadian and sometimes one more American, that will resolve disputes based on American law in complaints against American trade remedies, and Canadian law in complaints against Canadian trade remedies. A five to seven year process to arrive at some form of genuinely binational criteria for resolving disputes has also been established — the ultimate success or failure of which may well remain a mystery until the mid-1990s.

Even strong supporters of the agreement will allow that this is less than an optimal arrangement from Canada's point of view. Some Canadian critics of Part Six (and not just Ontario Premier David Peterson) have branded it the Achilles' heel of the Mulroney trade deal. Even in Western Canada, *The Vancouver Sun* has suggested: "It's difficult to imagine Trudeau blundering into a free trade deal that does not provide secure access to U.S. markets."

Yet, as the great bulk of mainstream business opinion has tended to argue, in the short run it is at least equally plausible that, given the wolf of U.S. trade policy that has recurrently appeared at Canada's door in the past, the Part Six which has actually been negotiated is much better than nothing at all. And it holds out some prospects for more reliably secure Canadian access to U.S. markets in the future.

These prospects themselves, however, raise another class of issues — beyond the real world of economics, and with longer-term implications for a restructuring Canadian Confederation, in the new world of the 21st century.

Chapter 14

AGAINST THE AMERICAN GRAIN?: WHAT DOES CANADIAN SOVEREIGNTY MEAN?

The U.S.-based *Business Week* has described the final compromise that Canadian Finance Minister Michael Wilson and U.S. Treasury Secretary James Baker forged over the dispute-settling mechanism of Part Six in the early fall of 1987, before the initialing of the preliminary Mulroney-Reagan agreement:

"On the basic issue — how to handle trade disputes — Wilson and Baker struck a deal. Ottawa had been demanding what Congress was sure to reject: an independent tribunal that could override current laws. Instead Ottawa accepted a last-resort arbitration panel that will use current law to resolve disputes in return for a standstill on new trade laws affecting Canada.

"The pact will work something like a trial marriage. For the first five years, with a two-year extension, Canadian and U.S. industries will be able to appeal trade rulings to the bilateral panel. Meanwhile, the countries will work toward a common code on unfair trade practices. If the partners can't agree on new rules by the end of the trial, they can 'divorce' with six months notice.

"This escape hatch calmed U.S. anxieties over sovereignty enough to let other changes in trade relations move ahead."

For Americans as well as Canadians, in other words, the effort to secure Canadian access to U.S. markets through the processes established by the new Canada-U.S. Free Trade Agreement has already raised issues that go beyond the real world of economics, and into the equally real world of political sovereignty. U.S. politicians are reluctant to completely surrender their rights to safeguard the economic interests of their constituents to a binational panel with ultimately equal representation from the two countries.

From one Canadian standpoint, like the apparent absence of Erastus Wiman's old commercial or customs union option from current discussions, this reflects historical progress in Canadian-American relations . It used to be that only Canada saw Canada-U.S. free trade as a potential threat to its national sovereignty .

From another Canadian standpoint, however, any further progress in the development of the dispute-settling mechanism during the 1990s can only raise further questions about just what both Canadian and American national sovereignties will mean in the 21st century.

Moreover, it is arguable that Parts Three, Four, and Five also raise at least a few queries about political sovereignty on both sides of the border — and particularly on the side that has only slightly more than one-tenth the population of the other.

In a footnote to his influential early 1987 background report on the negotiations, even Paul Wonnacott compares Trudeau's 1970s metaphor of living next door to an elephant with a remark of the Mexican president Porfirio Diaz in the early 20th century: "Poor Mexico! So far from God, and so close to the United States."

The Social Base in Canada and the United States

Sovereignty is a complicated term, perhaps especially in the late 20th century. A literal definition, in English, is "supremacy in respect of power...authority, or rule."

Serious claims on this kind of supremacy within particular geographic boundaries, it is often assumed, presuppose serious claims on some kind of distinctiveness within the same boundaries. Henry Ford II was once asked about Canadian sovereignty by a CBC TV reporter: he confessed that he was sceptical, on the grounds that he found it hard to tell the difference when he crossed the border from the United States to Canada.

If we think of a national society as an underlying social base, with a particular guiding institutional structure on top of it, there is a strong sense in which Canada is in fact a place with a very similar social base to the United States, guided by a somewhat different institutional structure. Yet even in the late 20th century, even the social bases of the two countries have some straightforward differences, flowing from somewhat different histories and geographical circumstances.

To take some brief highlights, in the early 1980s close to one-half the Canadian population was Roman Catholic, compared with somewhat less than one-quarter in the United States. Just over 25% of the Canadian population reported French as its mother tongue in 1981; just under 17% reported French as its official language; and an additional 15% reported its official language as both French and English, or English and French.

From a still more ancient heritage, in the 1980s there are some half a million statistically recognized Indians, Inuit, and Métis in Canada, in a total population of somewhat more than 25 million people. In the United States the number of similar peoples is less than a million — in a total population of more than 235 million.

In the late 20th century both Canada and the United States are ethnically heterogeneous national societies. Yet the historical development and modern form of social heterogeneity in Canada is somewhat different than in the United States — as reflected in the old idea of a "Canadian mosaic" as opposed to an American "melting pot," and the rather vague but much-discussed modern concept of Canadian "multiculturalism" (officially endorsed in the early 1970s by the Canadian federal government).

The French aside, immigration from the United Kingdom and other more northern and western parts of Europe both began and peaked later in Canada, while immigration from the more southern and eastern parts of Europe became important earlier in the United States. Though there were a few blacks in Canada even during the French regime, the great bulk of Canada's modern black population (which is still smaller proportionately than in the U.S.) has roots in much more recent migrations from the exotic old British Empire, and new Commonwealth of Nations, in the Caribbean Sea.

Before the Second World War America was no doubt a much, much brighter beacon for international migration than Canada. Yet after the Second World War immigration played a proportionately greater role in Canadian than in American development.

Some 4.5 million immigrants entered the United States in the 1970s, while some 1.4 million entered Canada. With somewhat less than one-tenth of the total population of Canada and the United States together, Canada received close to one-quarter of all new immigrants to the two countries. The largest numbers of recent immigrants to the United States have come from other parts of the Americas. The largest numbers of recent immigrants to Canada have come from Asia (like the Indians of the Americas perhaps 15,000 to 20,000 years ago).

Finally, though there are important internal variations in the geography of both countries, that spill across the undefended border, Canada generally has a more arduous northern geography, and (as even Henry Ford II would probably concede) a colder northern climate — both of which can have an effect on you, after you have been in the place for a while.

Institutional Structures & the Role of Government

Stronger and longer-lasting legacies from France and especially the United Kingdom and the British Empire are the most commonly noted elements that distinguish the modern institutional structure of Canada from that of the United States. The whole truth, however, is more subtle and, to Canadians at least, more intriguing. And it relates to the subtle differences in the modern social bases of the two countries.

Today institutional structures in both countries are quite complex. Government has played a somewhat more important role in Canada than in the United States. From the Great Lakes canals in the early 19th century, to the transcontinental railways in the late 19th and early 20th centuries, the Canadian Broadcasting Corporation in the 1930s, and John Diefenbaker's regional development activism in the 1950s and 1960s, even Canadian conservatives have not been reluctant to use government as an agent of national economic development, and Canada today has a richer assortment of publicly-funded social and development programs than the United States.

Ronald Reagan's free market evangelism notwithstanding, however, government is a key thread to the institutional structure in both places. From Henry Clay's American System in the early 19th century to the post-Civil-War high tariff regime in the late 19th century, Roosevelt's New Deal in the 1930s, Eisenhower's "military-industrial complex" in the 1950s, and Lyndon Johnson's Great Society in the 1960s, government has played a more important role in U.S. development than some strains of American opinion sometimes pretend. Other threads include financial institutions, and many kinds of voluntary organizations.

As has often been suggested in Canada, the somewhat different thrusts of the two institutional structures at large probably are hinted at by the difference between the bold enthusiasm for "Life, Liberty, and the pursuit of Happiness" in the American Declaration of Independence of 1776, and the more restrained aspirations for "peace, order, and good government" in the Canadian Constitution of 1867.

Whatever broad judgements you choose to make, it is the particular impact of the institutional structures in both countries on economic activity (or, more strictly, of those elements in them which flow directly from the authority of government) that is fundamentally at issue in Part Six of the 1987-88 trade agreement.

Drawing on a quite broad caricature of the discussion that has developed over the past several years, the U.S. is prepared to curb the use of *ad hoc* trade remedy laws against Canada (or anywhere else, for that matter), so long as American and Canadian business compete on "a level playing field." It reserves the right to continue using such remedies whenever Canadian governments tilt the field to the advantage of Canadian business, through policies and programs that amount to unfair trade subsidies.

In principle (if not necessarily in practice), this particular set of terms for debate could open up a Pandora's box of issues about the respective roles of government in both countries. On a very rigorous interpretation of the level playing field, it could be that to finally satisfy American criteria for completely stable Canadian access to U.S. markets, Canadian and American business would have to face virtually identical (or at least, as the current jargon has it, extremely "harmonized") commercial regimes.

In some limiting case, this could have implications for virtually everything government does in both countries. It could even raise a new form of the late 19th century Canadian anxiety over commercial union.

In this context, Abraham Rotstein, an economic nationalist at the University of Toronto, has given voice to the most profound Canadian pessimism about future Canada-U.S. discussions toward a common code on unfair trade practices. The "chances of arriving at something other than existing American countervail laws as the common code for the two countries," he has suggested, are very slim. In the end: "we will gracefully incorporate the American rules I suspect and call it the new common code."

A cold climate and a vast arduous geography have helped give Canada a particular tradition of government intervention in the interests of national economic development. Historically at least, the tradition has also been more warmly embraced by Conservatives than by Liberals. In this Sam Hunter cartoon Jack Canuck is lecturing the Liberal Wilfrid Laurier on the importance of public ownership in Canada's railway system. It would be the Conservative Arthur Meighen, however, who would finally take Jack's message to heart, and create the modern Canadian National Railways.

There are historical precedents for this depth of emotion in Canada about the limiting political implications of Canada-U.S. trade relations. In May 1948 Harold Innis, who only a few years later would be elected president of the American Economic Association, told an British audience that the "tariff is an instrument in American imperialism" — an imperialism that "has been made plausible and attractive in part by the insistence that it is not imperialistic." It was also one of Innis's half-serious beliefs in the late 1940s and early 1950s that some Canadians who had felt most comfortable as part of the old British Empire were uniquely susceptible to seeing the country's future after the Second World War in terms of membership in some new American imperial design.

On a more optimistic view of both Canadian and American human nature, Canada's best defence against such a fate may well be that the U.S.A. (which is at its very bottom, like Canada, a North American democracy) is in fact incapable of devising and executing any genuinely successful imperial design — for all the very best reasons. Whatever the ultimate truth may prove to be, even before the negotiations leading to the 1987-88 agreement began, Brian Mulroney himself made an effort to set some unmoveable parameters for any wider Canada-U.S. trade discussion, when he told a Chicago audience that "our political sovereignty, our system of social programs, our commitment to fight regional disparities, our unique cultural identity, our special linguistic character...are not at issue in these negotiations."

A balanced assessment of what followed will allow that the United States showed both some respect for this particular Canadian position, and even some parallel concerns of its own. In the end, however, Mulroney's clarification by itself proved inadequate to the task of forging a common code on exactly what kinds of specific government policies and programs do amount to unfair trade subsidies. The result is the process for continuing to discuss the question in Part Six of the agreement.

Even if Abraham Rotstein in his most profoundly pessimistic moments is quite wrong, just what this may or may not mean, for either of the real worlds of both economics and political sovereignty, is unclear. A White House summary of the agreement has described the process in terse bureaucratic prose: "for up to seven years...a bilateral working group attempts to develop new approaches to unfair pricing and government subsidies that would ensure effective discipline over unfair trade practices and minimize unfair trade disputes within the new free trade area."

Political Sovereignty & Trade in Services

There is also some no doubt inevitable lack of clarity about the broader political implications of the more innovative parts of the 1987-88 agreement on trade in services.

Part Two of the agreement, for instance, requires each country (or "Party" as the legal language puts it) to extend "national treatment" to goods from the other country, subject to various specific limitations for particular goods. Part Four extends this requirement to a selected list of services provided by "persons of the other Party."

The Canadian federal government's commentary on the agreement stresses that though "Canada and the United States have agreed not to discriminate between Canadian and American providers of these services...this is not an obligation to harmonize. If Canada chooses to treat providers of one service differently than does the United States, it is free to do so, as long as it does not discriminate between Americans and Canadians. Each government also remains free to choose whether or not to regulate and how to regulate."

At the same time, persons who provide services have a political existence that mere goods lack. And there does seem a sense in which extending national treatment to persons providing certain services (broadly agriculture and forestry, mining, construction, distributive trade, insurance and real estate, and general commercial services), will also extend what amount to some rights of national citizenship.

The Part Four chapters on "Temporary Entry for Business Persons" and "Investment" help to clarify the limits on these rights. Yet it may be that, in principle, internationally mobile service sectors ultimately imply some broader degree of internationally mobile citizenship as well.

Because the social bases of Canada and the United States are as similar as they are, and because Canadians and Americans have for so long been moving in both directions across the undefended border for a wide variety of purposes, this may not raise quite the kinds of practical difficulties between Canada and the United States that it seems to be raising for the wider, multilateral GATT discussions. Even between the friendly North American cousins, however, it has already raised concerns about political sovereignty.

Some, for a national-security conscious U.S. federal administration, are reflected in Part Three of the agreement on government procurement. Here it seems clear that the current regime in Ottawa was prepared to be more innovative than the current regime at Washington. Despite the most recent trends, even in the United States the growth of government has been a key ingredient in the 20th century development of the service economy. Yet Part Three provides only modest liberalization of trade in government-purchased goods, and largely excludes the broad range of services included in Part Four altogether.

On the other hand, it can and has been argued that in Canada Parts Two, Three, Four, and Five of the agreement taken together have implications for the linkage that is sometimes made between political development and economic diversification.

On at least one theory of economic growth, a national economy focused on only a few resource products that must be exported will typically be a captive to destabilizing international economic fluctuations that frustrate ambitions to establish a stable political regime — a classic dilemma of what used to be called "underdeveloped countries". A national economy with a more diversified

A traditional Canadian complaint about the traditional resource-dominated Canadian economy has been that it makes Canadians mere hewers of wood and drawers of water for others elsewhere. This early 20th century cartoon is suggesting that Wilfrid Laurier's penchant for free trade with the United States would keep more advanced manufacturing industry south of the border. By the late 20th century Canada in fact has a strong manufacturing base. But — in a new variation on the traditional argument — some opponents of Canada-U.S. free trade argue that it will keep more sophisticated or "higher order" service industry south of the border.

economic base, including strong manufacturing and service sectors, is more able to cope with international fluctuations and generate its own political stability.

In Canada this same logic has also been urged in a regional setting, as illustrated by the Mulroney government's recently established Western Diversification Agency. Similarly, one of the Ontario provincial government's objections to the 1987-88 free trade agreement seems to be that the agreement appears most advantageous for the least sophisticated resource elements in Canada's economic structure, and least advantageous for its most sophisticated higher-order service elements (the often unloved Canadian banks being one obvious case in point).

The apparent concentration of U.S. domestic opposition among resource producers in the American West lends some weight to such objections (though there has been some notable opposition as well from auto parts producers and the state of Michigan).

On the other hand, in the U.S. it also can and has been argued that by stressing its service economy to the detriment of its resource and manufacturing sectors, the American Republic itself may be running significant risks for its longer-term stability and political development.

Necessary Compromises?

Like the ancient Reciprocity Treaty of 1854, the Canada-U.S. Free Trade Agreement of 1987-88 began with Canadian overtures to the United States. Under such circumstances, in the 1850s the political embryo of what is now the Canadian Confederation had to offer some special incentives to the United States, to make a deal possible : Atlantic fishing rights and free navigation of the Canadian Great Lakes-St. Lawrence waterway.

In the same spirit, there are a few parts of the Mulroney trade agreement of the 1980s that could be described as calculated infringements on Canadian political sovereignty, willingly sustained by the Government of Canada, in the larger interests of striking an otherwise quite positive deal with historically sly Yankee traders.

One example that has raised some concern is the investment provisions of Part Four. In particular, Canada has ultimately agreed to limit its screening of U.S. direct takeovers of Canadian corporations to deals involving $150 million or more. Put another way, the Canadian federal government has forgone any responsibility it might otherwise assume for monitoring and influencing U.S. investment in all but larger, more established Canadian business enterprises.

Opinions on how important an abridgement of Canadian sovereignty this is can vary. Two particular points on the side that argues against exaggerating its consequences are worth noting.

First, strictly speaking the U.S. (though it quite arguably has much less interest in such things, as a result of its much greater population weight) has sustained an even greater abridgement of its sovereignty with respect to Canadian investment. As the Ottawa-based Institute for Research on Public

Policy has summarized the relevant provisions: "No general controls on cross-border investment will be permitted, except on the Canadian side."

Second, even its supporters have argued that the Foreign Investment Review Agency of the Trudeau era was never an altogether convincing element in Canadian development strategy. Moreover, even among such supporters there is a growing body of evidence and opinion that challenges many of the assumptions on which earlier concepts of foreign investment review were based.

William K. Carroll's recent *Corporate Power and Canadian Capitalism*, for instance, contends that Canadian corporate development between 1946 and 1976 reflected "the internationalization of industrial capital rather than growing dependence on the American metropole." Similarly, "the growth of foreign-owned corporate capital" in Canada has had very little to do with some "process...whereby Canadian-owned firms were 'gobbled-up' by foreigners." According to the political scientist James Bickerton, "Carroll is arguing for a greater cognizance...of the internationalized form of contemporary capitalism and the need to direct energies and attention away from the (misplaced?) nationalist struggles of the 1970s to more salient concerns."

In a rather different setting, Part Five of the agreement on financial services has some negative implications for an important non-governmental supporting apparatus of Canadian sovereignty. Unless or until the Glass-Steagall Act governing the relationship between banks and securities industries in the U.S. is changed, Canadian banks will not have quite the same advantages in the United States as American banks will have in Canada. Except for the Bank of Nova Scotia's mildly-voiced reservations, however, Canadian banks themselves seem to have taken the position that they are strong enough to overcome the handicap.

The most unambiguous restriction on Canadian sovereignty in the 1987-88 agreement involves the specific provisions regarding what U.S. government commentary describes as "energy sharing" in Part Two on trade in goods. These provisions have been the subject of some debate, but it seems clear enough that, broadly, they will make it impossible for the Canadian federal government to set a price for Canadian energy products in Canada that is different from the price for Canadian energy products in the United States — and vice-versa for the U.S. federal government and American energy products in Canada. Whatever else, this will also make impossible any future Canadian National Energy Policy of the sort established by the Trudeau government in the early 1980s.

It is equally clear, on the other hand, that there is significant Canadian domestic support for this particular curbing of Canadian federal government authority, most notably in Western Canada (and especially in the province of Alberta).

Despite such calculated lapses, supporters of the agreement can justly claim that it entails no major and fundamental abridgements in such traditionally crucial underpinnings of national sovereignty as currency and monetary policy, or foreign policy and international affairs.

At the same time, some domestic opposition to the agreement in the U.S. suggests that the value of the Canadian dollar could become an issue as and if the Part Six discussions toward a common code on unfair trade practices unfold in the 1990s.

Similarly, in foreign policy and international affairs Brian Mulroney's government can take some credit both for its recent efforts to strengthen Canada's traditional ties to the Commonwealth of Nations, and for its role in the development of the new international organization of la Francophonie — presumably in an effort to demonstrate that while Canada is for the moment devoting much energy to updating its relationship with the United States, it still places a very high value on its historic relationships and commitments outside North America.

Shortly after his election in 1984, however, the new prime minister of Canada also put the world on notice that in the complicated struggles of international politics his particular Canadian government would be giving Canada's good neighbours and cousins in the American Republic "the benefit of the doubt."

"The radio crosses boundaries which stopped the press."

Whether you finally look on the sum of these particular slights on Canadian sovereignty as a series of modest necessary compromises in the interests of a greater good, or something much more alarming for the Canadian future, partly depends on your wider political views.

Some Canadian critics have complained that the Canada-U.S. Free Trade Agreement taken as a whole has profound strains of free market evangelism that will, in effect, lock Canada in to a particular anti-government form of public policy, very much out of step with its traditional attachments to a mixed economy. This, it has been claimed, is the most fundamental explanation for much of the strong business backing that the Mulroney trade agreement has won.

In one sense, the criticism contains, virtually by definition, at least a half-truth. In the nature of things, any "free trade" agreement implies a judgement against certain kinds of government intervention in economic life. At a minimum it prescribes that governments ought not to place tariffs or duties against the products of the countries which are party to the agreement. And the 1987-88 agreement between Canada and the United States implies that, with respect to the economic relationship between the two countries, government ought to be taking a back seat to the private sectors of the two economies on a rather wider range of issues than mere tariffs.

At the same time, this in itself does not imply that the December 1987 document signed by Reagan and Mulroney is by definition a strident manifesto for a permanent anti-government political and economic regime in Canada. The actual text of the document refers to *reducing* "government-created trade distortions while preserving the Parties' flexibility to safeguard the public welfare." On the face of things, even Brian Mulroney's Chicago statement of December 1985, about what is "not at issue" in Canada-U.S. free trade, stakes a rather broad claim for government involvement in Canadian national life.

As evidence that some even in America have been listening to this particular Canadian voice in the negotiations, shortly after the 1987-88 agreement was initialed *Business Week* advised its readers: "Canadians worry that their sovereignty and cultural identity will be eroded by closer economic ties with the U.S. It's important that the U.S. recognize — as the trade pact does, in effect — that these are legitimate concerns for a bilingual country that is still struggling to define its sense of nationhood."

Moreover, as Harold Innis informed an audience at the University of Maine in the late 1930s: "The radio crosses boundaries which stopped the press." In the late 1980s we can confirm that television is an even more potent force. And people who pay as much attention to events in the U.S.A. today as most Canadians do cannot fail to notice that in the late 20th century Canada is not the only place in North America that is struggling to define a new sense of nationhood for the 21st century.

Against the American Grain is itself the title of a 1960s book of essays by the American writer, Dwight Macdonald. Even in the late 1980s, a recent survey reported on in *Rolling Stone* magazine found that among Americans between 18 and 44: "Only 33 per cent of the men would willingly fight alongside our allies to defend Western Europe. Only 19 per cent of the men would be willing to serve in a war to keep a Third World nation from falling to communists. Only 22 per cent would enlist to defend our sources of oil in the Persian Gulf."

The Washington Post columnist Haynes Johnson has recently observed: "National opinion on major issues is sufficiently fragmented to raise questions about what the country collectively believes and what it is willing to do about several obvious problems: Central America, economic competitiveness, the deficit." As the New York liberal finacial guru Felix Rohatyn has pointed out, the late 20th century free-trading U.S.A. already has "a review mechanism for foreign acquisitions of companies with defense-related activities." It also has "statutory limits on foreign acquisitions of U.S. airlines and U.S. television stations."

In *Trading Places: How We Allowed Japan To Take The Lead*, Clyde Prestowitz, former "point man in the Reagan Administration's trade skirmishes of the early 1980s," has argued that "the United States and Japan have fundamentally different understandings of the purposes and workings of a national economy." And, as U.S. business journalist Robert Neff has recently put it: "Prestowitz seems less intent on persuading Japan to change than on convincing Americans that we need an industrial policy, albeit one that preserves U.S. openness and most free-trade principles."

The great practical challenge for the Canadian Confederation in the late 20th and early 21st centuries may well be to avoid simply being swallowed up by some such new American industrial policy. Yet this would be true even without a free trade agreement between the two countries. Even with a free trade agreement, if the United States can have a distinctive national industrial policy, so can a resolute and determined Canada.

As Pierre Trudeau put the ultimate point in one of the hard and clear essays he wrote before he became prime minister of Canada: "more than language and culture, more than history and geography, even more than force and power, the foundation of the nation is will."

Chapter 15

REGION & CULTURE

At least a considerable number of the Canadian opponents of Canada-U.S. free trade who have raised concerns about its potential impact on political sovereignty have also raised concerns about its impact on, as *Business Week* has put it, Canada's "cultural identity."

Many among the native intelligentsia active in Canadian cultural industries have argued that this concern flows from different understandings of the word "culture" in Canada and the United States. In the U.S., it is said, the word is most often used strictly as a synonym for entertainment: in Canada it more often refers to the sum of a country's creative endeavour, that ultimately adds up to its national "distinctive voice."

Beyond the intellectual fringes of Canadian life, the cultural concern raises broader issues. Moreover, Canada is not the only country where the concern itself has become mixed up in trade negotiations with the United States. The American expert on Japanese education, Merry White has recently explained how the Japanese "are alert to the need to maintain their own cultural values at the core of any new system adopted. They regard culture as an integral, dynamic part of their society and economy. For Americans bred on Adam Smith and Thomas Jefferson, culture is what's left only after the market economy and attendant social mobility have worked their will."

Particularly for culture in the sense of popular or even highbrow entertainment, Canada largely shares with the United States a common North American culture of the New World (which itself has roots in Europe and — as we are only now beginning to allow — in Africa as well). Yet there is also a sense in which Canadians have slightly more appreciation than Americans of why trade discussions between Japan and the United States in the late 20th century so often develop into arguments about Japanese culture. And when Americans complain that it is hard to see all that much difference between the modern United States and modern Japan when you visit downtown Tokyo, Canadians can detect at least faint echoes of familiar themes.

The response of Brian Mulroney's Canada-U.S.Free Trade Agreement of 1987-1988 to concerns about Canada's cultural identity is that "cultural industries" have in fact been exempted from the provisions of the bargain that has been struck. In the specific language of the agreement, cultural industries include enterprises involved in: "books, magazines, periodicals, or newspapers in print or machine readable form"; "film or video recordings"; "audio or video music recordings"; "music in print or machine readable form"; "all radio, television and cable television broadcasting undertakings and all satellite programming and broadcast network services."

This exemption partly reflects the successful domestic lobbying efforts of Canada's native intelligentsia — a branch of the modern Canadian political and economic system that while still in its infancy in any comparative international context, is much more robust and energetic today than it was a generation ago. Yet the exemption itself is not without its ambiguities. Some of the harshest Canadian critics of the 1987-1988 trade agreement have come from the among the native intelligentsia, who have tended to view the Mulroney government's claims about the exemption of cultural industries with strong cultural memories of the ancient injunction to beware of Greeks bearing gifts.

"The Toronto Literati"

No nation that has been even only partly whitewashed by an Anglo-Saxon brush takes its intelligentsia altogether seriously, and Canada confirms the rule with particular conviction. "Culture" is often a term that large numbers among the sovereign electorate view sceptically. As Frank Underhill complained in the early 1950s: "There is no other country in the world where intellectuals suffer from such low repute as in Canada."

In the spring of 1988 the Newfoundland wit John Crosbie — to whom Brian Mulroney had entrusted the job of selling the new Canada-U.S. Free Trade Agreement in its most crucial domestic phases, urged that at bottom, it was only the "Toronto literati" who were deeply worried about the agreement's impact on such things as Canada's cultural identity. In a political nation at large where Toronto is even less popular than culture, this is a cunning enough argument.

But Toronto is not the only city where culture is a concern. Along with rival national intelligentsias in Montreal or even Vancouver, Canada has regional intelligentsias focused on such places as Halifax, Quebec City, Thunder Bay, Winnipeg, Regina, Edmonton, Victoria, and certainly St. John's, Newfoundland. Less than 50% of the head offices of the members of the Association of Canadian Publishers are concentrated in Toronto.

Moreover the distinctive voice of the Canadian intelligentsia has been noted in other places. In the early 1960s the American literary critic Edmund Wilson, from a base in the village of Talcottville in upstate New York, intermittently visited with both French and English Canadian colleagues north of the border. On returning from one of his journeys, he confided to his journal: "Strange how different Talcottville looks from Canada, which is another country, dark and special... . The literary and academic people are interesting in a way quite

Concern over the excessively arduous conditions facing native cultural industries in the Canadian Confederation has a longer history than is sometimes recognized. This late 19th century Hunter cartoon focuses on the early struggles for a Canadian copyright law. As Hunter implies, both Uncle Sam and John Bull were involved in the problem. The drawing also seems to anticipate the late 20th century concept of a "level playing field" — though it adds a horse and buggy labeled: "This ambulance is reserved for injured authors and publishers."

distinct from ours.... . Morley Callaghan may seem, like his novels, common-place when you first encounter him, but, like them, he is deeply sensitive and understanding of human processes... . Marie-Claire Blais, who writes such gloomy and eerie novels, is an altogether unique phenomenon.... . None of these people seems to me in the least to resemble any type in the United States."

Since the advent of the Canada Council in the late 1950s, the fortunes of the distinctive voice have become linked with modest programs of government cultural patronage that owe more to models in Europe than in the United States (which has been able to depend on the cultural patronage of colossal private foundations — some of which have also been, especially in an earlier era, active in Canada).

In this context, both the national and regional intelligentsias have made a few suitably grateful noises for the exemption of cultural industries from Mulroney's trade agreement. But they have expressed alarm at the lacunae and ambiguities in the exemption. Some have argued that the Canadian federal government will be under pressure either from the U.S. government or large U.S. entertainment conglomerates to forestall new programs to encourage the development of Canadian culture. They have also raised concerns about potential U.S. harmonizing pressures on the growth of Canadian culture under bilateral free trade, and the possible disappearance of at least some such enterprises as publishing houses and film production companies, which link the cultural producer with his or her audience.

In fact, the characteristic problem of especially English-speaking Canadian cultural industries has not been gaining access to U.S. or other outside markets, but gaining access to the Canadian market itself. (Even today books published in Canada account for less than a quarter of the domestic book market.) Since the 19th century the United Kingdom as well as the United States has played a part in the problem. And the political evolution from colony to nation has been accompanied by slow steps of progress down a long road.

In 1850 Henry Thoreau from Massachusetts could somewhat critically observe that except for "schoolbooks and the like" the bookstores of Montreal "got their books from the States." But by 1890 Goldwin Smith, the expatriate English intellectual of Toronto (and late 19th century partisan for Canadian-American free trade, whatever it might bring), was at least complaining about the "arduous and costly" exertions of himself and others "to give Canadian intellect an organ in the shape of a magazine or a literary paper."

There was, Smith went on in the final issue of his own *Bystander,* "no use in denying the fact that the literary products of a dependency are at a discount in the dependency itself. The struggle against the literary journalism of the mother country and still more against that of the United States is almost desperate.... . Those who have been unsparing in their efforts...may fairly plead that they have shown patriotism in their way, albeit their way may not be that of the Jingo."

Desperate or otherwise, the struggle continued. As the political nation began to emerge, the Canadian federal government increasingly played some part. A Conservative government established the Canadian Broadcasting Corporation in the 1930s. A Liberal government established the Canada Council in the 1950s

Trudeau came to power just after a wave of patriotic celebrations surrounding the Centennial of the 1867 Confederation. His regime took a few steps in the 1970s — such as allowing Canadian cable television operators to replace U.S. commercials on programming from U.S. border stations with Canadian commercials — that were chauvinistically unfair to U.S. cultural industries in the Canadian market, and did not much help the growth of any notable kind of Canadian culture.

Despite the cultural exemption, Mulroney's government has agreed to curb such excesses in its new trade arrangement with the United States. It has also agreed to "the elimination of tariffs on any inputs to, and products of, the cultural industries, such as musical instruments, cassettes, film, recording tape, records and cameras." Moreover, it seems clear enough that U.S. governments and U.S. interests have other concerns about Canada's modern efforts to strengthen and energize its national communications system.

Under a U.S. administration headed by Ronald Reagan it is not surprising that the movie industry has been a particular sticking point. The Hollywood-based American industry, which has traditionally regarded Canada as part of its own domestic market, has been particularly irked by the past efforts and future plans of Canadian federal governments to make the Hollywood-dominated distribution system for the Canadian movie market more open to Canadian-based producers.

All this flows from longstanding arguments in both countries. Even to some Canadians who are not cultural or any other kinds of nationalists, it seems somehow less than democratic that U.S.-based distributors — with no attachments to, interests in, or understandings of Canada, should largely decide what movies are shown in the Canadian market (and in the process exclude producers who want to make movies on Canadian subjects). Even the few movies on Canadian subjects of the past decade or so have only appeared since governments began to intervene in the economics of the movie business in Canada, in the interests of national development.

From an American free market continental point of view, Canadians have done well enough in North American show business. The Canadian movie theatre operator Garth Drabinsky's Cineplex chain has recently become a force of some account in both Canada and the United States. Especially since the fall in the Canadian dollar, North American movies are being made in Canada (even if their scripts pretend that the locale is in the U.S). Moreover in the late 1980s the Toronto region is the third largest movie market in the United States and Canada taken together (after New York and Los Angeles), and in the U.S.A. today internationally popular American movies are important earners of foreign exchange and relievers of deficits. Washington is eager to defend whatever shares of foreign movie markets it already enjoys.

In its own house, the U.S. federal government has made clear that it is not altogether happy with the broad exemption of cultural industries in the Canada-U.S. Free Trade Agreement. "Regrettably," Trade Representative Clayton

Yeutter told Congress early in 1988, "a cultural exemption was essential if we were to reach an agreement." The issue was "enormously sensitive for our Canadian friends."

Bilaterally, the practical expression of U.S. concern is the somewhat mysterious hedge on the cultural industries exemption that declares its impact for either party may be, in effect, countervailed by "measures of equivalent commercial effect." Just what this may eventually come to mean is unclear.

Not surprisingly, in this setting, many Canadian critics of the agreement have not been reassured by the exemption of cultural industries. In response, it seems, John Crosbie (who no doubt understands practical politics somewhat better than most Canadian intellectuals) has concluded there is more advantage to be gained from dismissing their concerns as the colourful exaggerations of the Toronto literati.

Political Culture, Regionalism & National Communications

If the concerns of the intelligentsia constituted the only pressure for a cultural exemption from Canada-U.S. free trade, it is unlikely that Brian Mulroney's government would have worked so hard at the matter. Yet beyond culture as entertainment, and culture as a quest for a distinctive voice, there is political culture — the values, organizations, and communication networks that support and sustain the distinctive institutional structure of the Canadian political system itself. Even the American business press has been able to grasp the broader logic behind Margaret Atwood's comment: "I don't see how you can have a country if all your information is coming from somewhere else."

It has been said in the past that the great difference between the political cultures of Canada and the United States is that Canada has had no War of Independence. There is a sense in which this still has some meaning. Even after the new Constitution of 1982 Canada retains a symbolic constitutional monarchy presided over by the Queen of Canada (who, strictly by accident on the current doctrine, just happens to be the same person as the Queen of the United Kingdom).

But today the American War of Independence itself does not seem quite as significant an event as it may have seemed once. In its own way, Canada (along with many other countries) long ago embraced the one major political innovation that the American Republic pioneered — democracy in de Tocqueville's sense of equality of opportunity and social mobility. The archaic feudal symbolism of the constitutional monarchy in Canada may remain forever, in an exotic tribute to the tradition of compromise and the richest meaning of gradualism and moderation. It is also possible, however, that in the 21st century Canada will become a Commonwealth republic, on the consitiutional model of India (which the Canadian Prime Minister Louis St. Laurent in fact had a hand in devising in the late 1940s).

In any event,whatever other kind of culture different from that of the United States it may or may not have, Canada does have an unambiguously distinctive political culture. And the very heterogeneous and pluralist character of Canadian society makes a strong and effective national communications system crucial to the growth and development of a robust and energetic Canadian Confederation in the 21st century.

As matters stand, the current Toronto-centred English and Montreal-centred French media add up to less than a genuinely effective national communications system. Yet, in a continental setting where the national communications system of the much larger American Republic has exerted enormous influence on Canada (and has itself been increasingly dominated by large corporate oligopolies since the late 19th century), even making Canada's national communications system more regionally sensitive can only mean moving, in this particular sector, in the opposite direction from Canada-U.S. free trade.

For both the intelligentsia and the sovereign electorate at large, that is to say, Canadian political culture has a profoundly regional as well as a national edge. A concern to resist certain kinds of harmonizing pressures from "Central Canada" implies a parallel concern to resist similar pressures from New York or Southern California. A regionalist is only a nationalist who takes the subject very seriously.

Put another way, a major difference between the political ethos of Canada and the United States is that Canada has never had a Civil War. It had its best chance in the 1960s and 1970s, but even this never got beyond Trudeau's brief October 1970 invocation of the War Measures Act. The practical implication is that the Canadian Confederation of 1867 has evolved into a notably decentralized federal system, much more like the United States of the first half of the 19th century than the United States of today.

The Distinct Society in Quebec

There are various factors behind this evolution, but a crucial one has been the survival of French-speaking Quebec. The French fact itself has also meant that Canada has evolved into a place with an officially bilingual political culture (reflected *a mari usque ad mare* in things as disparate as bilingual corn-flakes boxes and bilingual academic journals). Above all else, however, French remains a language of daily life in Canada because it has been geographically concentrated in the region of Quebec.

The late 1980s career of Jacques Parizeau as third leader of the Parti Québécois suggests that it would be wrong to imagine the spectre of the Quebec independence movement has altogether vanished from the modern Confederation. The Meech Lake Accord, by recognizing Quebec as a "distinct society" within Canada, has finally prompted Robert Bourassa's current Quebec Liberal provincial government to agree to sign the new 1982 Constitution. Yet not all provincial legislatures have ratified the Accord, and it remains less than an accomplished fact — especially since the election of Frank McKenna as Premier of New Brunswick (and Sharon Carstairs as leader of the official opposition in Manitoba).

While conceding the significance of cultural and related concerns for English-speaking Canada, Parizeau himself has suggested that the French language shields the Quebec of the independantist's dreams from any serious worries about such issues in Canada-U.S. free trade. His widely admired acute intellect notwithstanding, this seems to underrate the historical significance of the fate of the French language in the U.S. state of Louisiana — which originally conducted debates in its state legislature in both English and French.

It also likely underestimates the extent to which the survival of a more limited French Canadian culture in such places as the Windsor region of southwestern Ontario (but not across the river in Detroit, Michigan) acts as a forward defence for the more pristine distinct society in Quebec itself.

Moreover, the more fantastic continental political implications of a genuinely independent new nation of Quebec were suggested, in a provocative rather than a serious way, by the American journalist Joel Garreau's *The Nine Nations of North America,* published in the United States in the midst of some mild American speculation prompted by the 1980 Quebec referendum in Canada. Garreau's book also suggests how the regionalism of the Canadian Confederation reflects underlying economic, geographic, and cultural realities in North America at large, and not just in Canada: "North Americans are a bunch of tough, resilient, imaginative smart people who are not waiting around for New York or Washington or Ottawa or Los Angeles to tell them what to do — how to get into the 21st century."

Regionalism, however, has developed a vigorous political expression in Canada that the Civil War thwarted in the United States. Moreover, Quebec has been a primary creator of Canada's particular variation on the regionalism of the continent, and it is highly unlikely that it could ever be truly happy anywhere else.

For the restructured Canadian tradition of compromise in the 21st century, on one side of the coin — as a matter of practical politics in North America, Quebec needs Canada as much as Canada needs Quebec. This was implicitly recognized even in René Lévesque's "sovereignty association" formula. On the other side, the modern history of Canada begins with the acceptance that, as a matter of concrete historical fact, Quebec is the birthplace of the Canadian as well as the post Second World War Québécois nationality. The modern English-speaking Canadian majority cannot suppress Quebec in a civil war, without destroying Canada itself.

Western Canada Rising

If Quebec has been the great anchor for regionalism throughout the country, the original warrior for provincial rights and the regional state in English-speaking Canada was the province of Ontario. Especially since the Second World War — and more generally, no doubt, as Toronto began to supplant Montreal as the country's undisputed financial capital — Ontario provincial governments have increasingly moderated historic regionalist instincts with stronger concerns for "the national interest."

Though there are some signs that this too could change again, in the late 20th century the torch of provincial rights lit by Oliver Mowat of Ontario in the late 19th century has fundamentally passed on to particularly the most western provinces of Western Canada. In some ways Western Canada and Quebec have the least in common among the modern regions of the Confederation. (Both Atlantic Canada and Ontario, for instance, have larger French Canadian minorities.) Taken together, however, Western Canada and Quebec account for some 54% of the Canadian population in the late 1980s.

In the modern democracy of the Canadian Confederation, this is politically significant because support for the new Canada-U.S. Free Trade Agreement — in opinion polls and among provincial premiers, is strongest in Quebec and Western Canada. And this is perhaps the best reason for believing that the agreement has at least a potentially durable popular base for the future in Canadian domestic politics.

Especially in Western Canada enthusiasm for Canadian-American free trade also has roots in the history of the Confederation's regional political culture. Alberta and Saskatchewan were the strongest provincial supporters of Laurier and reciprocity in the federal election of 1911.

In 1988 B.C.'s opposition to reciprocity in both 1911 and 1891 continues to be reflected in a somewhat higher percentage of B.C. opponents over supporters of the Mulroney trade agreement in opinion polls. Here as elsewhere, the Confederation's "Pacific region," whose premier has recently announced plans "to make British Columbia Canada's strongest and most prosperous province," is unique.

But even in B.C. at least initial popular support for the agreement remains higher than in Atlantic Canada or Ontario. And support for Canada-U.S. free trade in the prairie provinces in 1988 is stronger than anywhere else except Quebec.

ANGUS REID'S REGIONAL OPINION POLL ON THE CANADA-U.S. FREE TRADE AGREEMENT, January 1988

Region	% Undecided	% Oppose	% Support
Quebec	19	26	55
Prairies	14	39	47
B.C.	6	49	45
Atlantic	20	37	43
Ontario	13	50	37
ALL CANADA	14	41	45

It may be mistaken to overemphasize the potential for the future in the obvious enough streaks of free market economy evangelism that some have criticized in the new Canada-U.S. Free Trade Agreement. But it is not surprising that a bargain struck between Canadian Conservative and U.S. Reaganite Republican governments in the late 1980s should have such streaks.

In this context, it is somewhat ironic that the Western Canadian provinces of Manitoba, Saskatchewan, and British Columbia are also the only jurisdictions in North America, in the sense of "Canada and the United States," that have been governed by an avowedly socialist or social democratic political party. (Though it can also be urged that, at bottom, the socialism of the Canadian New Democrats has more in common with the liberalism of Jesse Jackson in the U.S., than with the socialism of François Mitterand in France or Neil Kinnock in the United Kingdom.)

At the same time, Canada-wide polling data suggests that as many as 30% of New Democrats support the Confederation's new trade agreement with the United States. Support in Western Canada no doubt owes more to the Social Credit-Conservative side of the regional political culture. Yet it also seems to ring some responsive chords for those who still remember the old western agrarian democratic protest against Canada's miniaturized heejous monsters back east.

Similarly, Toronto can in some senses be said to have used strengthened relations with New York via the ancient Reciprocity Treaty of 1854 to get out from under the shadow of Montreal. In the same way, Calgary and perhaps Vancouver (and perhaps Montreal and Halifax as well) seem to see strengthened relations with the U.S. via the new treaty of the late 1980s as a way of getting out from under the shadow of Toronto (and, particularly in Alberta, from Central Canada's perceived use of the federal government in Ottawa to exploit the regions — as in Trudeau's National Energy Policy of the early 1980s).

Regional Disparities in Atlantic Canada

Brian Mulroney himself has linked the agreement with the aspirations of a different kind of historic regional protest in Atlantic Canada.

Virtually since 1867 Atlantic Canada has been the slowest growing and least prosperous region of the Confederation. In this respect it is somewhat and in some cases markedly different from the West. The western regional economic problem, from the wheat economy drought and Depression of the 1930s to the oil boom and bust of the 1970s and 1980s, has broadly had much more to do with the volatility of its resource-dominated economic base than with low or "lagging" income.

Nonetheless, as in the case of the rather different problems of the West, a long tradition has perceived slow growth in Atlantic Canada as at least partly the result of Central Canadian economic domination — or even, as the Manitoba theorist of *Regional Disparities,* Paul Phillips, has argued, "in large measure, the result of Macdonald's 1879 National Policy of protection."

To the extent that this tradition does connect with real political and economic forces, it is logical enough to argue that movement away from the historic protection of the National Policy in the new Canada-U.S. Free Trade Agreement will improve the regional circumstances of Atlantic Canada, as well as those of Western Canada (and, so the argument goes, even Quebec).

Perhaps like all such traditions, however, this one has its ambiguities. In the late 20th century some of the most obvious are suggested by even a simple look at changes in provincial average family income rankings between the mid-1970s and the mid-1980s.

PROVINCIAL AVERAGE FAMILY INCOMES, 1975-1984.

$1975		$1982		$1984	
Ontario	17,772	Alberta	38,834	Ontario	37,721
B.C.	17,520	B.C.	34,501	Alberta	37,062
Alberta	16,878	Ontario	33,716	B.C.	35,248
Sask.	15,784	Sask.	31,586	Quebec	33,561
Quebec	15,273	Manitoba	30,554	Manitoba	33,269
Manitoba	14,869	Quebec	30,075	Sask.	32,487
N.B.	13,283	N.S.	26,412	N.S.	29,833
N.S.	13,068	N.B.	25,988	N.B.	29,247
Nfld.	12,359	Nfld.	25,554	P.E.I.	28,134
P.E.I.	12,032	P.E.I.	25,113	Nfld.	26,187
CANADA	16,368	CANADA	32,447	CANADA	35,092

Partisans for the regional cause of Alberta can and have argued that its decline from highest to second-highest income province between 1982 and 1984 owes a great deal to the Trudeau regime's National Energy Policy — the likes of which will become, in effect, "illegal" under the new free trade agreement. Apologists for Ontario, on the other hand, can and have argued that the notable similarities between the economic bases and recent economic performances of Alberta and Texas point to quite different factors at work.

Similarly, it is true enough that the four provinces of Atlantic Canada are invariably in the bottom half of provincial average income rankings. At the same time, in 1984 the average income of the two highest income states in the U.S. (Alaska and Connecticut) was some 85% higher than that of the two lowest income states (West Virginia and Mississippi); but the average income of the two highest income provinces in Canada (Ontario and Alberta) was only some 38% higher than that of the two lowest income provinces (P.E.I. and Newfoundland).

It is often said, with much truth, that the trouble with regional development programs, in Canada and elsewhere, is that they simply have not worked. Yet the difference between state and provincial income rankings in Canada and the United States suggests that Canada's federal-provincial equalization grants and

On one Atlantic Canadian view, Confederation has been a Central Canadian plot to keep Atlantic Canada down. On one Central Canadian view it has been an Atlantic Canadian plot to extract "boodle" (or as the dictionary puts it, "money for political bribery") from Central Canada. The staunch Ontario free trader and North American free market enthusiast Richard Cartwright — pictured as the parrot in this late 19th century Sam Hunter cartoon — was a proponent of the second view. The gentleman Nova Scotia and the demure Miss Laurier are courting, but Miss Laurier complains: "No sooner does a young man show a disposition to stay than that parrot drives him off." (In the end Laurier would choose former Nova Scotia Premier W.S. Fielding over Cartwright for the job of finance minister in his first cabinet.)

regional incentives — a particular Canadian institutional response to national stresses and strains cast in bold relief by the 1930s Depression — may not have been altogether in vain.

So Prince Edward Island, the least populous and often lowest income province in the Confederation, has joined Ontario, the most populous and often highest income province, in opposing the Mulroney trade agreement.

It has also been reported that Premier John Buchanan of Nova Scotia only announced his support for the agreement after receiving written assurances from Brian Mulroney himself that Canada's "commitment to fight regional disparities" would not in any way be abridged by its new free trade pact with the United States.

Popular Culture: *A Mari Usque Ad Mare*

In the very end — beyond culture as entertainment, beyond culture as the quest for a distinctive voice, beyond political culture, national communications, and regionalism — there is the widest sense of the word: some incalcuable sum of individual experiences in the activities of daily life.

If you start out with an image of Canada as a very homogeneous place and then travel from the Atlantic to the Pacific (or vice-versa), you will be struck by the regionalism of the sovereign electorate, as it lives from day to day. On the other hand, if you start out with an image of Canada as a very regional place and then travel across the country, you will be struck by the similarities in the life of the electorate from region to region (and even, if you speak both French and English, in Quebec).

While the political culture of the Confederation nourishes its distinctive institutional structure, it is the concrete results that the structure produces for ordinary life on the ground that are at least subtly visible to the naked eye, and widely valued or otherwise by the electorate at large. From this standpoint, like equalization grants and regional incentives, Canada's federal-provincial public health insurance scheme, federal unemployment insurance program, and federal-provincial pension plan are at least as much parts of its modern culture as the Canada Council and the CBC (and account for much, much larger shares of federal and provincial government budgets).

There are still more subtle results on the ground. An American Broadcasting Corporation TV colour commentator at the 1988 Calgary Winter Olympics observed that he had always imagined Canadians and Americans were the same; but, having now spent some time in Canada, he concluded that Canadians were "more polite."

The observation can be broadened out. Just as the settlement of the Canadian West was not marked by the same recurrent violent conflict with Indians that punctuated the settlement of the American West, both comparative statistics and direct observation suggest that modern Canadian cities — *a mari usque ad mare* — have less crime, cleaner streets and public parks, more orderly local planning processes, and stronger civic pride than most cities in the modern American Republic. The ambience is captured in Peter Ustinov's quip that modern Toronto (also lately described in the U.S. business press as "the hottest market in North America") is like "New York run by the Swiss."

Almost no one in Canada carries a gun, except members of the Canadian Armed Forces, police officers, professional criminals, and licensed hunters in season. On the other hand, a U.S. CIA official has complained that you can in fact do anything you like in the country's leading cities, so long as you don't spit on the sidewalks. From another angle again, during the past few decades some three-quarters of the Canadian electorate have typically voted in Canadian federal elections, while only somewhat more than half the American electorate have voted in U.S. presidential elections.

A preference for preserving Canada's particular national style of life in these respects, as part of the larger enterprise of preserving Canadian political sovereignty, may finally be no more than a matter of taste. The Canadians who argued against the 1911 Reciprocity Treaty on the grounds that it would increase the number of divorces in Canada, for instance, reflect a quirky, moralistic side to the political nation's culture — never universally admired, even by Canadians. According to George Orwell, however, the partriot's primal belief about his or her country is: "However much you hate it or laugh at it, you will never be happy away from it for any length of time."

Besides, if you find you don't like Canada, you can always move to the United States; and since the very birth of the American Republic it has been equally true that if you are unhappy in the United States, you can always move to Canada. During the most recent full decade for which statistics are available (1971-1980), 169, 939 Canadians did move to the United States, and 178, 621 Americans moved to Canada. It has also been a particular attraction of Canadian culture, for Canadians of any origin, that you do not have to love Canada or leave it. If you chose, you can hate the place and stay, in comfort.

Whatever else they may have had in mind, when the Canadian provincial governments of Prince Edward Island, Manitoba, and Ontario declared their opposition to the new Canada-U.S. Free Trade Agreement late in 1987, they were affirming a belief in the worth of all these things. (And it seems that Manitoba's opposition may well survive even the election of a new Conservative minority government in April 1988.)

An editorial in *The Financial Post* (voice of another kind of Toronto intelligentsia) has condemned the Government of Ontario's opposition as "on the wrong side of history." Ironically enough, this notion of historical inevitability has a rather marxist tinge and like at least the more vulgar forms of marxism it is too simplistic, too rooted in the 19th century, and too insensitive to richer and even more conservative understandings of the human past, present, and future to be altogether convincing.

Opposition to Mulroney's trade agreement on the grounds of its merely potential implications for Canadian political sovereignty and cultural identity may not be, by itself, enough to outweigh the agreement's other advantages; but the positions taken by the provincial governments of P.E.I., Manitoba, and Ontario shortly after the agreement was first announced have implications for the long-term future. Ultimately, in the politics of Canadian democracy there is no right or wrong side of history; there is only the tradition of compromise.

Chapter 16

NEW NATIONAL POLICIES & THIRD OPTIONS

I n all regions of the country, strong positive feelings about the new Canada-U.S. Free Trade Agreement among both big and small business may be taken as evidence of its short to mid-term economic potential for the country at large; but this implies nothing about even strictly economic benefits in the long run.

Business in North America is not noted for its attention to the long-term future. In this respect at least, much of it still tends to agree with the economist John Maynard Keynes: "in the long run we will all be dead."

The most persuasive argument for the agreement in Canada may well be that in the short run there is no sensible alternative. Different politicians may have been able to negotiate a better agreement at a different time. But now that a particular agreement has been negotiated, it may in the end make most sense for everyone to at least start trying to make it work.

In the late 1980s, unlike in the late 1970s, Southern Ontario is one region where recent economic growth has been rapid enough to leave obvious room for doubts about how necessary Brian Mulroney's particular trade agreement actually is, even in the short run. Yet even inside Ontario, polling data suggests that there is considerably more support for the agreement in the Toronto region than in the province at large — no doubt less because it may be necessary than because it seems a possible positive boon.

Moreover, in Atlantic Canada, Quebec, and Western Canada (and even Northern Ontario), to varying extents, residues of the international economic stresses and strains of the early 1980s are still noticeable enough to make any new economic policy direction with some arguable potential for new growth seem attractive on the face of things.

At the same time, if we stand back and at least try to grasp the longer-term trends in Mackenzie King's evolving global economic system, "which has substituted world for local markets and interdependence for self-sufficiency in Industry and Trade," it is highly arguable that a Canadian Confederation which spent the next generation largely focused on a new trade agreement with the United States would run significant risks, not just for its political sovereignty but for its economic progress as well.

It seems clear enough, for instance, that the United States will continue to be the world's largest consumer marketplace for some considerable time yet. It seems equally clear, however, that the American market (or even a somewhat larger North American market) cannot indefinitely be the single great engine of world economic growth.

Along with Canada, such places as Japan, West Germany, South Korea, Taiwan, Brazil, and now even Mexico have been working harder and harder to win a place in the heart of the American consumer. Even with new generations of improved and innovative products, high technology, and a buoyant domestic U.S. economy, there is a practical limit to how much the American consumer can buy.

Canadian industry in particular already has considerable strength in U.S. markets. In the long run, at the very least, there is a limit to how much more Canadian (or even American) economic expansion the American marketplace can sustain.

These are prospects that have recently been troubling Japanese as well as U.S. policy makers. And they ought to be troubling the various federal and provincial policy makers of modern Canada as well. A new trade agreement with the United States could be a sensible first step in the development of a stronger, internationally restructured Canada, ready to face the challenges and take the opportunities of the 21st century; but, as the 1987-88 agreement itself implies when it looks to a wider "expansion of world trade," it cannot be the only step.

The Future of the Domestic Economy

Strictly speaking, to talk about "alternative" policies for the long run is misleading. The literal meaning of alternative implies "mutually exclusive" options: i.e., you take one but not the other, or others.

Yet all three federal political parties in late 20th century Canada agree that some form of new trade agreement with the United States (at least a successor to agreements negotiated in, for example, 1935 or 1938 or 1941 or 1965) is an important Canadian national policy objective.

The fundamental issue, apart from the specific provisions of any agreement with the U.S., is not what alternative but what "additional" broad long-term policies are important or, on some views of the matter, possible?

One obvious starting point is the recognition that though foreign trade accounts for more than 30% of Canada's national income in the 1980s, close to 70% of Canadian income is still generated within the country itself.

"I'd like well enough to get any cheese that may be in there," says Sam Hunter's Laurier mouse: "but I don't think it would be safe to get into it too far." Hunter himself would probably urge that the message is still relevant enough for whatever modern Canadian mouse leads the Confederation in the 1990s. Canada is part of North America, but it is also part of the world at large.

Nationalists in the tradition of William Caniff in the 1870s have argued that to sign any broad free trade agreement with the United States must ultimately mean abandoning Canadian political control over national economic development in Canada. This is not, however, quite the message suggested by the experience of the 1850s and 1860s — when the first free trade treaty between the political embryo of the modern Canadian democracy and the United States was accompanied by the first burst of Canadian national expansionism that led to the Confederation of 1867.

There is some evidence in this particular historical precedent for the Mulroney trade agreement of the late 1980s to suggest that a Canada which runs an especially vigorous national development policy in the context of a free trade agreement with the U.S. runs the risk of U.S. abrogation of the agreement. (An example would be American irritation with Galt's revenue tariff on manufactured goods in the United Province of the late 1850s.)

This is a risk that all parties to international agreements inevitably run as a matter of course. Whatever weight is given to the 1866 U.S. abrogation of the 1854 treaty in the final consummation of 1867, it is a fact that the "road to Confederation" began in the 1850s, along with Canada-U.S. free trade in resource products.

It is also quite clear that the particular kind of updated Canadian national development strategy reflected in the Trudeau regime's Foreign Investment Review Agency and National Energy Policy departs fundamentally from the spirit of the particular trade agreement that the Mulroney regime has negotiated with the United States. Yet, even for some nationalists of the 1960s and 1970s, it is at the very least arguable that these are in any case far from the most sensible policies for promoting strong Canadian national economic development in the late 20th and early 21st centuries.

It is clear as well that under the agreement of the late 1980s American nationals have rights, with respect to a quite broad range of economic activity, to participate in any Canadian national economic development policy, under rules of the game set by Canadian electorates through their governments. (And Canadian nationals have similar rights to participate in any similar U.S. policies, under the equivalent conditions.) As in the case of William Van Horne and the C.P.R., however (or U.S. investors and the International Nickel Company of Canada), in one way or another American nationals have been participating in Canadian national economic development policies since the earliest history of the Confederation — and vice-versa for Canadian nationals in the United States.

Finally, it is notable that most genuinely strategic political and economic sectors from the standpoint of national development have been excluded from the late 1980s agreement. Beyond the obvious untouched heights of federal fiscal and monetary policy, for example, much of the communications sector falls under the exemption of cultural industries in Part Seven .

Similarly, as the Canadian federal government commentary stresses, in Part Four on trade in services: "Transportation services (marine, air, trucking, rail and bus modes) are not covered by the agreement." Whatever the exact limitations on national and provincial energy policies may prove to be, the

Canadian federal government still has its hands on the ancient east-west pathways of the transcontinental fur trade that began the modern national economy in Canada.

Trade Barriers Inside Canada & An Elected Senate

There are at least two obvious items on the agenda of any future national economic policy for Canada, with or without a free trade agreement between Canada and the United States.

The first starts with a by now well-established albeit enormously difficult issue at federal-provincial conferences over the past decade: the need to rationalize or give some dynamic national shape to a wide variety of inter-provincial barriers to trade within the Canadian domestic market, prompted by a diverse assortment of "un-harmonized" provincial government development policies.

To no small extent, the issue is so difficult because the restructuring Confederation has yet to achieve real consensus on the national limits to its historic regionalism. Any rapid progress on the rationalization of inter-provincial trade barriers within Canada is unlikely. Yet a serious start on addressing the issue becomes increasingly urgent, insofar as the various phases of the new Canada-U.S. Free Trade Agreement do move ahead over the decade of the 1990s.

There are, of course, those who argue that the east-west Canadian market will gradually disappear into the larger North American continental market, if and as the new agreement moves ahead. For practical purposes, however, the North American market is not really one single market, but a variety of often overlapping regional markets (which form one element in the logic of Joel Garreau's *Nine Nations of North America*).

For many purposes, the Canadian market has already long been a regional market in the North American economy. And, while there can be no doubt that the Mulroney trade agreement sets new parameters for its future, there are pragmatic and even geographic reasons for believing it can and will not only survive, but even grow and develop, in an increasingly new form.

Thus it is true enough, for instance, that even before and after the Reciprocity Treaty of 1854 an opportunistic Toronto used New York to get out from under the shadow of Montreal — much as the late 20th century cities of Western Canada see the Canada-U.S. Free Trade Agreement of the late 1980s as an opportunity to get out from under the shadow of Toronto. On the other hand, Toronto has also used Montreal and the east-west Canadian economy to, as much as possible, stay out from under the much wider and more potent shadow of New York.

Both north-south and east-west sides of the geographic equation, in other words, have been important in the gradual evolution of the late 20th century "hottest market in North America" (or, in the Canadian idiom, "the city with the heart of a loan shark"). In a late 1980s variation on a recurrent Central Canadian north-south theme, the American business press has declared: "Toronto now provides financial backup and other services unequalled anywhere between New York and Chicago"— pointing the city's attention to a region of the United States loosely comparable to the old lost French Canadian southwest in the Quebec Act of 1774.

At the same time, in the late 1970s the modern Canadian historian Carl Berger summarized part of Harold Innis's message in *The Fur Trade in Canada* almost a half century before: "behind the pattern of separate regions" in Canada — each linked to an analogous region of the United States — "there existed a countervailing tendency toward unity," based on the east-west French and Indian canoe waterways that took Alexander Mackenzie to the Pacific Ocean in the late 18th century, and that became the Canadian transcontinental railway system in the late 19th century. In one sense at least, "Canada developed not in spite of geography but because of it."

With or without a Canada-U.S. trade agreement, Canada still has an east-west transcontinental transportation and communications infrastructure, to which the fate of virtually all its larger cities is in some degree linked. And it is in Canada's modern east-west system of "liveable" cities and urban regions — *a mari usque ad mare* — that the growth of the future will be concentrated.

Beyond the historic transcontinental railways, there is already an extensive cross-Canada microwave network for transmitting telecommunications signals. *The Financial Post* has recently reported that all "major cities in Canada should be linked by fibre by the 1990s". Moreover: "Construction of the fibre lines, with a total cost of about $1 billion, has been compared to the building of Canada's national railway system."

Whatever else, it seems clear enough that the rationalization of inter-provincial trade barriers within the Canadian market of the future is fundamentally a problem of "political economy" rather than merely "economics," more narrowly defined. It raises Trudeau's concern for the "Canadian Economic Union," and his question to the most ardent regionalists of the Confederation: "Who will speak for Canada?"

It also raises the issues that the Mulroney regime has tried to address through the creation of the Western Diversification Agency and the Atlantic Opportunities Agency. And, as Trudeau sometimes seemed loath to fully recognize, it appears virtually certain that in the restructuring Canada of the late 20th century, the problem is insoluable without significantly enhanced regional representation in the exercise of the federal power within the Confederation. Put another way, an elected Canadian Senate is an urgent first step toward a new Canadian national economic policy for the 21st century.

This in turn raises the fate of the Meech Lake Accord. New Brunswick Premier Frank McKenna's recently voiced reservations about the Accord are linked, among other things (such as the fate of the heirs of the French-speaking Acadians), to its potential impact on the pace of Senate reform. The reservations of Sharon Carstairs in Manitoba raise still further questions about the Accord.

Whatever happens in this context, even in the short term Canada-U.S. free trade is far from the only fundamental issue that the restructuring Canadian Confederation of the late 20th century is working to resolve.

Multiculturalism & Immigration

Immigration policy (which has also figured in debate over the Meech Lake Accord) is a second obvious item on the agenda of any Canadian national development strategy for the future, with or without Canada-U.S. free trade.

One crucial historic weakness of the Canadian domestic market has been its relatively small population size — particularly as set beside its large geographic extent. The Canadian territory is actually somewhat larger than the territory of the United States. But even in the late 20th century the population of the country is only somewhat more than 10% of the U.S. population: roughly equivalent to the most populous modern U.S. state, California.

Much of Canada is in effect a cold-climate wilderness desert of rock, water, and rugged vegetation that is uninhabitable on any scale (though also still rich enough in natural resources). By the late 20th century it has become very clear that the country can never have a population that even approaches the size of the population in the much more benign southern regions of the American Republic.

On the other hand, the habitable regions of the country are also quite large, and not at all densely populated by international standards. In the early 1980s, for instance, Canada's population density amounted to only 2.5 persons per square kilometre, compared with 25.0 persons in the U.S., or (to look at somewhat more geographically similar northern places) 12.2 persons in the Soviet Union, and 18.4 persons in Sweden. Even the most populous and highly developed Canadian region of Southern Ontario had a population density of only some 90 persons per square kilometre, compared with almost 230 persons in the United Kingdom, more than 245 persons in West Germany, 320 persons in Japan, and more than 400 persons in South Korea.

Canada has something of a sobering early history of grossly exaggerating its population potential. Nonetheless, throughout the 20th century its population as a percentage of the U.S. population has steadily increased. Excessively gloomy academic experts of the late 1930s projected that the population of the Confederation "will not be above 18 million by the end of this century" — a number that was in fact reached by the early 1960s and has since been left rather far behind.

In a continental context, Canada's particularly strong population growth relative to the United States after the Second World War bears some comparison with parallel faster growth in the modern U.S. south, as opposed to the modern U.S. north. Canada's recent growth, however, has been much more driven by migrations from outside the Western hemisphere.

The most recent patterns of international migration also make clear that a national economic policy which stresses as high levels of immigration as the pace of economic growth will permit has continuing implications for the country's historic multiculturalism. From this standpoint, the Canadian federal government's new multicultural policy, pioneered by the Trudeau regime in the early 1970s, flowed from sounder intuitions about the future of Canadian national development than the Foreign Investment Review Agency.

Sources of Immigration to Canada, 1980-1985

Region	% Total Immigrants
Asia	42.7
Europe (excluding United Kingdom)	19.8
United Kingdom	10.4
Central America (including Mexico & Caribbean)	9.1
United States	7.8
South America	4.8
Africa	3.7
Australasia	1.7

From a related angle, it is only a coincidence that Canada should be seriously addressing the constitutional status of its Indian and Inuit first peoples (who migrated to the New World from Asia millenia ago), at about the same time that Asia has become the single largest source of migrants to the modern Confederation. The fundamental reason for the late 20th century constitutional debate on Indian, Inuit, and Métis rights is to at last give Canada's first peoples a role in the future of the country that flows in justice from their seminal (and still too often unrecognized) contribution to its past.

Another part to the urgency of resolving the issue, however, is that it will help us make clear to ourselves and anyone else who cares to pay attention that Canada is and has always been more than a white man's country, in either modern official language. In the broadest sweep of world history Canada, like other parts of the New World, has been and is once again a place for people from all parts of the Old World: not just in Europe, but in Asia and Africa as well.

Like Canada-U.S. free trade itself, this is not so much a possible option for the future, as a present priority. In the 1981 Census well over 40% of the population in Toronto, and not much under 40% in Vancouver, was born outside Canada. The comparable figure for such places as Montreal, Winnipeg, and Calgary was about 20%, and in such places as Halifax or Regina about 10%. In the country at large it was some 16% (or 4 out of every 25 residents). During the 10-year period from 1975 to 1984, 1,258,697 persons — a number larger than the individual populations of 6 of the 10 provinces — were granted Canadian citizenship.

It also says something about Canada's particular institutional structure that, theoretically, a Canadian citizen is all you have to be to become a Canadian prime minister (unlike in the United States, where to become president you must be born in the U.S.A.). John A. Macdonald, in fact, was born outside Canada, and so was John Turner, who briefly preceded and — despite a great many obstacles — may yet succeed Brian Mulroney.

Echoes of Old Empires

In some ways, the great wave of polyglot global migration that has left notable marks on Canadian life during the past generation, especially in large urban centres, is a kind of final legacy from the world of the old empire on which the sun never set.

This raises another obvious point of departure for additional strands of long-term Canadian development strategy in the 21st century — the Trudeau regime's Third Option (increasing trade with Europe, Japan and the Third World), itself a kind of update of the old Imperial preference of the late 19th century.

For the long run, the short-term failures of the Trudeau regime's own efforts to make this strategy work are not especially significant. It is in the nature of long-term policies that they are typically difficult and give only slender results in the short run: otherwise they would not be necessary.

The experience of the first three decades of the 20th century suggests that even with major new waves of immigration the Canadian market has limits as a vehicle for economic expansion. Improved access to U.S. markets can help, but the thrust of recent U.S. trade policy itself suggests the limits of the

Hunter would likely have agreed with the late 19th century nationalist William Caniff that modern Canada has aspired to treat the Indian as "a man and a brother." Yet many among the brothers themselves have not been persuaded. Here Hunter himself suggests how the great Canadian boom of the early 20th century brought grief to the Indian brothers' last refuge from the not always progressive pressures of European mass settlement. In this respect, as in others, the Confederation of the 21st century ought to do better: and the fate of Canada's first migrants from Asia and the Old World beyond Europe ought to set new precedents for the fate of its most recent migrants from the same wide regions of the globe. To start with, the Canadian Constitution of the late 20th century has at least begun to recognize that "the Indian and his culture" were in fact "fundamental to the growth of Canadian institutions."

American market. The leading enterprises of the modern Canadian economy are already aggressively pursuing more diversified international markets — as many of their predecessors have in the past.

Here as well, while the long-term goal remains difficult and off somewhat in the distance, there are urgent shorter-term priorities. In a recent speech at the opening of a new Calgary manufacturing facility, Northern Telecom president David Vice called for a Canadian "national crusade" to develop a new "competitive consciousness" about the pre-requisites "for our ability to prosper as a trading nation."

Government at all levels, he went on, must encourage capital formation and investment, stimulate private sector research and development, improve post-secondary education, and promote global trade as a national priority. "We in Canada have no choice but to think globally...in any and all products of Canadian culture and enterprise."

Recent judgements against Canadian domestic liquor-marketing and fish-processing policies under the General Agreement on Tariffs and Trade show that even in the here and now of the present Canada must deal with pressures on its trade policy from the global village outside North America, as well as from the United States.

The Mulroney regime itself has at least begun to respond to these pressures (though not at all with the energy and commitment it has put into its U.S. trade negotiations). A pamphlet on Canada's objectives in the current "Uruguay Round" of multilateral GATT negotiations, for instance, has been included with the marketing package the federal government has prepared on its new Canada-U.S. trade agreement.

The pamphlet tells us that Canada wishes to improve its international market access in five specific areas: "agricultural and food products"; "other natural resource products"; "energy-based...industries"; "a range of advanced-technology and transportation equipment"; and "trade in services".

The New World On Which the Sun Never Sets

Given the still rather cold political climate of the global village, and what the U.K.-based *Economist* has described as the ancient spirit of anti-free-trade "mercantilism" in the current GATT negotiations, there is perhaps little chance that even these modest objectives will achieve any more immediate success than the bolder Third Option strategies of the Trudeau era.

Moreover, whatever else, Trudeau's approach at least had the virtue of pointing clear paths to the future. One of the original paths led in the direction of the European Economic Community. The apparent profound failure of the so-called "contractual link" with the EC may suggest some important flaws in this side of Trudeau's vision. And even the American business press has expressed qualms about recent moves by the EC to eliminate internal commercial, financial, and customs barriers by 1992: "Such an EC will be a huge market for the U.S. but also a formidable rival."

Historically, Canada has had particularly close and deep European ties. In the current GATT discussions on freer world trade in services the EC takes a somewhat different position from the U.S. in stressing, like Canada, exemptions for cultural industries. Canadian Pacific Ltd., the modern diversified transportation, communications, and resource products heir of the old C.P.R. transcontinental railway, is one of several Canadian enterprises now said to be reaching out to Europe, after a rigorous restructuring at home.

Yet in the 21st century, especially with a new Canada-U.S. Free Trade Agreement, post-imperial Europe may be even more inclined than in the more recent past to see the Canadian Confederation as little more than an uninteresting northern extension of the necessary evil of the American Republic.

The "Third World" side of Trudeau's Third Option, on the other hand, still has all the hallmarks of the wave of the future. A late 1987 report by the Conference Board of Canada has urged, in the words of board Chairman James Nininger: "In spite of the international debt crisis, the long-term dynamism of the world economy will depend on the developing countries.... If Canada is to expand its trade, it has to be there."

The report notes that though a few Canadian companies, such as Alcan Aluminium, Lavalin, and SNC Group, are now doing well in Third World markets, in 1986 only 7% of Canadian exports went in these directions, compared with 20% of exports from the United States. And in the late 1980s there are, the Canadian Conference Board suggests, some quite straightforward short-term tactics available to any Canadian federal government concerned to improve the situation.

One is simply to reverse some more recent small-minded minor government economies: "The impression that a country is not important in Canada's external strategy...was particularly evident in Brazil, where the closing of the Rio de Janeiro consulate in 1985 left the impression that Canada was downgrading Brazil in its international priorities."

Another Conference Board proposal is to open government-seeded but private-sector operated and ultimately financed "storefront offices" in Third World countries, to advise Canadian enterprises on local opportunities and conditions, and to "offer the permanent presence that is considered essential in opening and retaining a new market."

From a somewhat different angle, "Third World" is a not altogether satisfactory term for the so-called newly developing but usually quite different and in some cases very ancient societies of Asia, Latin America, and Africa.

Like the United Kingdom in Europe in an earlier era, Japan has done some pioneering for the late 20th century developing economies of Asia and "the Pacific Rim." They are now growing at about twice the rate of the older industrialized nations, and it is estimated that Asia will have some two-thirds of the world's total population by the year 2000. If nothing else, Asia's modern role as the single largest source of new migrants to Canada is building new Asian connections into the future of the Confederation. Some already have significant economic implications. The Hong Kong billionaire Li Ka-shing recently purchased the site of Expo 86 in downtown Vancouver, from the provincial government of British Columbia.

Canada also has old Latin American connections — especially with the not exclusively Latin islands of the Caribbean Sea. The region plays a special role in the distinctive North American vision of Ronald Reagan. Canada has old qualms about such visions, reflected in its longstanding refusal to join the Organization of American States. But Canadian business also has old ties to Brazil as well as the Caribbean, and Trudeau himself worked hard to build Canadian relations with Mexico.

There have been suggestions in the U.S. that, if the new Canada-U.S. trade agreement succeeds, pressures on Mexico to somehow join in will be irresistible. This could raise some difficulties for Canada; but it could also have advantages — as one part of the longer-term quest for still wider international markets.

Canada's traditional ties with Africa, as with parts of both Asia and the Caribbean, have much to do with its more than three centuries of involvement in what has now become the Commonwealth of Nations. Robert Mugabe from Zimbabwe recently alluded to "my good friend Brian Mulroney." To its credit, the Mulroney regime has made efforts to show some leadership in the modern Commonwealth, and it has seconded France's leadership in the development of the new international organization of la Francophonie.

The old imperial metropolis of the United Kingdom seems to have lost interest in a Commonwealth dominated by new nations of the so-called Third World. Yet, though even its original proponents have grown increasingly sceptical about the comprehensiveness of the so-called "dependency model" of Canadian economic growth, in both its political and even economic development the Canadian Confederation remains, in several respects, a kind of new nation of the Third World itself.

Epilogue: Simultaneous Translation

The new world of the global village on which the sun never sets is enormously different from the old one. As before, it may not appeal equally to all Canadians. Yet, as George Orwell's unusually astute reflections on such things suggest, the distinguishing mark of any place with an instinct for survival is a "power to change out of recognition and yet remain the same."

In the same spirit, what the history of the Canadian Confederation since the 19th century suggests is not that the Confederation of the 21st century ought to pursue a new reciprocity treaty with the United States rather than a new National Policy, or a new "Imperial" preference rather than a new reciprocity treaty with the United States.

The complete wisdom from the past is that a Confederation which truly wants to succeed in "securing Canada's future" (as the current federal government marketing package puts it), now ought to pursue all three of its historic development strategies — in suitably updated forms — at once.

Somewhat more specifically:

(1) Whatever happens to Brian Mulroney's particular Canada-U.S. Free Trade Agreement, in the tradition of Canadian-American reciprocity, Canada needs to update and stabilize its short to mid-term trading relationship with its North American cousins in the United States;

(2) Though the historic protective tariff of John A. Macdonald's National Policy, and such more recent experimental successors as FIRA and the NEP, are obsolete, Canada needs a new generation of national policies to build and strengthen its domestic markets for the 21st century;

(3) The historic empires of Europe have ended forever; but in the old tradition of Imperial preference and the new tradition of the Third Option, Canada needs aggressive new long-term policies for reaching out to markets outside North America, in the rising global economy of the world at large.

All this is obviously complicated and difficult, requiring many kinds of skills, much hard work, and even some luck. Yet to say it is impossible is only to say that Canada is impossible. People have been saying this since the very earliest beginnings of the modern country in the 16th century. And they have been proven wrong over and over and over again.

CONCLUSION

Chapter 17

"GOOD FENCES MAKE GOOD NEIGHBOURS."

What Samuel Eliot Morison has described as "the old Ben Franklin doctrine that a division of North America was 'unnatural'" may have fewer genuinely dedicated disciples in the American Republic of the late 20th century than it did once. Yet many modern Americans with friendly feelings toward Canada still find it hard to understand, in any serious way, why there ought to be any real sort of a border between Canada and the United States.

Something of this sense of the relationship between the two countries is captured in some lines by the New England poet, Robert Frost, written on a different subject in 1913 — coincidentally the year when the Underwood Tariff signalled the first big wave of moderation in the relentlessly protectionist America that emerged from the Civil War:

> "Oh, just another kind of outdoor game,
> One on a side. It comes to little more:
> There where it is we do not need the wall:
> He is all pine and I am apple-orchard.
> My apple trees will never get across
> And eat the cones under his pines, I tell him.
> He only says, 'Good fences make good neighbors.'"

From an American point of view, such scepticism about the real importance of the border between Canada and the United States is understandable. For Canadians, however, the obvious question, and thus the resulting sense of the relationship, is somewhat different.

At bottom the question is: why should the Canadian Confederation disappear? (And if it's not going to disappear, in the venerable North American can-

Uncle Sam is saying: "It'd improve the look of things a hull lot if ye'd lower this fence Jack." With the 21st century in sight, tariffs have outlived their usefulness — and not just between Canada and the United States. From another angle the wise old North American adage about good fences and good neighbours will perhaps never be altogether obsolete.

do spirit shouldn't we in Canada be doing everything we can to make it a robust, energetic, and prosperous Confederation?)

It is true enough that in the mid-1980s Canada's estimated population was actually slightly less than that of the most populous U.S. state of California. (In an earlier era it was also for many years considerably less than that of the most populous U.S. state of New York.) Yet in any comparative international setting this only shows how vast and various a universe is embraced by the modern colossus of the United States of America.

Some 80% of the 159 current members of the United Nations, for instance, have a population that is smaller than that of Canada. Canada's annual assessment to the financial support of the UN is only exceeded by those of the United States, Japan, the Soviet Union, West Germany, France, the United Kingdom, and Italy. Even on a North American continent that reserves its highest respect for the colossal and is obsessed by superlatives, Canada can boast that it is, geographically, the second largest country in the world (next to the Soviet Union and, of course, in this one respect at least, incontestably ahead of the United States).

Especially in the past generation, the Canadian Confederation has actually begun to resolve many problems that even many Canadians once suspected might be beyond real solution. Since the Second World War enormous effort, energy, intelligence, and skill have gone into building a new post-colonial Canadian political nation, on deep foundations that have been constructed over several centuries. Particularly when it has been accompanied by a record of much more success than many thought possible, this seems an odd time to be setting it all aside.

By the late 20th century Canada has acquired a still somewhat hesitant but ultimately irresistible new sense of itself as a place with an interesting future in the global village of the 21st century: though obviously related to, it is different from the future of the United States. If economic competition is good for capitalism and freedom, political competition is at least equally good for pluralism and democracy.

On any balanced view, there is nothing at all decisive in the December 1987 free trade document that Brian Mulroney and Ronald Reagan signed to suggest that Canada is in fact about to disappear into the regional history of the American Republic. If we learn from our past, and work still harder to keep ourselves together in the present, we can have a future that combines the best of all worlds.

At the same time, if we look at the Canada-U.S. Free Trade Agreement of 1987-88 in its broadest historical perspective, and ponder the wider present-day political process that surrounds it, there are some reasons for concern about the fate of the Confederation in the 21st century. If we really are to have the best of all worlds, we will have to show some cunning and even on occasion some courage, and we will have to keep on working harder, and harder.

"Canada: A Story of Challenge."

According to Arnold Toynbee, a pioneering (and like all pioneers, controversial) student of world history, the need to respond to challenges has been a great engine of political development in the broad sweep of the global past. Assuming Mulroney's trade agreement does go into effect in January 1989, and does survive in some form for some significant length of time, its greatest benefit for Canada may prove to be the creative challenge it presents to the management of the Confederation.

Historically, the agreement is without doubt the broadest and most comprehensive arrangement of its sort that has ever been signed or even seriously proposed between Canada and the United States. At a point in the history of the world when the historically warring nations of Europe are also involved in trade arrangements of increasingly unprecedented breadth, this should not be alarming. Yet it can only be naive to imagine that it will not put some significant new pressures on the Confederation that, as ultimately healthy as they may be, will still have to be dealt with in some new ways.

The most challenging feature of the agreement is its unusually open-ended character. This applies not just to the potential future evolution of the dispute-settlement mechanism in Part Six, but to a variety of provisions, scattered throughout the text of the December 1987 document, for continuing bilateral discussion on such matters as technical standards, still unresolved issues of detail, and areas where further progress in reducing trade barriers is anticipated.

The ambiguities of the document are such that, when the U.S. Congress began to consider it in the early spring of 1988, even the notably pro-free-trade *Globe and Mail* explained how a detailed initial assessment of pros and cons from a Canadian standpoint would only be possible when American implementing legislation had been drawn up. On the Canadian side, similar implementing legislation was required from the federal parliament in Ottawa, and there were a few questions about implementation in what are provincial fields of jurisdiction under the Canadian Constitution (for instance in connection with Chapter Eight of the agreement on "Wine and Distilled Spirits"). The Government of Ontario indicated in the spring of 1988, that it was considering a court challenge to federal government authority in such matters.

Of perhaps greater consequence for the future, even with all this successfully resolved on both sides, because the agreement is both open-ended and even in its less ambiguous parts divided into several phases, the late 20th century debate on free trade between Canada and the United States will be far from over once the agreement begins to take effect in January 1989.

In late April 1988 Sam Gibbons, chairman of the foreign trade subcommittee of the ways and means committee in the U.S. House of Representatives, referred to the Canada -U.S. "problems" that lay at the bottom of the 1987-88 trade agreement, at a meeting of an international discussion group known as the Quadrangular Forum, held in Toronto. He suggested that the agreement "begins to start us along the way to solving some of these problems," and he went on:

"It doesn't attack them directly but it does create the environment in which we can work them out."

It reflects nothing but credit on Americans to say that in the continuing process of working these problems out over the decade of the 1990s, the federal government of the United States will stand up for and press its own national interests, which are at most indifferent to the ultimate fate of the Canadian Confederation. If Canada is in fact to grow more robust, energetic, and prosperous under these circumstances, it will have to be led by a Canadian federal government that is at least equally prepared to stand up for and press Canadian national interests, which will not always be the same as those of the United States.

Canada will have to be led by a federal government that, while always sensitive to the historic regionalism of the Confederation, is strong and vigorous in its own right, with some recurrent vision and courage to draw some bold and clear lines around the Canadian future.

An Example: Canadian Currency

As a concrete illustration of what could be at stake, in the limit Canadian political sovereignty is not just important for itself and for the social, cultural, and regional development programs it sustains. It is also an anchor for the more strictly economic benefits that Canada-U.S. free trade is expected to bring to Canadian business, big and small, and to Canadian consumers and job-holders.

Given the relative population weights of the two countries, for instance (and the historic inefficiency of much of Canada's traditional industrial base, viewed on a continental scale), Canada can only hope to adjust to its higher restructuring burden under the new agreement, in any fair way, by retaining a Canadian dollar below the value of the dollar in the United States.

At least in the initial phases, the only real alternative safeguard at Canada's disposal would be lower wages and salaries. In fact, the modern decline of the Canadian dollar in U.S. terms can be broadly traced to the modern equalization of Canadian and American manufacturing wage rates in the mid-1970s.

The story behind this says something about the character of the traditional bilateral economic relationship. As the Canadian economist J.H. Dales pointed out in his mid-1960s book *The Protective Tariff in Canada's Development,* historically both manufacturing wage rates and manufacturing productivity in Canada have been lower than in the United States — to no small extent as a result of the small scale of the Canadian domestic market. In the decade after the Second World War, average manufacturing wages in Canada ranged from just below 70% to just below 80% of average manufacturing wages in the United States. During the same period output per employed worker covered a similar range.

According to the academic theory, Canada-U.S. free trade should act to improve Canadian productivity over the longer term. But it is unclear just what the new agreement's early impact on international market perceptions and the value of the Canadian dollar might be. C.M. Harper, president of the Canadian appliance manufacturer Camco Inc. (in a Canadian industrial sector that is understandably nervous about free trade with the U.S.), has suggested: "Opinions range from 65 cents to par for the next five to 10 years."

Quite arguably, even in the longest term, the Canadian dollar will have to remain somewhat lower than the dollar in the U.S. For one thing, Canada will still have to bear the extra cost of supporting some continuing version of its traditional east-west transportation and communications infrastructure — in a large geographic area with a relatively small number of people. Apart from anything else, a Canadian Confederation that does not make some effort to keep something of this sort alive economically, cannot hope to survive politically.

Canada will arguably also need a lower dollar than the U.S. to accommodate its higher loading of publicly-funded regional development, social, and cultural programs. And it can be argued as well (as Simon Reisman sometimes seems inclined to do) that the results these programs produce on the ground constitute one of Canada's important competitive advantages as a North American business location.

In such contexts a distinctive Canadian currency can only forever remain a crucial attribute of Canadian political sovereignty. And a Canadian dollar that trades internationally at a value notably below that of the U.S. dollar is at least an important shock-absorber for Canada, in adjusting to the disproportionate restructuring burden it will take on in Canada-U.S. free trade.

The Zimmerman Telegram

As evidence that the situation does in fact bear watching, the value if not quite the fundamental existence of the Canadian dollar has already figured on the sidelines of the late 20th century bilateral discussion.

Paul Wonnacott's influential early 1987 background report on the negotiations, published by the Institute for International Economics in Washington, included an appendix arguing that "Canada make a 'contribution' to reducing the U.S. trade deficit by exerting upward pressure on the exchange value of its dollar." The value of the Canadian dollar also became something of an issue during discussions of the new agreement in Congress early in 1988.

Oddly enough, the exchange value of the Canadian dollar in terms of the U.S. dollar actually began to rise in early 1988. Moreover, *The Financial Post* reported: "The hand of Bank of Canada Governor John Crow is clearly evident behind the strength of the C$. Crow has severely restricted the growth of the money supply and raised interest rates in his battle to push down inflation."

At about the same time, the Canadian federal government began to scale down (though not completely abandon) previously announced special assistance programs for the clothing and textile industries in Canada, and new policies to bolster the access of Canadian-based producers to the Canadian movie market. Both the special assistance programs and the new policies were consistent with the spirit and the letter of the only recently negotiated Canada-

U.S. Free Trade Agreement. But U.S. interests had made clear that they might nonetheless prejudice Congressional ratification.

There are good enough short-term strategic reasons for such Canadian federal government tactics, in the difficult period between the negotiation and actual implementation of the agreement. Yet as and if the agreement unfolds over the 1990s, there will no doubt be other good enough short-term strategic reasons for continuing modest abridgements of Canadian national interests, in the larger interest of keeping the Canada-U.S. Free Trade Agreement intact. And this could raise some continuing difficulties for future Canadian federal governments.

To serve as a stable framework for new business investment the agreement must promote some longer-term confidence among investors. On the other hand, if, in the tough world of day to day bilateral politics, the only way for the Canadian federal government to ensure such confidence is to continually modestly abridge Canadian national interests, then it is very difficult to see how the agreement can be consistent with the growth of a strong Canada in the 21st century.

Adam Zimmerman, chairman of Noranda Forest Inc., was among a private Canadian-American group that met with various Washington officials late in March 1988. Zimmerman subsequently observed: "I do remain concerned — and it's not popular for a businessman to say this — that from an American point of view...we may find some intense pressure to consolidate...I did have a strong sense from the Americans we saw that their view of us in the free trade agreement (was) that we would become an appendage of the American economy and the American economic system."

Even beyond the question of becoming an American economic appendage, the issue of what has come to be called the "geopolitical significance" of the Canada-U.S. Free Trade Agreement has been raised by some U.S. spokesmen. Presumably on the theory that a good salesman always at least tells his customers what they want to hear, Brian Mulroney himself has thought it shrewd to mention in Washington that the agreement can indeed have geopolitical significance.

This is, of course, a phrase that could mean almost anything. Moreover, it is easy enough to imagine situations in which it will be in the national interest even of a rigorously post-colonial Canada to side with the United States in some international conflict or dispute — over trade or anything else. As a plain matter of fact, Canada has obviously done this many times in the past, and will no doubt do so many times in the future.

Yet to anyone whose ears are attuned to the strains of the Canadian past, talk about such things as geopolitical significance too easily recalls the pressures that the old imperial officialdom in the United Kingdom periodically used to bring to bear on the Confederation. In a Canada-U.S. Free Trade Agreement that had a great deal of geopolitical significance, Canada could easily enough revert to some updated North American version of its old status as a British dominion.

It sometimes seems that even well-informed and sympathetic opinion leaders in the United States do not quite appreciate the extent to which this is an unacceptable alternative for the new, bolder and more confident Canadian Confederation of the 21st century. More significantly, however understandable it may be in the real world of Canada-U.S. politics, it also sometimes seems that Canadian politicians who have the most at stake in seeing the new trade agreement succeed have not spent at all enough time making Canada's post-colonial ambitions clear. As Trudeau has observed in another context, it is not difficult to get agreements with people if all you do is give them almost everything they want.

Thinking the Unthinkable (or "David & Goliath")

All this gives particular force to the question of just how "necessary" Brian Mulroney's trade agreement really is to even short to mid term Canadian prosperity.

By the late 1980s, for instance, the Canadian economy had been growing faster than the American economy for some time. On any international criteria, Canada has one of the highest standards of living in the world.

When health care, unemployment insurance, pension systems, liveable cities, and other quality of life elements are factored into the equation, it is arguable that Canada already has a higher standard of living than the United States. In the late 20th century, if you travel from Cleveland or Detroit to Toronto, or from Mississippi to Prince Edward Island, or from Great Falls, Montana to Calgary, the notion that the United States is somehow more prosperous and affluent than Canada seems puzzling at best.

Similarly, a serious trade war between Canada and the United States would create real difficulties for significant numbers of Canadians. But, in one degree or another, so will a free trade agreement between the two countries.

It is also at least conceivable that, in the midst of the hardship, a trade war would prompt a much more rapid and reliable Canadian restructuring in the direction of the global markets that are customarily said to be the ultimate target even of the trade agreement with the United States.

If future Canadian federal governments are to face continuing serious U.S. pressures to gradually transform what is in fact the rather open-ended agreement of 1987-88 into what would be, in effect, a commercial union of the present two national political and economic systems (or "political economies"), then the Confederation can only survive (let alone grow and prosper) by being regularly prepared to risk actions that could result in U.S. abrogation of the agreement.

If at some point the U.S. government were to abrogate an implemented agreement, in response to what it considered unacceptable actions by the Canadian government, it would only repeat what has already happened in history, in 1866. The trauma of American rejection has proved creative for Canada in the past, and it could prove creative in the future. Despite the vast discrepancies in population, Canada's vast geography counts for something. Ultimately, the United States can no more completely reject Canada than Canada can completely reject the United States.

A New Image Of National Development

There are, no doubt, a great many other practical implications of putting the Canada-U.S. trade agreement of the late 1980s in historical perspective. In this book, most of them will have to be left to the deductions of the reader. For Canadians, there is never enough time to do the subject justice.

Two other crucial issues, however, beg to be made explicit. To begin with, it seems clear enough that if Canada-U.S. free trade really is going to help build a more robust, energetic, and prosperous Canada for everyone, it will have to be accompanied by some new and strong domestic Canadian consensus on the national limits to the historic regionalism of the Confederation.

One the one hand, we have to start to act much more positively on our understanding that if we pursue only our regionalism, we will soon find that we have lost the larger political instrument which makes our regionalism possible — socially, culturally, politically, and even economically. Whatever we may think of Trudeau himself, we have to be able to answer his question: "Who will speak for Canada?" And we must soon begin taking much bolder steps in this direction: *a mari usque ad mare* and, in varying degrees, in both official languages .

On the other hand, we have to act as well on our understanding that our national patriotism (or political nationalism) also expresses our regionalism and our vast heterogeneity — on our intuitive complex understanding that to be successful we do not have to try to be the same kind of North American nation as the United States. To start with here, we must simply get on with the urgent business of recognizing Quebec as a distinct society, establishing an elected federal Senate, and institutionalizing some workable form of Indian, Inuit, and Métis self-government.

This returns the wider debate on Canadian restructuring to the free trade agreement's companion constitutional innovation, the Meech Lake Accord.

In its present form the Accord has the singular and inestimable virtue of at last resolving the problem of the modern French Canadian cultural identity to the satisfaction of the province of Quebec. Yet, beyond the distinct society issue, it also goes a rather dangerously long distance toward locking in what might be called a more general continuing federal-provincial conference version of Canadian federalism.

Over the past quarter century, the uniquely Canadian institution of the federal-provincial conference has proved invaluable, in addressing the various constitutional problems of the new post-colonial political nation that began to emerge after the Second World War. There are still important items that remain on its agenda. Yet at some point the constitutional debate must at least subside for a generation or two. And, in the ordinary, day to day management of the Confederation, the federal-provincial conference has proved a highly ineffective forum for the development of any robust and energetic national policy.

In this context an elected Senate would entrench the regionalism of the Confederation not by mindlessly increasing provincial rights and decreasing federal power, but by giving all regions effective representation in the exercise of federal power. Its broad impact on the Confederation of the late 20th century would be to promote much-needed regionally sensitive forces of centralization.

Similarly, two key short-term problems with at least the 1987 version of the Meech Lake Accord are that it will make it very difficult to achieve provincial agreement on the details of an elected Senate, and equally difficult to at last resolve the problem of Indian, Inuit, and Métis self-government. (And, as the current appointed Canadian Senate has suggested, it will be easier for us to recognize Quebec as a distinct society outside the context of a more general mindless provincialization of Canadian federalism, if we recognize Indian, Inuit, and Métis rights to self-government at the same time.)

These problems with Meech Lake were less urgent before it became clear that the Mulroney and Reagan regimes had in fact reached agreement on a notably broad and open-ended free trade pact with the United States. It would also be foolish to claim that Meech Lake (wherever it may be) and Canada-U.S. free trade taken together threaten the survival of the country. In the tradition of moderation and compromise, however, if both Mulroney's trade agreement and the 1987 Meech Lake Accord were to become part of the new law of the land, then the Canadian national political climate would be ripe indeed for some very bold new movements in countervailing directions.

Standing Up for the Tradition of Compromise

The final crucial issue which begs to be made explicit relates to the continuing process of political and constitutional debate that both Mulroney's trade agreement and the Meech Lake Accord inevitably seem to place on the Canadian horizon — at least as the shifting sands of democratic politics appear to an optimistic observer in the early spring of 1988.

The 1960s and 1970s brought stormy times to the Confederation (though in a country less superficially dull and orderly they would no doubt be judged merely interesting). The 1980s have been a period of retrenchment and re-grouping. It seems likely enough, however, that the 1990s and the first decade of the 21st century will bring a new long season of interesting political weather.

Polling data, for instance, suggests that opposition to the Canada-U.S. Free Trade Agreement among the sovereign electorate is far from confined to Ontario and Prince Edward Island, with some reservations about Manitoba. Data from both late 1987 and early 1988 indicate that popular opinion in British Columbia is also somewhat more opposed than supportive, and that majority support is clear only in Quebec. It is intriguing as well that in 1911 British Columbia, Manitoba, Ontario, and P.E.I. were also the four provinces that gave the least support to Laurier and reciprocity — despite vast demographic changes in all places over the past three-quarters of a century.

The Canada-U.S. Free Trade Agreement and the Meech Lake Accord, in other words, do not finish an old debate in the Confederation: they begin a new round of an old debate that, for a while longer yet, goes on and on. After the 1987 New Brunswick election, Robert Bourassa's overtures to Frank McKenna on the New Brunswick premier's reservations about the Meech Lake Accord hinted at new momentum in the tradition of compromise. After the 1988 Manitoba election, Sharon Carstairs brought the new momentum out into the open.

No doubt,the the path ahead is arduous. Yet, as even David Peterson in Ontario has urged, whatever the future may hold, there is a new spirit in Canada, determined to bring the restructuring Confederation more securely into the mainstream of the global village, in the difficult early beginnings of a new era in human history on the planet.

One guiding light behind this spirit, it would appear, is the collectively reincarnated soul of William Lyon Mackenzie King. We should not always expect the spirit to speak in a clear voice. In the end, we do have to decide for ourselves: each generation must make its own history.

Yet the spirit reminds us that "the Canadian as he exists in the mind of God" did have some principles: "Industry exists for the sake of humanity, not humanity for the sake of industry." Whoever may lead in the future, the counsel of the incredible Canadian may also help sustain us through the interesting stormy weather that lies ahead.

Legend has it that he was once walking along the winding banks of the Ottawa River with a friendly colleague. He pointed to a distant church spire beyond a bend in the river — once the first great stretch of the ancient French and Indian transcontinental fur trade route from Montreal to the Northwest. And he explained: "If I try to reach that point directly I shall drown. I must follow the curves of the bank and ultimately I shall get there, though at times I may seem to be going somewhere else."

Chapter 18

EPILOGUE:
ON THE EDGE OF A NEW ERA

The appearance of a second edition of this book—after the Canada-U.S. Free Trade Agreement has survived the Canadian federal election of November 21, 1988, and been duly passed by both houses of Parliament at Ottawa and the American Congress at Washington—offers an opportunity to update the story told in the first edition.

Because the perspective is so short-term, the opportunity is fraught with risks. In Canada as elsewhere, however, any knock of opportunity worth hearing has risks. For commercial purposes alone, to say nothing of humanity's typically more diffuse aspirations, it would be wrong not to seize the occasion in a confident pose.

In this spirit, whatever the ultimate significance of the Canadian political events of late 1988 and early 1989, already they have signalled the start of an era in Canadian history.

For almost 100 years, Canada had, when pressed, gently turned its back on a renewal of the first Canadian-American free trade agreement, that preceded both the modern Canadian Confederation and the American Civil War. Now, according to the long-accepted conventions of its national political system, Canada has reversed this historic posture. And, until at least the next Canadian federal election at some point in the early 1990s, or until some as yet unforeseen event in either Canada or the United States, that might trigger the treaty's six-month abrogation clause, the evolution of the quite open-ended Canada-U.S. Free Trade Agreement negotiated late in 1987 has begun to unfold.

Few in the United States imagine that the agreement will have much impact on the future of America, despite polite rhetoric to the contrary on ceremonial occasions. Yet inside Canada, the voters who went to the polls on November 21 could much more logically believe that they were, for a vital moment, real actors in the drama of their national history.

In the end, the decision that the sovereign people of the true north made, in all their collective wisdom, might be described as characteristically Canadian, or perhaps even incredibly Canadian. If the spirit of Mackenzie King is the spirit that guarantees Confederation's survival, then the immediate significance of what has happened is that Canada will survive.

"North to Argentina": The Canadian Federal Election of 1988

By the middle of the summer of 1988, it had become more or less clear that, as in the last full round of the debate in 1911, there would be a Canadian federal election, whose central issue was a recently negotiated Canadian-American free trade agreement.

Brian Mulroney's Progressive Conservatives, still with their overwhelming majority from the 1984 election, had no decisive difficulty sending the 1987-88 agreement through the federal House of Commons. (As widely predicted, despite some localized American opposition, the document would also have no fundamental trouble in the United States Congress.) But John Turner, leader of the Liberal opposition at Ottawa, indicated that he would ask the appointed Canadian Senate to precipitate an election, that would allow the voice of the people to resolve the issue. What's more, appointees of the previous long federal Liberal regime of Pierre Trudeau and Lester Pearson dominated the Canadian Senate.

Mulroney waited until early October to call the November 21 election, after it had become certain that the Senate would indeed create problems. In the ensuing campaign, Canada enjoyed a few uncharacteristic brief moments in the limelight of the American mass media—especially after it appeared that the Canadian electorate might actually vote Brian Mulroney's Progressive Conservatives out of office.

As evidence that the issue could for a moment become as emotional in America as it was in Canada, the *Wall Street Journal* published an editorial entitled "North to Argentina," at the height of the Canadian campaign. It compared Liberal leader "Juan Turner" to the nationalistic populist dictator of post-World War Two Argentina, Juan Peron. Appealing to ancient 'gringo' prejudices in both countries, the *Journal* suggested that if Canada rejected free trade with the United States this time, it could only ever become a far northern variation on a South American 'banana republic.'

In both French and English versions of televised leaders' debates among Mulroney, Turner, and Ed Broadbent of the New Democrats, John Turner did briefly manage to focus the diffuse concerns for Canada's future that the concept of Canadian-American free trade has traditionally raised, at least since the

American Civil War. More than Ed Broadbent, who also opposed Mulroney's trade agreement (but did not speak French at all well), Turner at last became a tall-in-the-saddle man of the northern wilderness, who stood up for both his country and its right to a place of its own in the 21st century.

Opinion polls immediately after the debate put the Liberals significantly ahead of the Conservatives. Yet in the end, Turner could not remain equally convincing as the leader of an effective national political party. And he failed to project a serious alternative vision for starting to address the economic dilemmas that, as the free trade debate itself was making clear enough, Canada, like many other places, had to confront in the late 20th century. Recovering from a lame performance in the televised debates, Mulroney managed to claim that he too was standing up boldly for "our beloved Canada"—only in a more practical way.

When the ballots were counted on November 21, Brian Mulroney's Progressive Conservatives had won 43% of the national popular vote, Turner's Liberals 32%, and Broadbent's New Democrats 20%. The remaining 5% was distributed among assorted minor parties and independents.

Had the vote been strictly a referendum on the free trade issue, the Canada-U.S. Free Trade Agreement would have been defeated, by a margin not too much different from the one that had defeated "sovereignty association" in the Quebec referendum of 1980. Yet it was not a referendum: it was a contest for seats in Canada's single-member-constituency, elected House of Commons. Five ministers in Mulroney's cabinet were defeated, but his Progressive Conservatives nonetheless held on to 169 seats at Ottawa, compared with only 83 seats for the Liberals, and 43 for the New Democrats. In terms of votes in the elected House of Commons, Mulroney had won a clearly workable majority government. By all the conventions of Canadian parliamentary democracy, his free trade agreement with the United States was at least entitled to proceed.

As Mulroney himself had bemoaned during the televised leaders' debate, the agreement was, after all, no more than a commercial treaty, that could be cancelled by either side on six months notice. With a new House of Commons in place, in which the Conservatives still commanded a majority of more than 20 seats, the appointed Senate abandonned its earlier reservations. By the end of December 1988 both houses of Parliament had passed Canadian legislation implementing the Canada-U.S. Free Trade Agreement in time for the original January 1989 deadline, agreed on by both Canada and the United States late in 1987.

Is the War Over?

In the 1988 election, at least 52% of the Canadian electorate voted for parties clearly opposed to Mulroney's free trade agreement with the United States. This is actually a slightly higher percentage than had voted against Laurier and reciprocity in 1911. And this raises obvious questions about the agreement's longer-term evolution and stability.

Among its most strident opponents and supporters, the election was seen as a profoundly polarizing event, with a legacy of deep internal division for Canadian political culture. Some strong opponents have left no doubt that they will continue to oppose Mulroney's deal with the United States, through to the next federal election and beyond.

At the same time, in at least the immediate wake of the election, a continuing struggle over Canada-U.S. free trade did not obsess the mainstream of Canadian national politics. A Gallup poll taken early in January 1989 indicated that as many as 45% of all Canadians supported the Canada-U.S. Free Trade Agreement that had just begun to be implemented, up from only 34% in October 1988, before the election. Early in February, the Liberal Premier of Ontario, David Peterson, a prominent early opponent of the deal, told reporters: "In my business you've got to make lemonade when you've got a lemon." (He was reacting to comments by his provincial Treasurer, Robert Nixon, in a speech to overseas investors in London, England, touting the Mulroney trade agreement as "a great business advantage and a great trade advantage" for Canada's most populous province.)

The signs did not all point in this direction. At about the same time, the federal New Democratic notable, and former Premier of British Columbia, David Barrett, was announcing that the New Democrats would hold public hearings on free trade across the country, to demonstrate that Canada "is not for sale," and that Canadians "have charge of our own economic destiny." Nonetheless, a few weeks later, both the Winnipeg-based federal Liberal notable, Lloyd Axworthy, and the Montreal-based Paul Martin, made noises to the effect that the Liberal party in Ottawa was "softening its opposition to the trade deal."

In this immediate context, the most convincing interpretation of the more than 50% popular vote against the deal in the 1988 election was that there were limits to the potential evolution of the quite open-ended agreement that had been negotiated.

Late in September 1988, for instance, Giles Gherson, Washington correspondent for the Toronto-based *Financial Post,* had reported on the Canada-U.S. Free Trade Agreement "so overwhelmingly ratified in the U.S. Senate." The "huge success from the U.S. vantage point," he urged, "was not the phase-out of border tariffs over 10 years." It was the prospect of a new "North American colossus ... in which Americans rightly believe they are the dominant partner ... as senator after senator made clear, the task ahead is to use the agreement to eliminate remaining particularist Canadian policies ... that still interfere with the single market."

Gherson then observed: "Whether Canadians will see the evolution of the free trade area in the same way, remains to be seen." And, whatever else, the 1988 Canadian election some two months later made clear that any evolution of the agreement which effectively dismantled Canada's national economy would indeed prove fundamentally unstable in Canadian domestic politics. Commitments from strong supporters of the deal during the 1988 election, regarding the preservation of Canadian social programs, regional development incentives, cultural industries, and linguistic duality, will be remembered in future Canadian election campaigns.

The election held surprises as well for observers who had been overimpressed by the ideological wars about economic geography that natives of the country enjoy so much. As widely prophesied, the working majority that Mulroney won owed much to support in Western Canada, and, above all else, in French-speaking Quebec, where the Tories took 63 of the distinct society's 75 federal seats. But the election did very little to confirm the extreme regionalist theory that the Canadian Confederation, reputedly warped in a fundamental way by the old protectionist National Policy, was deeply valued only in the opportunistic Province of Ontario.

Mulroney's Tories themselves won 47 of Ontario's 99 seats at Ottawa. The Liberals, on the other hand, took 20 of Atlantic Canada's 32 seats, and the Progressive Conservatives only 12, suggesting that the people of Atlantic Canada were less convinced than Brian Mulroney about the benefits of Canada-U.S. free trade for Canadian regional development.

Similarly, though the Conservatives took 48 of Western Canada's 86 seats, their western representation leaned profoundly on 25 of the 26 seats in Alberta. In Manitoba they won only seven seats, compared with five for the Liberals and two for the New Democrats. In British Columbia the New Democrats took 19 seats, compared with only 12 for the Tories, and one for the Liberals. And in Saskatchewan the New Democrats took 10 seats, and the Tories only four.

Though there were certain broad continuities with the past, in this as in other respects things had changed since 1911. Both Prince Edward Island, which gave none of its four seats to Mulroney, and British Columbia showed marks of their more ancient history. But Ontario was no longer the strident leading opponent of Canada-U.S. free trade. In 1988 the former Conservative Justice Minister, Ramon Hnatyshyn, who lost his Saskatoon area seat to New Democrat Chris Axworthy, explained: "Saskatchewan was the centre of the anti-free-trade movement in Canada, so it was a real uphill battle."

Canada's Export Profile in the Third Quarter of 1988

During the 1988 election one apparently hard fact was stressed, in different ways, by both opponents and supporters of Mulroney's trade agreement. In the late 20th century, Canada was already sending more and more of its exports to the United States of America. However, in December 1988 Statistics Canada released data that confirmed the potential beginnings of a somewhat different picture, already dimly discernible in trade statistics since the mid 1980s.

This data made it possible to compare changes in export destinations for at least the first three quarters (January to September) of 1986, 1987, and 1988. It showed that the percentage of all Canadian exports bound for the United States actually fell from 77.8% in the first three quarters of 1986, to 75.9% in the same period of 1987, and 73.4% in the same period of 1988.

Three years of only nine months each do not make any longer term trend. Yet they may signal some intriguing developments. The single best explanation for the modest late 1980s diversion of Canadian exports away from the United States, and toward Asia and Western Europe, is a dramatic fall in the value of the American dollar: from some 260 Japanese yen in late 1985 to only 125 yen in late 1988.

This began with the so-called "Plaza accord" among the United States, Japan, West Germany, France, and the United Kingdom, in September 1985. It was meant to strengthen American exports, and improve the American trade deficit. Inevitably, even though the Canadian dollar traded significantly below the U.S. dollar in the 1980s, it remained linked to its American cousin in international money markets. And the late 1980s fall in the U.S. dollar had the effect of making Canadian as well as American products more competitive, in markets outside North America.

Changing Destinations of Canadian Exports
January-September 1986 / January-September 1988

To	% J-S 86	% J-S 88	Change
United States	77.8	73.4	-4.4
South America	1.3	0.9	-0.4
Eastern Europe	1.1	0.9	-0.2
Central America & Antilles	1.3	1.2	-0.1
Middle East	0.9	0.9	-
Oceania*	0.7	0.7	-
Other Africa**	0.7	0.9	+0.2
Western Europe	7.4	8.9	+1.5
Other Asia**	8.8	12.2	+3.4

* Australia, New Zealand, Fiji, Tonga, Western Samoa, Guam, and 15 other South Pacific island groups.

** Africa or Asia outside the Middle East. Some 60% of all Canadian exports to "Other Asia" in the first three quarters of 1986 went to Japan, and about 53% in the first three quarters of 1988.

In 1986, 1987, and 1988 the cheap Yankee dollar did increase U.S. as well as Canadian exports offshore. Alas, it did not improve the American trade deficit significantly, because American imports tended to rise virtually as fast as exports. Nonetheless, the experience cast a strong light on the mutual interests of both Canada and the United States, in making North American products more competitive in world markets.

If Mulroney's trade agreement, or anything else, can contribute to this objective, Canada-U.S. free trade could be accompanied by a continuing trend toward declining shares of Canadian exports destined for the United States; oddly enough, this would match the historical irony of the 1911 Canadian election, which was followed by a period of increasing exports to the United States. In this sense, Canada has a strong national as well as a "North American" interest, in seeing the United States come to grips with its particular global trading problems in the decades that lie ahead.

A somewhat different cut at the statistics of the late 1980s also suggests some of Canada's own particular global trading problems in the coming decades, as well as part of the parallel logic involved in the quest to secure its trading relationship with its friendly American cousins.

During the 1988 election, some argued that free trade would only strengthen lamentable historic trends toward "specializing in resources—what we do best," in the Canadian national economy. This had unhappy implications as well, it was claimed, for the pristine northern wilderness cause of environmental protection. Yet as the Liberal free trade advocate Donald Macdonald had tried to urge, this view paid too little attention to what the Canadian economy of the 1980s, as opposed to the economy of the 1880s or even 1950s, was actually doing best.

Canadian Exports by Commodity Category
January-September 1988: To U.S.A. and All Other Countries

Category	% To All Other Countries	% To U.S.A.
End products, inedible	15.9	51.2
Fabricated materials, inedible	41.6	33.9
Crude materials, inedible	21.9	9.4
Food, feed, beverages, & tobacco	20.1	4.0
Live animals	0.2	0.5
Special transactions	0.3	1.0

In at least its trading relationship with the United States, Canada was at last drawing closer to the status of an industrial producer in its own right. For the first three quarters of 1988, more than half of all Canadian exports to the United States fell into a category described by statisticians as "End products, inedible" (industrial machinery, agricultural machinery and tractors, transportation equipment, and other equipment and tools). Another third involved "Fabricated materials, inedible" (wood and paper, textiles, chemicals, iron and steel, and non-ferrous metals). "Crude materials, inedible" (assorted metal ores and concentrates, and such things as raw hides and skins, pulpwood, other crude wood products, crude petroleum, and natural gas) accounted for less than 10%, and "Food, feed, beverages, and tobacco" for less than 5%.

Canada's export profile with all other countries displayed notably different patterns. Here the most processed goods ("End products, inedible") accounted for only somewhat better than 15% of all trade. The proportion of the least processed goods ("Crude materials, inedible") was more than twice as large as in the profile with the United States alone. Though continuing diversification of Canadian exports away from overdependence on the American market remains an obvious objective of Canadian national development policy, in the late 20th century it was Europe and Japan who were most unwilling to see Canada develop into something more than a mere hewer of wood and drawer of water for others elsewhere.

Early Implementation

During the first few months of 1989, it seemed that one murky cloud on Canada's industrial horizon under Canada-U.S. free trade could be continuing American concerns over the incorporation of the mid-1960s Auto Pact into the new agreement. More broadly, it is still not possible to say a great deal about progress in implementation. Initial tariff reductions have taken effect, the agreement's administrative apparatus has begun to breathe, and there are a few signs of what the more open-ended future might involve.

On January 1 both Canadian and American tariffs on such items as fur and fur garments, whiskey, motorcycles, and computers were completely abandonned. One-fifth of tariffs on such things as furniture and subway cars, and one-tenth of those on such things as steel and textiles and apparel, were more gently removed. Differences in federal, state, and provincial taxes still complicated matters: some ordinary travellers on both side of the border were surprised at how little difference the initial implementation of free trade made in their customs transactions.

Simple tariff reductions on goods quickly proved the easiest part of the agreement to implement, just as they had earlier been the easiest to negotiate. Late in February the Canadian Department of External Affairs indicated that, in pursuit of an option provided for in the original document, Canada and the United States would be negotiating accelerated tariff reductions on at least 50 items, later in the year. This was in response to requests from interested parties on both sides of the border.

The development of the five to seven year process for negotiating common dispute-settlement criteria was much slower. In Canada it was urged that, if negotiators wished to take continuing advantage of "fast-track" procedures for trade issues in the United States Congress, the process probably had to be completed within as little as two and a half years—according to the deeper technicalities of the implemented agreement. Even so, in late February 1989, the Canadian Department of External Affairs would only say that "Canada hopes to name its senior negotiator and start the process some time before the end of the year."

Progress in establishing the interim dispute-settlement mechanism, that would merely apply the domestic law of each country—and in establishing some initial disputes—was more rapid. Canada had named its roster of 25 potential dispute-settlement panelists even before the agreement went into effect. The United States named its 25 panelists during the second week of the new year. (Actual dispute-settling panels of five will be drawn from these lists, as required.) When the new agreement was barely four days old, Canada filed complaints about the U.S. definition of wool, and continuing American tariffs on Canadian softwood plywood. A day later, American pork producers filed a domestic complaint against alleged unfairly subsidized exports of Canadian pork products.

Early in February, Canada appointed former justice department lawyer Ellen Beal to head the Canadian section of the joint secretariat administering Canada-U.S. trade disputes. The transition from the Reagan to the Bush administration had complicated the American picture somewhat. The United States appointed an acting official to the secretariat, which was to have offices in both Ottawa and Washington.

The inaugural meeting of the Canada-United States Trade Commission, a forum for the top two trade officials to oversee implementation of the agreement as a whole, was held in Washington on March 13, 1989. In the United States Carla Hills had replaced Clayton Yeutter as the American Trade Representative, but John Crosbie continued as her Canadian counterpart. Crosbie and Hills blessed the forthcoming discussions on accelerated tariff reductions, but made only modest progress on plans "to pick a select panel to advise Ottawa and Washington to improve the competitiveness of the North American auto industry." Among other things, the panel would be bound to address sensitive concerns about branch plants of Asian and European multinational automakers in Canada.

On a different front, Ontario and Ottawa had jousted throughout the earliest part of 1989, over Ontario's initial refusal to implement fully the wine and distilled spirits provisions of the new agreement. This had been resolved by the time Hills and Crosbie met on March 13. But Hills had words to say in public about continuing eruptions of an earlier, GATT-related Canadian-American dispute over herring exports on the British Columbia coast.

On a different front again, late in February 1989 the U.S. Department of Commerce announced a tentative duty of 103.5% on exports of steel rails by Sydney Steel of Nova Scotia, on the grounds of "initial evidence that Sydney benefits from federal and provincial subsidies." A week later, in early March, the Commerce Department announced a much more modest tentative duty of 2.72% on both Sydney Steel and Algoma Steel in Northern Ontario, on the grounds that "the Canadian companies were exporting rails at unfairly low prices."

The unfair pricing tentative duty was so low that one Algoma official described it as "more of an irritant than a barrier to trade." But the unfair subsidization duty on Sydney Steel in Nova Scotia, an obvious beneficiary of Canadian regional development policy, was unusually high. Some in Canada read it as a strong indication that, whatever Brian Mulroney might think about the legitimacy of Canadian regional development incentives, on Washington's view they will always be subject to countervailing duties, even under the Canada-U.S. Trade Agreement.

On the one hand, it could be said that already, in the first round of the new struggle to give Mulroney's notably open-ended trade deal with Canada's American cousins some clearer definition, the cousins had bared their sharpest teeth. On the other, only some 3% of Sydney Steel's total output went to the United States. Nova Scotia Premier John Buchanan's reaction was that the markets that Sydney Steel was most concerned about were in Canada and the Third World.

To help keep the side up in another direction, while John Crosbie was meeting with Carla Hills in Washington on March 13, Revenue Canada back in Ottawa announced a final punitive duty of 25% on perfumed American clothes hangers "after a complaint that U.S. firms were dumping the padded wooden hangers in Canada at less than the cost of production."

Industrial Restructuring & Economic Geography

Even after implementation had begun, the most mysterious aspect of the new Canada-U.S. Free Trade Agreement remained its potential impact on economic restructuring and economic geography, within the Canadian Confederation.

When the agreement was still less than two weeks old, industrial managers at a Toronto seminar on "Planning to Profit From Free Trade" were told that a seven-cent rise in the Canadian dollar in 1988 had largely offset its immediate positive impacts. When it had seemed that John Turner might actually deprive Brian Mulroney of a majority government, in November 1988, international money markets had bid the Canadian dollar down. When Mulroney's victory became clear, however, the dollar resumed its earlier ascent—also stimulated by the Bank of Canada's continuing policy of high domestic interest rates.

Here Canada, like other places, confronted the not always obviously rational impulses of an increasingly "globalized" international financial system. World money markets, it increasingly seemed clear, saw the free trade deal as a distinct advantage for the Canadian economy. They bid the Canadian dollar up when it appeared that the deal was likely to be accepted by the local electorate, and down when it appeared likely to be rejected. Yet the more they bid the dollar up, the less advantageous the deal became, and vice-versa. The experience suggested that, in an arrangement so sensitive to Canadian currency fluctuations, any longer term restructuring or geographic impacts were extremely difficult to predict.

Early 1989 nonetheless saw a few highly visible changes in Canadian corporate organization. In the third week of January the domestic brewing giants Molson and Carling O'Keefe announced plans to merge their operations, "reducing," as a newspaper article put it, "the three major players in the Canadian industry to two." One day later, Pacific Western Airlines announced plans to purchase Wardair, "leaving only two major players in Canada's airline industry." Then, in the energy sector, "Imperial Oil Ltd., Canada's largest oil company, bought fourth-ranked Texaco Canada."

All this was only part of at least a decade of increasing corporate concentration in Canada, following restructuring trends in the United States, Western Europe, and elsewhere. (A Royal Commission on Corporate Concentration in 1978 had made the particular Canadian policy case.) There were those who argued, however, that the free trade agreement had quickened the pace of earlier trends. Harvie Andre, the federal Consumer and Corporate Affairs Minister at the time, urged that "mergers in the oil, beer and airline industries won't be the last as Canadian industry gears up to compete in the United States and the rest of the world."

At about the same time, the Mulroney government gave preliminary approval to a request from American Express, a strong and highly visible American supporter of the new free trade agreement, to establish a Canadian bank. Both the new agreement and earlier domestic changes in Canadian banking legislation made this theoretically possible. It brought a major protest from the major Canadian chartered banks, who at last broke their stoical reserve over their treatment in the original negotiation of free trade with the United States.

In the final week of January, Chicago-based Stone Container Corp. bought Consolidated-Bathurst Inc., one of Canada's largest pulp, paper, and packaging enterprises, from the Montreal-based Power Corp. This was followed by a report in the *Globe and Mail,* suggesting that "foreign investors view stock prices for many Canadian companies to be significantly undervalued." This, in turn, raised some traditional Canadian anxieties about Canadian-American economic relations.

On the other hand, a week before *Business Week* had reported that the Vancouver-based Canadian businessman, Jim Pattison, was exploring the prospects of acquiring an interest in a Chicago-based consumer products company, Whitman Inc. A week before this, *Business Week* had reported that the multinational branch operation, Du Pont Canada Inc., had announced plans to increase its 1989 capital budget by 50%. It noted as well that in "Alberta alone, U.S. and Canadian companies have announced more than $2 billion in new pulp and paper mills since the Canadian election," and that "Big deals are also brewing in natural gas."

Very late in January, a Hong Kong company controlled by the Toronto-based microelectronics entrepreneur, James H. Ting, made a bid for SSMC Inc. of Shelton, Connecticut, the old Singer sewing machine enterprise. This, it seemed, was meant to become part of a much less traditional Canadian-based corporate empire, including 89 Consumers Distributing retail stores in five eastern states, and two Canadian data processing companies Ting had acquired in 1988. Early in February, Royal Trustco of Toronto announced that it was taking over Pacific First Financial Corp., the largest savings and loan bank in the northwest United States.

With special reference to traditional perceptions of Canada's unique economic geography, in March the Toronto real estate analyst Frank Clayton told a seminar of chartered accountants: "Free trade is likely to take away Toronto's trading dominance within Canada." Canada's only highbrow monthly magazine, *Saturday Night* (under its new owner, Toronto tycoon Conrad Black), advised that "Central Canadian nationalists can no longer claim to be acting in the broad interests of the country while manipulating the levers of power to their own narrow advantage."

Yet what *Saturday Night*'s advice meant for the "nationalists" in Saskatchewan, Atlantic Canada, and British Columbia, who had proved more effective than their Central Canadian counterparts in the 1988 election, was not clear. In March 1989 the Province of Quebec, staunchest supporter of Brian Mulroney's trade agreement, made sure that the headquarters for a new, federally funded Canadian space agency would be located in Montreal, the former economic capital of the old Dominion of Canada. In another part of the new Confederation, the legal firm, Bennett Jones, ran ads boosting its ability to satisfy "the demand for legal services under the Canada-U.S. Free Trade Agreement and growing multinational business activity," at offices in Calgary, Edmonton, Saskatoon and Ottawa.

As evidence of how Wall Street viewed the future, Salomon Brothers in New York issued a report on the attractions of commercial and industrial real estate in Toronto. Prospects for long-term investment in Canada's most populous metropolitan region of the late 20th century were strong, "because free trade is expected to boost its economy." According to Salomon Brothers: "The United States has no single city that approaches the dominant market position that Toronto occupies within Canada.... It functions effectively as the combination of Chicago, Los Angeles and New York relative to the United States."

Canada & the United States in the Global Village

When the dust from the 1988 Canadian election finally settled, it was clear that, whatever else, fragments of the American media had learned a few new things about Canada.

Business Week's immediate reaction was headlined "A Giant Step Closer to North America Inc." It then declared: "Mulroney's victory virtually assures a continental bloc to rival a unified European market." But, it also suggested, Mulroney may seek written assurances from Washington that Canada's heavily subsidized social and medical programs which benefit industry are not subject to attack. "In doing so, he'll be asking the U.S. to take the same leap of faith as Canadian voters."

Speaking for those Americans who cannot seem to help feeling that the desire of the vast majority of Canadians to remain Canadians is somehow a criticism of the United States, the editor of the *New Republic* delivered a short psychological meditation. This argued that Canada's too strident determination to remain separate from the United States actually concealed deep-seated Freudian, and even sexual, desires for annexation.

Such more mainstream voices as *Time* magazine, however, accepted that Canada was "anti-American," in only the benign sense that it had decided to have a country of its own at least as long ago as the American Civil War. Canada need not worry about its cultural integrity, *Time* argued. It was "the major constitutional monarchy in the Western Hemisphere," and thus forever unique. If this was not quite how Canadians themselves saw the world, it was a form of progress. And, as *Time* also suggested, the 1988 election did reflect both "the voters' proclamation of devotion to Canadian values," and "the country's growing confidence."

Against all this was the stubborn fact that Canada still had only somewhat more than 10% of the North American market. Given the blunt edges of power politics among nations, all Canada can hope to be is a junior partner in "North America Inc.," and it will no doubt have to work hard to avoid becoming the wrong kind of junior partner.

Yet the latest free trade debate in Canada has also made clear that in the late 20th century we are looking out on a much different world from the one which the late 19th century looked out on. Asian winds are now blowing in the global village. The ancient history of the mysterious East, which the West is only starting to appreciate dimly, may hold some provocative messages for the mysterious spirit of William Lyon Mackenzie King.

Japan, for instance, has only about 10% of China's population. In the more remote past, it has had a peculiar special relationship with China. At certain points in history, China has been a kind of overlord of Japan. The classics of Chinese literature have been, and are a staple of traditional Japanese education. Even today, some American Orientalists jibe that Japanese culture is only a pale imitation of Chinese culture. The *Kodansha Encyclopedia of Japan* itself tells us that historically "the Chinese elite were indifferent or condescending to the Japanese. China always loomed very much larger in the minds of Japanese rulers and thinkers than did Japan in Chinese official circles." In the early 15th century the shogun Yoshimitsu negotiated a trade agreement with China, that involved his accepting "the tributary title 'king of Japan,' in his dealings with the Chinese court." And Yoshimitsu's "pragmatic acceptance of the title ... earned him censure in his own day and since."

In the late 20th century, it seems absurd to suggest that, several centuries hence, the relationship between Canada and the United States could evolve into anything at all like the present relationship between Japan and China. Yet the history of the world is a rich treasure house of human experience. It can at least be said that even stranger evolutions have actually taken place.

From any remotely sane sense of forward vision today, it is ridiculous to contemplate such a prospect. The best Canada can hope for in the 21st century is to become the kind of aggressive and ambitious North American junior partner, who works hard both for the partnership and for herself, and keeps all options for the future wide open. A Canada that even began to approach some modest approximation of widely recognized political and cultural parity with the United States, would be a much bolder place than the still somewhat hesitant second largest country in the world, that walks into the 1990s.

Nonetheless, among the no doubt many cunning passages of the history that lies before us, this could be the kind of Canada for which Brian Mulroney's free trade agreement with the United States has actually set the stage—if that is what Canadians want and work for. And the events of late 1988 and early 1989 seem to suggest that Canadians do indeed want something of this sort, along with peace, health, prosperity, and stable, good relations with their friendly next-door neighbours, in the United States.

In the wider world of the global village, even more than in the past, it will be increasingly important for Canada to stand by itself, and not in tandem with the United States. In this context, the bilateral decision of both countries to erect a free trade area in North America, north of the Rio Grande and the Gulf of Mexico, could prove to be only one more stitch in an emerging international pattern.

This includes earlier trade agreements between Israel and the United States and Australia and New Zealand, and quite dramatic new agreements among the members of the European Community, scheduled to take effect in 1992. Canada may be especially intrigued by how relations develop between the new, more unified EC and the European Free Trade Association (which includes such smaller nations as Sweden, Austria and Switzerland, and all told accounts for only about 10% of the larger EC's total population).

Less clearly, there are important on-going trade discussions and piecemeal agreements between the United States and Japan. Washington also has increasingly strong concerns over its trade deficits with Taiwan and South Korea. In a speech in New Zealand late in March 1989, John Crosbie expressed Canada's interest in some form of Asian-Pacific trading arrangement that would include Canada, the United States, Japan, Australia and New Zealand. He also noted that Canadian economists were studying the 1987 report of a New Zealand parliamentary committee that had urged New Zealand to "enhance its existing close link with Canada."

Crosbie stressed as well Canada's continuing concern for and commitment to the General Agreement on Tariffs and Trade. A few weeks before, Canadian External Affairs Minister Joe Clark had announced additional restrictions on trade with South Africa, and an easing of controls on Canadian sales to Warsaw Pact countries, Vietnam and North Korea.

In the best of all possible worlds, the Canada-U.S. Free Trade Agreement will finally become only a stepping stone to a wider Canadian national future, in a wider and more interesting world. On the other hand, if the Canada that has come through the fire of the 1988 federal election really does know its own mind, the worst that can happen is that the agreement will not even last as long as the ancient Reciprocity Treaty of 1854.

SELECT BIBLIOGRAPHY.

General.

Berger, Carl. *The Writing of Canadian History*. Toronto: Oxford University Press, 1976.

Bernard, André. *La Politique au Canada et au Québec*. Montreal: Les Presses de l'Université du Québec, 1976.

Bliss, Michael. *Northern Enterprise*. Toronto: McClelland and Stewart, 1987.

Brebner, John Bartlet. *North Atlantic Triangle*. New York: Columbia University Press, 1945.

Careless, J.M.S. *Canada: A Story of Challenge*. Toronto: Macmillan of Canada, 1963.

Dales, J.H. *The Protective Tariff in Canada's Development*. Toronto: University of Toronto Press, 1966.

Morici, Peter. *The Global Competitive Struggle: Challenges to the United States and Canada*. Washington: Canadian-American Committee, 1984.

Morison, Samuel Eliot. *The Oxford History of the American People*. New York: Oxford University Press, 1965.

Rostow, W.W. *The World Economy*. Austin: University of Texas Press, 1978.

Stairs, Denis and Gilbert R. Winham, eds. *The Politics of Canada's Economic Relationship with the United States*. Toronto: University of Toronto Press for Minister of Supply and Services Canada, 1985.

Ancient History.

Axtell, James. *The European and the Indian*. New York: Oxford University Press, 1981.

Beck, J. Murray. *Joseph Howe*. 2 vols. Kingston and Montreal: McGill-Queen's University Press, 1982 and 1983.

Berger, Carl. *The Sense of Power*. Toronto: University of Toronto Press, 1970.

Careless, J.M.S. *Brown of the Globe*. 2 vols. Toronto: Macmillan of Canada, 1959 and 1963.

_____. *The Union of the Canadas*. Toronto: McClelland and Stewart, 1967.

Creighton, Donald. *John A. Macdonald*. 2 vols. Toronto: Macmillan of Canada, 1952 and 1955.

_____. *The Empire of the St. Lawrence*. Toronto: Macmillan of Canada, 1956.

Eccles, W.J. *Canadian Society During the French Regime*. Montreal: Harvest House, 1968.

_____. *The Canadian Frontier 1534-1760*. New York: Holt, Rinehart and Winston, 1969.

Fisher, Robin. *Contact and Conflict*. Vancouver: University of British Columbia Press, 1977.

Hatch, Robert McConnell. *Thrust for Canada*. Boston: Houghton Mifflin, 1979.

Howay, F.W., W.N. Sage and H.F. Angus. *British Columbia and the United States*. Toronto: The Ryerson Press, 1942.

Innis, Harold A. *The Cod Fisheries*. Toronto: University of Toronto Press, 1954.

_____. *The Fur Trade in Canada*. Toronto: University of Toronto Press, 1956.

Morton, W.L. *The Critical Years*. Toronto: McClelland and Stewart, 1964.

_____. *Manitoba, A History*. Toronto: University of Toronto Press, 1967.

Smith, Goldwin. *Canada and the Canadian Question*. Toronto: University of Toronto Press, 1971.

Stanley, George F.G. *Canada Invaded 1775-1776*. Toronto: Hakkert, 1973.

Thoreau, Henry D. *A Yankee in Canada*. Montreal: Harvest House, 1966.

Trigger, Bruce G. *Natives and Newcomers*. Kingston and Montreal: McGill-Queen's University Press, 1985.

Waite, P.B. *Canada 1874-1896. Arduous Destiny*. Toronto: McClelland and Stewart, 1971.

Whitelaw, William Menzies. *The Maritimes and Canada Before Confederation*. Toronto: Oxford University Press, 1934.

Winks, Robin W. *Canada and the United States: The Civil War Years*. Montreal: Harvest House, 1971.

Wrong, George. *Canada and the American Revolution*. New York: Cooper Square, 1968.

The Twentieth Century.

Brady, Alexander. *Democracy in the Dominions*. Toronto: University of Toronto Press, 1958.

Brown, Robert Craig and Ramsay Cook. *Canada 1896-1921. A Nation Transformed*. Toronto: McClelland and Stewart, 1974.

Carroll, William K. *Corporate Power and Canadian Capitalism*. Vancouver: University of British Columbia Press, 1986.

Clement. Wallace. *Continental Corporate Power*. Toronto: McClelland and Stewart, 1977.

Conway, J.F. *The West*. Toronto: James Lorimer, 1983.

Cook, Ramsay. *The Maple Leaf Forever*. Toronto: Macmillan of Canada, 1971.

Creighton, Donald. *Canada's First Century*. Toronto: Macmillan of Canada, 1970.
_____. *The Forked Road. Canada 1939-1957*. Toronto: McClelland and Stewart, 1976.

Forsey, Eugene. *Freedom and Order*. Toronto: McClelland and Stewart, 1974.

Fowke, Vernon C. *The National Policy & the Wheat Economy*. Toronto: University of Toronto Press, 1957.

Garreau, Joel. *The Nine Nations of North America*. Boston: Houghton Mifflin, 1981.

Grant, George. *Lament for a Nation*. Toronto: McClelland and Stewart, 1965.
_____. *Technology and Empire*. Toronto: Anansi, 1969.

Granatstein, J.L. *Canada 1957-1967. The Years of Uncertainty and Innovation*. Toronto: McClelland and Stewart, 1986.

Hutchison, Bruce. *The Incredible Canadian*. Toronto: Longmans Canada, 1952.

Innis, Harold A. *The Bias of Communication*. Toronto: University of Toronto Press, 1951.
_____. *Essays in Canadian Economic History*. Edited by Mary Q. Innis. Toronto: University of Toronto Press, 1956.

Johnson, Harry G. *The Canadian Quandry*. Toronto: McClelland and Stewart, 1977.

Lévesque, René. *La Solution: Le Programme du Parti Québécois*. Montreal: Editions du Jour, 1970.

Lukacs, John. *Outgrowing Democracy*. New York: Doubleday, 1984.

Marshall, Herbert, Frank Southard Jr. and Kenneth W. Taylor. *Canadian-American Industry*. Toronto: McClelland and Stewart, 1976.

Phillips, Paul. *Regional Disparities*. Toronto: James Lorimer, 1982.

Rawlyk, G.A., ed. *The Atlantic Provinces and the Problems of Confederation*. St. John's: Breakwater Books, 1979.

Scott, F.R. *Canada Today*. London: Oxford University Press, 1938.

Smiley, Donald V. *The Canadian Political Nationality*. Toronto: Methuen, 1967.

Thompson, John Heard and Allen Seager. *Canada 1922-1939. Decades of Discord*. Toronto: McClelland and Stewart, 1985.

Trudeau, Pierre. *Federalism and the French Canadians*. Toronto: Macmillan of Canada, 1968.

Underhill, Frank H. *In Search of Canadian Liberalism*. Toronto: Macmillan of Canada, 1960.

Wilson, Edmund. *O Canada*. New York:
    The Noonday Press, 1965.
    _____. *Upstate*. New York: Farrar,
    Straus and Giroux, 1971.
Woodcock, George. *Canada and the
    Canadians*. Toronto: Macmillan of
    Canada, 1970.

The Issue Today.

Axworthy, Thomas S., ed. *Our American
    Cousins*. Toronto: James Lorimer,
    1987.
Canada. *The Canada-U.S. Free Trade
    Agreement*. Ottawa: The International
    Trade Communications Group, 1988.
    _____. *The Canada-U.S. Free Trade
    Agreement Synopsis*. Ottawa: The
    International Trade Communications
    Group, 1988.
Canadian Institute of International Affairs.
    "The North American political
    economy". *International Journal*. Vol.
    XLII No. 1., Winter 1986-87.
Laxer, James. *Decline of the Superpowers*.
    Toronto: James Lorimer, 1987.
Magun, Sunder, Someshwar Rao and Bimal
    Lodh. *Impact of Canada-U.S. Free
    Trade on the Canadian Economy*.
    Ottawa: Economic Council of Canada,
    1987.
Riggs, A.R. and Tom Velk, eds. *Canadian-
    American Free Trade: Historical,
    Political and Economic Dimensions* .
    Halifax: The Institute for Research on
    Public Policy , 1987.
Smith, Murray G. and Frank Stone, eds.
    *Assessing the Canada-U.S. Free Trade
    Agreement*. Halifax: The Institute for
    Research on Public Policy, 1987.
United States. *Summary of the U.S.-Canada
    Free Trade Agreement*. Washington:
    Office of the United States Trade
    Representative, 1988.
Wonnacott, Paul. *The United States and
    Canada: The Quest for Free Trade*.
    Washington: Institute for International
    Economics, 1987.

NOTES ON THE ILLUSTRATIONS

The illustrations used throughout the book are derived from two separate collections of Sam Hunter's original drawings.

The first collection belongs to the Canadian Decorative Arts Department of the Royal Ontario Museum. The cartoons in this collection appeared mainly in the *Toronto Daily Star* and the *Globe*.

The second collection is found in the Baldwin Room of the Metropolitan Toronto Library and contains cartoons covering an earlier period beginning about 1894. The drawings in this collection were published in the *World*.

In both collections, the original Sam Hunter drawings are almost universally undated. In some instances, the original captions are present; in many others, only the original drawing remains.

In working with the collection there have been several instances where we have taken the liberty of cropping the original drawings. In such cases we have indicated this by including an asterisk before the reference number.

The cover illustration is an engraving by C. Butterworth Jr. of F.A. Hopkin's painting "Running a rapid on the Mattawa River, Canada" (C-13585) from the collection of the National Archives of Canada.

INDEX